WITHDRAWN

GARLAND STUDIES IN ENTREPRENEURSHIP

edited by
STUART BRUCHEY
University of Maine

A GARLAND SERIES

DO SKILLS PREDICT PROFITS?

A Study of Successful Entrepreneurship

―――――――――――
LANNY HERRON

GARLAND PUBLISHING, Inc.
New York & London / 1994

Copyright © 1994 by Lanny Herron
All rights reserved

Library of Congress Cataloging-in-Publication Data

Herron, Lanny, 1943–
    Do skills predict profits? : a study of successful entrepreneurship / Lanny Herron.
        p.   cm. — (Garland studies in entrepreneurship)
    "A Garland series."
    Includes bibliographical references and index.
    ISBN 0-8153-1677-1 (alk. paper)
    1. Success in business—Psychological aspects.   2. Creative ability in business.   3. Entrepreneurship.   I. Title.   II. Series.
HF5386.H436   1994
658.4'21—dc20   93-48509
                                                                                 CIP

Printed on acid-free, 250-year-life paper
Manufactured in the United States of America

To Dor
...

Contents

Preface xvii

Acknowledgements xix

Chapter One: Introduction 3

    The Importance of New Ventures and Their Performance 3

    The Lack of Correspondence between the Results of Academic Research and Current Theory and Practice 4

    Research Questions 6

    Outline and Structure for this Book 6

Chapter Two: Model Development 11

    Introduction 11

    Economic Theories of Entrepreneurship 12

        Early European Entrepreneurial Theories 12

        Neo-Classical Entrepreneurial Theories 14

        Earlier American and Neo-Austrian Contributions to Entrepreneurial Theory 14

Modern American Contributions to Entrepreneurial
  Theory...16

Previous Research into the Characteristics of the Entrepreneur....18

   Definition of the Entrepreneur... 18

   Previous Studies Linking the Psychological
  Characteristics of the Entrepreneur to New Venture
  Performance...19

      Risk-Taking Propensity... 19

      Need for Achievement...21

      Locus of Control.. 21

      Other Psychological Characteristics...........................22

   Previous Studies Linking the Experience Characteristics
  of the Entrepreneur to New Venture Performance.............23

      Managerial Experience... 23

      Managerial Experience in the Line of Business............ 24

      Startup Experience... 24

      Education... 24

   Previous Studies Linking the Demographic
  Characteristics of the Entrepreneur to New Venture
  Performance...25

   The Possibility of Other Characteristics of the
  Entrepreneur Being Linked to New Venture
  Performance...25

- The Possibility of Behavioral Characteristics of the Entrepreneur Being Linked to New Venture Performance..26

- Possible Contingency of the Characteristic-Performance Link..27

- Teams as Contributing to Entrepreneurial Characteristics.... 27

- Possible Non-linearity of the Characteristic-Performance Relationship.. 28

- Synopsis of the Entrepreneurship Literature...................... 28

Important Directions Suggested by the Strategy Implementation Literature on Matching Managers to Jobs...... 29

- Review of the Strategy Implementation Literature on Matching Managers to Jobs... 29

- The Szilagyi - Schweiger Model...................................... 32

- A Synthesis of the Relevant Strategy Implementation Literature with the Entrepreneurship Literature................33

Important Directions from the Psychology, Psychological Testing, and Related Literature..33

- Personality Traits and Their Effect on Behavior and Individual Performance...33

    - Selecting Personality Traits for Study.......................35

    - The Stability of Personality Traits...........................36

    - The Causal Relation between Personality Traits and Performance... 37

Other Variables Affecting Behavioral Propensity................39

    The Causal Relationship between Self-efficacy and
    Behavioral Propensity...39

    The Causal Relationship between Values and
    Behavioral Propensity...41

The Relationship Between Behavioral Propensity,
Skills, and Performance...41

Mental Aptitudes.. 43

    Introduction to Intelligence...................................... 43

    Differential Theories...45

    Information Processing Theories..............................46

    A Synthesis of the Differential and Information-
    processing Paradigms...46

The Further Development of Katz' Skills Typology and its
Synthesis with Guilford's Structure of Intellect Model............48

    Extending Katz' Skill Typology.....................................48

        Technical Skills...48

        Human Skills..49

        Conceptual Skills... 49

    Reviewing Guilford's Structure of Intellect Model.............. 50

        Operations..50

        Contents... 51

    Products..51

    Matching Aptitudinal Elements from Guilford's Model
        with Elements from Katz' Skills Typology................. 52

        Technical Product/Service Skill................................ 52

        Technical Organizational Skill.................................52

        Technical Industry Skill.. 52

        Leadership Skill...52

        Networking Skill..53

        Administrative Skill...53

        Entrepreneurial Skill..53

        Summary.. 53

    The Current Research Model... 54

    Summary of the Literature Review..................................54

Chapter Three: Research Design..73

    Introduction.. 73

    The Holistic Construal Approach to Doing Research................ 73

    Development of General Hypotheses from the Current
        Research Model.. 74

    Operationalization of Variables..77

    Operationalization of Strategy..................................... 78

        Operationalization of Scope Strategy........................ 78

        Operationalization of Aggressiveness of Growth Orientation.. 81

        Operationalization of Entry Wedge............................ 81

    Operationalization of Industry Structure...........................84

        Operationalization of Industry Life Cycle....................84

        Operationalization of Industry Differentiation.............. 84

    Operationalization of Aptitudes, Skills, Skill Propensity and Training...87

        Operationalization of Skills..................................... 87

        Operationalization of Skill Propensity....................... 87

        Operationalization of Aptitudes................................87

        Operationalization of Training................................91

    Operationalization of New Venture Performance.................91

The Research Design... 92

    The Study..92

    Main Sample.. 95

    Secondary (SBDC) Sample.. 95

    Preventure Sample.. 96

Methodology...97

Chapter Four: Analysis and Results..101
   Introduction...101
   Data Gathering..101
      The Main Sample...102
      The SBDC Confirmation Sample................................. 102
      The Preventure Aptitude Test Subsample........................ 102
      The Resultant Subsamples.. 102
   Reliability Issues... 103
      Questionnaire Construction and Pretest............................103
      Structure of Intellect Pretest and Test Construction........... 103
      Item Reliability... 105
      Construct Validity.. 107
      Validity of Skills Measures... 111
   Test of Hypothesis: H1 through H2G.................................115
      Test of the Main Hypothesis: H1................................... 115
      Tests of the Secondary Hypotheses: H2A through H2G... 121
   The SBDC Confirmation Sample.. 134
      The Sample...134

Item Reliability... 135
Construct validity..135
Confirmation of Hypothesis H1................................. 140
    Skills Factors.. 146
    Confirming Hypothesis H1.................................. 146
    Individual Skill Factors....................................... 149
Tests of Secondary Hypotheses: H2A through H2G.......... 158
Test of Hypotheses H3A Through H3G.............................. 173
The Preventure Confirmation Sample................................176
Derivation of Specific Normative Propositions..................... 179
    The Importance of Contingency Relations to Prediction of NVP...179
    Regarding the Investigation of Specific Contingency Relations... 185
    Development of Specific Normative Propositions Concerning Possession and Use of Skills.....................186
    Development of Specific Normative Propositions Concerning Skill Interactions with Venture Context...... 192
Summary of Analysis and Results Chapter..........................199

Chapter Five: Conclusions..203
    Introduction...203

    Conclusions 203

        Conclusions Involving Hypothesis H1 204

        Conclusions Involving Hypotheses H2A through H2G 205

        Conclusions Involving Hypotheses H3A through H3G 206

        Conclusions Involving the Specific Normative Propositions 207

    Implications 207

    Limitations 210

    Directions for Future Research 212

        Overcoming Limitations of this Research 212

        Expanding Knowledge in the Skills Area 213

        Studying the balance of the "Full" Model 213

        Expanding the Full Model 213

        Addressing Issues Derived from this Study's Findings 214

Appendix 219

Bibliography 229

Index 261

Preface

The motivation for this study was partly philosophical. One instrumental issue was that of will versus determinism: whether individuals tend to succeed at independent economic endeavors through the application of their wills to their own talents and environments (versus whether their capabilities and successes are largely predetermined by events beyond their own control).

I have long been fascinated by the relation between the individual and economic organization. I grew up in mid-century in an environment of increasing societal and economic massification, and was educated in "Eastern establishment" schools. There it was often implied that only individuals endowed with "the right stuff" were capable of creative entrepreneurship. By contrast, Management was a science. Managers, having once mastered a limited set of administrative principles, were believed capable of managing going concerns in any industry. Further, it was taught that all economic endeavors were fraught with the twin dangers of too few jobs and inherent limits to growth.

Fortunately, most of this hog-wash has proven to be just that. We have now moved into an era of the rampant growth of entrepreneurship and its extension (or re-extension) to large portions of our population. Jobs, while not as easy to come by as they could be, are available in abundance to those willing to push to extend their creativity. The attendant de-massification of society and the growth of many new sectors of our economy has been startling indeed. At the same time, it is becoming widely recognized that, while certain management principles are widely applicable, the ability of most managers to productively jump across industries has been greatly exaggerated.

Unfortunately, academia, at least in the social sciences of which Management is a part, often seems to badly lag changes in the world of practice. In the case of Entrepreneurship, academicians are continuing to churn out studies based on the premise that entrepreneurial success is closely linked to a limited set of personality characteristics; no matter that these studies have universally failed to correlate the two. Meanwhile, these same academicians imply that those possessing the mantle of entrepreneurial success can profitably navigate the economy in almost any area that they wish with only a few universal principles at their command.

In entering academe relatively late in life and career, I soon began to wonder why management researchers were unable to link success in entrepreneurship with characteristics of the individual. Was it a reaction to this failure which led so many management theorists to the conclusion that deterministic models on a larger scale were the only ways to predict the causes of economic success? Had Management, still rooted in the depths of Economies of Scale and Management Science, gone the way of Neoclassical Economics in its abolition of a place for the individual entrepreneur?

In the course of my studies it began to dawn on me that, strange as it may seem, few scholars had attempted to investigate the *skills* of entrepreneurs or to investigate contingency relations in the practice of entrepreneurship. Skills are combinations of inborn and learned abilities, and are fruitfully employed by individuals only when circumstances warrant. It seemed to me that their study promised to show productive relationships with entrepreneurial performance.

This study bears a witness to the potential of that relationship.

Lanny Herron

University of Baltimore

Acknowledgments

This study would not be complete without extending thanks to certain of those who have helped me so much along the way.

First, I would like to thank Richard Robinson who has been my guide, mentor, and friend for the eight years since I have returned to academia. He has been extremely generous to me not only with his valuable time but also with his resources, his good advice, and, most of all, with his encouragement. He has served as my example as teacher, researcher, theoretician, and business practitioner. I simply would not have accomplished what I have without him.

My thanks also goes to my other colleagues at the University of South Carolina who helped with this study in so many ways.

The sense of humor and the personal companionship of both Jesse and Sandi Teel have often stood me in good stead. They are very personal friends whom I will always remember often:

Jesse Teel has served as my special friend and statistical mentor since first we met. Jesse possesses one of the most astute mathematical minds that I have ever known combined with an ability to empathize and communicate, and a willingness to take the time to do both. The fact that he has never once, in eight years, lost his patience in the face of much "why-ning", is ample proof of these strengths.

Sandi Teel was my boss in the Division of Research at South Carolina as well as my friend and facilitator. I will never be able to repay her for either the shelter or the kindness which she provided me while I was in the throes of this study. I would not have been able to keep body and mind together during the transition period to academia were it not for her continued and constant support.

Bill Sandberg has helped me in such multitudinous ways that I could not enumerate them. His book served as the foundation and starting point for this study, and his help and kindness throughout the task were constant.

Dave Schweiger's and Kendall Roth's good advice have not only helped to mold this study but have also have had a positive impact on my thinking about the field and about research in general.

John Logan's constant assistance, empathy, and friendship will always be remembered. John contributed immensely to the productive atmosphere of my initial academic experience.

Jim Chrisman was always willing to take his time to help me over the rough spots. Jim has a wonderful understanding of the strategic management field, and his influence as both a teacher and researcher has helped in many ways to mold this study. The opportunity to work with him has been a real pleasure and his friendship will always be highly valued.

There were of course many others who provided assistance too numerous to list. I would be remiss, though, if I did not offer particular thanks to my family who have molded my existence and made it all worthwhile.

My mother, though she did not live beyond my childhood, might perhaps recognize some of the values which she tried so hard to teach me in the short time we had together.

I thank my father for many, many things, but mostly for never, ever losing his confidence in me.

I thank my brother Chip for sharing with me a common heritage.

I thank my daughters Bec and Deb, and my sons-in-law Chris and Joey, for their total love and support which they have always given me no matter how long or how difficult the tasks I've confronted.

Most of all, I thank my best friend and wife Dor, who has been my very special life-support system for 30 years, through a bit of "thick" and a lot of "thin". I love you...

Do Skills Predict Profits?

Chapter One:

Introduction

THE IMPORTANCE OF NEW VENTURES AND THEIR PERFORMANCE

"America is, right now, in [a] great entrepreneurial age".

This quote, from the lead article by Ronald Reagan in the inaugural issue of the Journal of Business Venturing, was generally recognized as true when it was published in late 1985.[1] Today, nearly 10 years later, we recognize that our entrepreneurial age is probably only in its infancy.

New business ventures are playing an increasingly important economic and societal role in America as time goes on. During the twenty years from 1965 to 1985, the economy of the U.S. increased its net employment by approximately 49%, or 35 million new jobs. In no other peacetime period has the United States created as many new jobs, whether measured in percentages or in absolute numbers.[2] Of this net, government jobs combined at all levels stayed relatively constant while big business lost approximately 5 million jobs. However, small and medium size businesses added approximately 40 million jobs, many of these in the form of new ventures.[3] While in the post-World War II economy, Americans created fewer than 100,000 businesses annually, they were starting over 1,000,000 per year by 1987.[4] By contrast, during the period 1970 through 1982, net jobs in Japan grew by only 10%, or less than half the U.S. rate, and total employment in the Common Market decreased by over 3 million jobs.[5] These trends are continuing into the 1990s with IBM, General Motors, and other Fortune 500 companies shrinking while new business start-ups continue to increase in proportion to our economy. Meanwhile, the Japanese economy is shrinking and the European economy struggles with the absorption of the former Communist states. American new business ventures are not only driving our economy now, but are keeping us competitive in the world community.

In 1980, Alvin Toffler, in his provocative publication "The Third Wave"[6], noted that the world economy is moving away from the mass-production era for the first time and into an era of "de-massification", a time more suited than the recent past to the creation of new ventures. John Naisbitt, in his 1982 book "Megatrends"[7], put forth ten major directions in society currently "transforming our lives". At least five of these are favorable to increasing entrepreneurship and new ventures. The information revolution is decreasing set-up and transactions costs within the economy, and in the process is breaking down the hierarchies of large companies and changing the way we do business. We are becoming more and more a nation propelled by entrepreneurs and their new ventures, and the trend is increasing and likely to persist.

Unfortunately, the failure rate for new ventures in our economy is quite high. Van de Ven, Hudson, and Schroeder[8], in commenting on the short life expectancies of new organizations, observed that about one fourth of all business firms in the U.S. are one year old or less, with the median age of all firms only about seven years. They further stated that only 54 per cent of all newly formed or acquired businesses survive one and a half years. Other scholars[9] [10] have reported both higher and lower mortality rates; however, a widely accepted estimate is 60 per cent failure by the second year after start-up and 90 per cent by the tenth year.[11]

These dual phenomena, the impact of successful entrepreneurship upon our economy combined with the high cost of entrepreneurial failure, lend impetus to the search for understanding of the causes of new venture performance. An understanding of these causes is of vital importance to our business community, to academicians, and to our society as a whole.

THE LACK OF CORRESPONDENCE BETWEEN THE RESULTS OF ACADEMIC RESEARCH, AND CURRENT THEORY AND PRACTICE.

Considerable progress has been made by academic researchers in management over the last 15 years in determining the causes of new venture performance. Much of this research has concentrated on the effects of strategy and industry structure on new venture performance.[12] [13] [14] [15] [16] In fact, some of this research purports to statistically explain such a high level of variance in new venture performance (NVP) [17] that the question arises as to whether the entrepreneur him/herself has any appreciable effect on NVP apart from the initial determination of strategy and industry structure.

In an attempt to determine the causes of new venture performance, Sandberg[18] developed a new model of new venture performance and tested it empirically. His model stated simply that new venture performance is a function of the characteristics of the entrepreneur, the structure of the industry in which the venture competes, and its business strategy [NVP=f(E,IS,S)]. In his testing of the model, Sandberg was able to find ample support for effects of industry structure and business strategy upon new venture performance. Unfortunately, as with many before him, he was able to find little evidence that the characteristics of the entrepreneur affect that same performance. In spite of this, however, he was unwilling to drop the "E" from his model for several very valid reasons. First, the caliber and depth of a venture's management are the traditional focus of venture capitalists' evaluations.[19] Thus the wisdom of the venture capitalists provides strong support for the inclusion of the entrepreneurial variable, the superior performance of ventures backed by venture capitalists in general being well known.[20] Second, the theory implicit in much academic research on entrepreneurship has been that the performance of new ventures is largely determined by the entrepreneur himself [NVP=f(E)][21], even though the results of that research have generally been tenuous. Third, the practitioner literature has been largely oriented toward this same concept. Fourth, Sandberg was necessarily limited in the type of study he did to looking solely at entrepreneurial characteristics defined by objective biographic data. Fifth, the sample size in Sandberg's study was only 17, limiting the power and generalizability of his tests. He was thus reluctant to recommend a radical departure from the past based upon his data alone.

Sandberg, of course, has not been alone in his inability to explain significant variance in new venture performance based upon empirical study of various entrepreneurial characteristics. Many excellent research studies have been conducted over the past thirty years with similar results.[22, 23, 24, 25, 26, 27, 28]

Thus, despite unquestioned strides in determining the causes of new venture performance, we are faced with a serious lack of correspondence between research results, and theory and practice. On the one hand, a long history of academic studies has failed to confirm empirically the existence of a strong and significant link between the characteristics of the entrepreneur and new venture performance even though academic theory has always proceeded on the basis of the existence of that link. On the other hand, venture capitalists and others who deal daily in the practical prediction and evaluation of the causes of new venture performance continue to hold to the dictum that it is the quality of the entrepreneur that ultimately determines the decision to fund a new venture.[29]

RESEARCH QUESTIONS

It is this disparity between theory and practice on the one hand and past research results on the other which has generated the first two major research questions guiding this study:

1. Do characteristics of the entrepreneur have a significant impact upon new venture performance in addition to strategy and industry structure?

2. If so, what characteristics are important and what is their relationship with new venture performance?

Based on the importance of new ventures to our economy and society as put forth above, answers to these questions are of great importance. However, for this research to be useful both in the practitioner arena and as a springboard to future research, it is believed that the normative implications of the answers to these questions should be explored as well. This leads to the third major research question guiding this study:

3. What specific normative relationships are implied between characteristics of the entrepreneur and new venture performance?

OUTLINE AND STRUCTURE FOR THIS BOOK

The remainder of the book will establish the theoretical base for the analysis, the research design, the findings, and the implications of the research project. Chapter 2 establishes the theoretical underpinnings of the study. First, the development of economic theories of entrepreneurship is reviewed to establish a foundation for further conceptualization about the entrepreneur. Next, a comprehensive review of the management literature attempting to link the characteristics of the entrepreneur to NVP is presented, along with some probable reasons for its failure to establish such a strong and significant link. Next, the strategic management implementation literature is reviewed for the illumination it provides to those seeking to link characteristics of the entrepreneur with NVP. Finally, the psychological and psychological testing literatures are selectively reviewed for their relevance in identifying and measuring characteristics associated with the role of "E" in NVP.

Chapter 3 operationalizes the research model and discusses the research and sample design. Chapter 4 then presents the results of empirically examining the research model. Specifically, the data analysis procedure and the hypothesis tests are presented. Chapter 5 then derives normative propositions from the analysis and discusses research conclusions, limitations, and implications derived from the model analysis.

Notes:

[1] Reagan, R. (1985). Why this is an entrepreneurial age. *Journal of Business Venturing, 1* (1), 1-4.

[2] Drucker, P.F. (1985). Entrepreneurial strategies. *California Management Review, 27,*(2), 9-25.

[3] Ibid

[4] Birch, D.L. (1988). The truth about start-ups. *Inc.*(Jan.), 14-15.

[5] Drucker, P.F. (1985). Entrepreneurial strategies. *California Management Review, 27,*(2), 9-25.

[6] Toffler, A. (1980). The third wave. New York: Random House.

[7] Naisbitt, J. (1982). *Megatrends.* New York: Warner Books.

[8] Van De Ven, A.H., Hudson, R., & Schroeder, D.M. (1984). Designing new business startups: entrepreneurial, organizational, and ecological considerations. *Journal of Management, 10* (1), 87-107.

[9] Cochran, A.B. (1981). Small business mortality rates: A review of the literature. *Journal of Small Business,* (Oct), 50-59.

[10] Dickinson, R. (1981). *Business Failure Rate. American Journal of Small Business, 2* (2), 17-25.

[11] Timmons, J.A. (1985). *New venture creation.* Homewood, IL: Richard D.Irwin, p. 4.

[12] Biggadike, R. (1979) The risky business of diversification. *Harvard Business Review*,(May-June). 103-111.

[13] Miller, A. & Camp, B. (1985). Exploring determinates of success in corporate ventures. *Journal of Business Venturing, 1*, 87-105.

[14] Cooper, A.C., Willard,G.E. & Woo,C.Y. (1986).Strategies of high-performaning new and small firms: A reexamination of the niche concept. *Journal of Business Venturing, 1* (3), 247-260.

[15] MacMillan, I. C. & Day, D. (1987). Corporate ventures into industrial markets: Dynamics of aggressive entry. *Journal of Business Venturing, 2* (1). 29-39.

[16] McDougall, P. (1987). *An analysis of new venture business level strategy, entry barriers,and new venture origin as factors explaining new venture performance.* Unpublished doctoral dissertation. Columbia, SC: University of South Caroloina.

[17] Ibid.

[18] Sandberg, W. R. 1986). *New venture performance: The role of strategy and industry structure.* Lexington, MA: D.C. Heath & Co.

[19] Ibid.

[20] Ibid.

[21] Ibid.

[22] Brockhaus, R.H. (1980). Psychological and environmental factors which distinguish the successful from unsuccessful entrepreneur: A long study. *Academy of Management Proceedings.* 368-372.

[23] Brockhaus, R.H. (1980). Risk-taking propensity of entrepreneurs. *Academy of Management Journal, 23,* 509-520.

[24] Begley, T.M. & Boyd, D.P. (1987). Psychological characteristics associated with performance in entrepreneurial firms and smaller businesses. *Journal of Business Venturing, 2*(1), 79-93.

[25] Hull, D., Bosley, J., & Udell, G. (1980). Renewing the hunt for the heffalump: Identifying potential entrepreneurs by personality characteristics. *Journal of Small Business,18*(1), 11-18.

[26] Hoad, W. & Rosko, P. (1964). *Management factors contributing to the sucess and failure of new small manufacturers.* Ann Arbor, Mich: Bureau of Business Research, University of Michigan.

[27] Smith, N.R. (1967). *The entrepreneur and his firm: The relationship between type of man and type of company.* East Lansing, MI: Bureau of Business and Economic Research, Michigan State University.

[28] Roure, J. (1986). *Success and failure of high-growth technological ventures: The influence of prefunding factors.* Unpublished doctoral dissertation. Stanford, CA: Stanford University.

[29]MacMillan, I., Seigel, R., & Narasimha, S. P. (1985). Criteria used by venture capitalists to evaluate new venture proposals. *Journal of Business Venturing, 1*(1), 119-128.

Chapter Two:

Model Development

INTRODUCTION

The purpose of this chapter is to review both the theoretical and empirical literatures which bear upon the characteristics of the entrepreneur and upon how those characteristics may be related to the performance of the entrepreneurial venture. This literature review is divided into four parts.

The first part examines the history of the concept of entrepreneurship as seen through the view of the economic literature bearing on the subject. This literature is by far the oldest on the subject, going back as far as the eighteenth century. A review of the historical development of this literature is critical for setting the stage to answer such questions as: Who is the entrepreneur, and what are the functions that he/she performs?

The second part of the literature review covers those studies that have been done concerning the entrepreneur, both theoretical and empirical, with a view toward discovering what characteristics are crucial to the conduct of entrepreneurship, and how they relate to the performance of the entrepreneurial venture. The review of this literature, looking back nearly thirty years, attempts to answer such questions as: What characteristics of the entrepreneur have been studied and why have these studies failed to confirm a strong relationship between those characteristics studied and the performance of the entrepreneurial ventures?

The third part of this literature review examines the strategic implementation literature bearing upon matching managers to managerial situations. This literature is reviewed for the purpose of integrating its relevant findings and theoretical underpinnings with those of the aforementioned entrepreneurship literature. This integration, a task which apparently has not been undertaken heretofore, sheds light upon the question: Why has the literature attempting to link entrepreneurial characteristics to performance of the entrepreneurial firm failed to do so?

The fourth and last part of this literature review delves into the relevant psychological and psychological testing literatures in an attempt to shed further light upon questions arising in the previous three sections of the literature review such as: What psychological characteristics have been shown empirically or theoretically to link with various task performances in humans; how are these characteristics interrelated; and how might they be measured?

ECONOMIC THEORIES OF ENTREPRENEURSHIP

As explicated by Hoselitz[1], the various economic theories which explain or differentiate the activities of the entrepreneur qua entrepreneur should attempt to determine those aspects of entrepreneurial behavior which are most significant and which are independent of a particular social framework as well. This goal of economic entrepreneurial theory becomes evident as the history of that entrepreneurial thought unfolds.

Early European Entrepreneurial Theories

The concept of the entrepreneur has been developing for many hundreds of years. The term "entrepreneur" comes from the French verb "entreprendre" with the connotation "to do something", and can be traced to the 12th century; by the fifteenth century the corresponding noun had developed.[2] Throughout the sixteenth and seventeenth centuries the most frequent usage of the term connoted a government contractor, usually of military fortifications or public works.[3]

The academic study of entrepreneurship originated with the study of economics. Economists have been writing about entrepreneurs since Richard Cantillon's "Essai sur la Nature du Commerce en Géneràl" was first published in 1755,[4] and "yet there is perhaps no other area of economic analysis where there exists less agreement than on the nature of the entrepreneurial function and the identification of the entrepreneur".[5]

Richard Cantillon (1680? - 1734) authored the first economic theory of entrepreneurship,[6] and his central concept was that of risk. The entrepreneur, said Cantillon, is one who buys at a price which is certain and sells at a price which is uncertain. Thus, for Cantillon, the entrepreneur is anyone who has the foresight and willingness to assume such monetary risk and takes the action requisite to making a profit (or loss).

Another major step in the economic theory of entrepreneurship was taken by the Abbé Nicolas Baudeau (1730 - 1792), a disciple of the physiocrat Quesnay. Baudeau envisioned the entrepreneur as not only a risk bearer but also as an innovator who reduced risk through invention.[7] He thus emphasized the entrepreneur's need for knowledge, information, and skills.

At about this same time, Anne-Robert Turgot (1727 - 1781) began to weave the threads of capitalism and of management into those of entrepreneurship. Turgot saw the entrepreneur primarily as a rich merchant or industrialist who advances capital to the enterprise and who plans and supervises the work in order to accumulate more capital.[8]

Jean-Baptist Say (1767 - 1832) was the man of nineteenth-century economics most identified with the theory of entrepreneurship.[9] Say divided human industry (the "production of wealth") into three distinct operations: the acquisition of scientific knowledge, the application of this knowledge to a useful purpose, and the physical production of a product.[10] It is this second step which is essentially "entrepreneurial" and which must meet the "market test" of leading to utility.[11] To Say therefore, the entrepreneur is a matcher of scientific knowledge with human desires, taking costs into account. Thus for Say, sound judgement is the main distinguishing characteristic of the entrepreneur lest "he might produce at great expense something which has no value."[12]

While this expansion of entrepreneurial theories was taking place in France, the English economists, led by Adam Smith [13] and David Ricardo (1772-1823), and continuing through the close of the classical period with John Stuart Mill (1806 - 1873), did very little to advance the idea of entrepreneurship. Instead, they basically regarded the entrepreneur as a mere capitalist who acted rationally to maximize profits.[14] Mill, however, was largely responsible for the introduction of the term "entrepreneur" into English economics.[15]

Meanwhile in Germany, the tradition developed in France by Baudeau of considering the entrepreneur to be both a risk-taker and an innovator, was taken up and further developed by J. H. von Thünen (1783 -1850) and H. K. von Mangoldt (1824 - 1868). Thünen in particular emphasized the development of innovation skills by the entrepreneur as he sought to avoid business failure.[16]

Thus the period of classical economics ended with the entrepreneur firmly ensconced, at least in Continental economics, as either a risk-taker, an innovator, or both.

Neo-Classical Entrepreneurial Theories

The neoclassical period of economic theory again showed the same geographic pattern of development of entrepreneurial theory with considerable progress being made on the European continent accompanied by relative stagnation in England. Alfred Marshall (1842 - 1924), A. C. Pigou (1877 - 1959), and John Maynard Kaynes (1883 - 1946) all did very little to advance the concept of the entrepreneur beyond that of a rational decision-maker. But on the continent, Carl Menger(1840 - 1921) established himself as the founder of the Austrian school of economics, and, in so doing, became an intellectual precursor to numerous (and sometimes conflicting) schools of entrepreneurial thought. Menger and the Austrian school taught that goods further up the economic chain (that is, more removed from direct human satisfaction but instead leading to production of goods which in turn directly satisfied human needs) were the milieu of the entrepreneur.[17] The function of the entrepreneur in this view was to transform these goods into lower order goods and, as such, the entrepreneur needed to deal in information, economic calculation, an "act of will", and supervision.[18] Menger further stated: "After what has been said, it will be evident that I cannot agree with Mangoldt, who designates 'risk bearing' as the essential function of entrepreneurship in a production process, since this 'risk' is only incidental and the chance of loss is counterbalanced by the chance of profit".[19] As will be seen shortly, Menger thus laid the major groundwork for Kirzner's[20] and Schultz's[21] more modern theories of entrepreneurial perception and adjustment,[22] and established an argument about the risk-bearing function of entrepreneurship which still goes on today and which has spilled over into the management literature.[23][24]

Earlier American and Neo-Austrian Contributions to Entrepreneurial Theory

In general, American economists have been much more successful than their English counterparts at conceptually separating the entrepreneurial from the capitalist functions.[25] The American economist Hawley (1843 - 1929) returned to the theory of Cantillon with his view that entrepreneurship was the bearing of risk, but he strictly separated this function from that of the capitalist. J.B. Clark

Model Development

(1847 - 1938), on the other hand, argued with Hawley that risk bearing was not an entrepreneurial activity but rather a capitalist activity.[26] For Clark, the entrepreneur was a coordinator and decision maker, but, interestingly enough, quite distinct from being a "mere manager".[27] In fact, Clark's entrepreneur is the force which serves to move the economy back to equilibrium after a disturbance:[28]

> In a dynamic state [of the economy] the entrepreneur emerges from the passive position. He makes the supreme decisions which now and again lead to changes in the business. 'Shall we adopt this new machine?' 'Shall we make this new product?' 'Shall we enter this new market?' are questions which are referred to him, and on the decisions he reaches depends the prospects of profit for the business.[29]

This view of the entrepreneur, as may be seen, is very close to that of Menger's described above, and in that regard Clark was also a precursor to Kirzner's (1979) and Shultz's (1980) more modern developments. Clark's view of the separation of the management and entrepreneurial functions, however, also make him a precursor to Frank Knight (1855 - 1972) and Ludwig von Mises (1881 - 1972).

Frank Knight[30] held that a manager only became an entrepreneur when he assumed the responsibility for exercising judgement involving liability to error. As Knight stated: "...the only risk which leads to [entrepreneurial] profit is a unique uncertainty resulting from an exercise of ultimate responsibility which in its very nature cannot be insured nor capitalized nor salaried".[31]

Thus Knight, in his turn, fell back on the basics of Cantillon as had many before him. However, it should be noted that Knight saw entrepreneurs as a subset of managers.

Von Mises was a student of Böhm-Bawerk (1851 - 1914), who was in turn a disciple of Menger, founder of the Austrian school. Mises, in his ponderous but influential tome entitled "Human Action" stated: "The term entrepreneur ... means: acting man exclusively seen from the aspect of the uncertainty inherent in every action."[32]

And he also stated: "In the imaginary construction of an [equilibrium] system nobody is an entrepreneur... In any real and [dynamic] economy, every actor is an entrepreneur... .[33]

This also reflects some of the ideas of Knight, but leaves one with a feeling of futility toward the concept of risk-bearing entrepreneurship as an isolator of human actors as opposed to human actions. As Shultz[34] later maintained: "The bearing of risk is not a unique attribute of entrepreneurs. Whereas entrepreneurs assume risk, there are also people who are not entrepreneurs who assume risk."

Schumpeter (1883 - 1950) represented an integrating figure in the history of entrepreneurial thought.[35] He was also a pupil of Böhm-Bawerk and thus had his roots deep in the Austrian school of economics. Schumpeter's entrepreneur was the opposite of Clark's in that he was a disrupter of equilibrium rather than a force leading to equilibrium.[36] Schumpeter's entrepreneur was also the opposite of Knight's and von Mises' in that: "Risk obviously always falls on the owner of the means of production or of the money-capital which was paid for them, hence never on the entrepreneur as such.[37]

Schumpeter's entrepreneur was an innovator, and Schumpeter defined innovation in terms of the production function itself: "...[The production] function describes the way in which quantity of product varies if quantities of factors vary. If, instead of factors, we vary the *form* of the function, we have an innovation:[38]

> This innovation must consist of producing and marketing a new [product], otherwise the innovation would represent a cost-reducing adaptation of knowledge, which leads only to a new supply schedule".[39] For Schumpeter, the innovation often consists of utilizing scientific knowledge which is already available, an idea which coincides with Say's. Schumpeter's entrepreneur was not necessarily an independent businessman, however, but could be an employee such as a hired manager.[40]

Thus, prior to the modern period, American and Austrian economics had established the entrepreneur as an innovator and manager, while still not resolving the risk-bearing function of the entrepreneur nor whether he must be an independent businessman.

Modern American Contributions to Entrepreneurial Theory

Three modern American economists have made particularly noteworthy contributions to the theory of entrepreneurship, building variously upon the ideas of von Mises, Schumpeter, and Clark. These are G. L. S. Shackle, Israel Kirzner, and Theodore Schultz.

Shackle, an economist at Harvard University, has further developed the concept of the entrepreneur as risk taker, following in the tradition of Cantillon, Knight, and von Mises.[41] Shackle, rejects equilibrium economics with his emphasis on "bounded uncertainty" and ascribes to the entrepreneur two interrelated roles, those of decision-maker and bearer of uncertainty.[42] This definition of the entrepreneur, however, shares with von Mises' definition the inability to distinguish itself from other actors in the field of economic endeavor though it does establish the entrepreneur as a manager.

Kirzner, a former pupil of von Mises, has maintained that the essence of entrepreneurship consists in the "alertness" of market participants to profit opportunities[43] and that risk bearing per se is not an essential ingredient.[44] Kirzner derives his concept from another aspect of the writings of von Mises than does Shackle. Kirzner points out that von Mises : "...recognizes that men are not only calculating agents but are also *alert to opportunities*....This alertness is the entrepreneurial element in human action."[45]

For Kirzner, in contradistinction to Schumpeter and in line with Clark, the entrepreneur is the agent which moves the economy toward equilibrium: "At the same time that it transforms allocative decision making into a realistic view of human action, entrepreneurship converts the theory of market equilibrium into a theory of market process."[46]

Though, as pointed out by Hébert and Link[47], the differences between Kirzner and Schumpeter on this point are more apparent than real. Both men believe that when a market in equilibrium is disturbed, it will move back toward equilibrium. Schumpeter believes the entrepreneur is responsible for the disturbance, but he is silent on the mechanism for re-obtaining equilibrium. Kirzner, on the other hand, believes that the entrepreneur provides the mechanism for moving the market back toward equilibrium, but is silent on how the disequilibrium is established in the first place. Further, Kirzner believes, as Schumpeter before him, that the entrepreneur need not be a capitalist and that he may even be a paid employee who sells his services for a wage.[48] Still, Kirzner likens the entrepreneur to an "arbitrager"[49] and downplays the "innovation" factor which Schumpeter emphasizes.

Perhaps the epitome of logical integration and extension of the above ideas from the economic literature has come about through the writings of the American Nobel laureate T. W. Schultz.[50] Rather than focusing on "alertness" as the entrepreneurial ability as does Kirzner, Schultz[51,52] defines entrepreneurship as the reallocation of resources and thus focuses on the entrepreneurial ability of dealing with disequilibrium. Schultz believes that this entrepreneurial ability is not only innate, but may be enhanced by experience and education.[53] He further states that risk bearing is not a unique attribute of entrepreneurs and that others besides business persons may function entrepreneurially and in fact may learn entrepreneurship.[54][55] He also believes that the demand for entrepreneurship is a function of economic disequilibria[56] which tends to explain why the modern economy has seen such a recent upsurge in entrepreneurship. He further believes "that the comparative advantage of schooling rises relative to that of learning from experience as technology becomes more complex.".[57]

Thus modern American economic theory has established the entrepreneur as a subset of manager, has emphasized his unique mental function of "alertness" or "innovation" or "coping with disequilibrium", has suggested that these mental skills can be learned or at least enhanced by learning, and has tended to de-emphasize the unique risk-bearing activities of entrepreneurship while at the same time acknowledging that the the entrepreneur makes decisions under uncertainty.

PREVIOUS RESEARCH INTO THE CHARACTERISTICS OF THE ENTREPRENEUR

Having reviewed the history and development of the economic theories of entrepreneurship, we now turn to previous management research into the characteristics of entrepreneurs and how those characteristics effect the performance of the enterprise.

Definition of the Entrepreneur

As was seen in the review of the economic literature above, there is disagreement among economists as to what an entrepreneur is or does. This ambiguity has extended into management and entrepreneurship research circles as well as into common usage. Most modern, common dictionary definitions include the starting of a business venture among the distinguishing attributes of the entrepreneur. Certainly the founder of a business would fit under the "umbrella" of most of the economic views of the entrepreneur presented above. However, many researchers and theorists see entrepreneurship as a way of thinking and believe that one does not have to start a new business to be an entrepreneur, nor does starting a new business per se make one an entrepreneur. This idea has recently been amplified by Stevenson and Gumpert[58] who believe that entrepreneurship is a state of mind or a set of behaviors characterized by innovation, flexibility, and creativity.

The fact that there is no generally agreed upon definition of the term "entrepreneur" has led to considerable confusion in the literature. Whenever a researcher wishes to build upon the work of predecessors, he must take great care to examine the nature of the sample and methodology of the work so as to be sure that any conclusions drawn are applicable to that group which he is calling "entrepreneurs" in his own research. Because of this problem, he will more often than not be forced to accept much previous research as applicable to his own work only with considerable qualification and much skepticism.

The objectives of this study are to study the impact of the characteristics of the entrepreneur upon new venture performance. Therefore this study will follow the lead of Gartner[59] and consider an entrepreneur as simply anyone who creates a new business organization "from scratch". To this extent, the entrepreneur will also necessarily be both an innovator and a risk taker in the terms of Schumpeter[60] although the extent of his innovation may be limited to the creation of the new organization per se, and the risk involved may be no more (and no less) than the time he spends in that task and his reputation for such creation. Since the entrepreneur is the primary mover of the creation of the new venture, his task must necessarily involve its management over time, since such creation is never instantaneous. Defining the exact period of time over which his management *must* extend is an unnecessary and overly restrictive effort. In most cases studied herein, management will have taken place over several years, the length of which is subject to any number of situation specific factors.

Previous Studies Linking the Psychological Characteristics of the Entrepreneur to New Venture Performance

Much of the earlier research, and indeed much of the current research on the characteristics of the entrepreneur involved attempts to find personality traits which differentiated the population of existent entrepreneurs from the general population at large. Presumably, such traits could then be used to predict entrepreneurial success.

Risk-Taking Propensity

In line with the theories of Cantillon (1755) and many of his predecessors, one of the earliest such characteristics explored by entrepreneurial researchers was risk-taking propensity. However, most such exploration took the form of theorizing without direct empirical support. One of the earliest empirical studies involving propensity to take risks was conducted by Meyer, Walker, and Litwin.[61] They found that shop managers (selected to represent jobs which required "entrepreneurial" characteristics) showed a greater preference for intermediate risks on a risk preference questionnaire than did shop staff specialists (representing "non-entrepreneurial" job-types) of comparable age, education, and job level. Brockhaus[62], conducted an actual empirical study comparing the risk-taking propensity of entrepreneurs with that of managers. Unfortunately for purposes of the present study, he defined entrepreneurs as owner-managers of businesses. However, since these subjects had become owner-managers during the previous three months, it may be inferred that many new ventures were involved. The results showed that there was no statistically significant difference between the risk taking propensities of the entrepreneurs versus that of the managers. Further, comparison with the Kogan-Wallace study of 1964[63] showed that neither group differed significantly in risk preferences from the general population at large. This was a critical study in light of the controversy in the economic literature over risk-taking as a distinguishing characteristic of entrepreneurs.

In addition, a later study by Brockhaus[64] found that, when the entrepreneur group was divided into a group whose businesses later failed within three years of taking the risk preference test versus a group whose businesses did not, there was no significant difference between the risk preferences of those two groups!

A more recent study by Begley and Boyd[65] comparing managers of small businesses who were previous founders of those businesses (entrepreneurs) with managers of small businesses who were not founders (non-entrepreneurs), did show a statistically significant higher risk-taking propensity among the entrepreneurs, but the absolute difference (and thus the practical significance) was small (29.08 vs. 27.00 on a scale of 8 to 40 with a standard deviation of 4.64). Perhaps more importantly, when risk-taking propensity was regressed on return on assets (ROA) for the entrepreneur group, it was found that a non-linear result ensued. Risk-taking propensity predicted increased ROA up to a point but then, when increased further, predicted decreased ROA. This non-linearity will be discussed in more detail later.

Overall then, empirical research has largely failed to confirm a significant link between the risk-taking characteristics of the entrepreneur and new venture performance, a finding which might have startled many early economists.

Model Development

Need for Achievement

Another characteristic that has been investigated in conjunction with entrepreneurs is that of need for achievement. Some of the earliest empirical work which was done linking this characteristic to entrepreneurs was that of McClelland[66]. In this and several subsequent studies,[67,68] however, McClelland defined the entrepreneur as anyone holding an "entrepreneurial occupation" such as a salesman, consultant, or officer of a large company as well as owner-managers of businesses. His finding, that need for achievement influenced the decision to enter entrepreneurial occupations, is therefore not directly applicable to the research involving new venture performance.

A 1972 study somewhat more relevant to new venture performance was done by Komives,[69] measuring the need for achievement of 20 founders of high-technology businesses. Komives found a high need for achievement among this group, but unfortunately his sample size was small and he had no control group with which to compare them except the general population.

More recently, Begley and Boyd[70] showed that need for achievement was higher for entrepreneurs than for non-entrepreneurs. However, the difference, while statistically significant, was again quite small in absolute terms (21.52 vs. 20.84 on a scale of 5 to 25 with a standard deviation of 2.22). Further, among entrepreneurs, need for achievement had no statistically significant correlation with either growth or ROA.

In short, little relevant research has been done concerning the effects of the need for achievement of the entrepreneur on the performance of new ventures and no demonstrable linkage has been found. In fact, even the causal link between choice of entrepreneurship itself and a high need for achievement has not been proven.[71]

Locus of Control

A more promising characteristic for linking the entrepreneur to new venture performance seems to be that of locus of control. This characteristic measures the extent to which an individual considers his own fate to be within his own control (internal locus of control) versus outside of his control (external locus of control).[72]

Borland,[73] Shapero,[74] Brockhaus,[75] and Brockhaus and Nord,[76] all did studies which, to different degrees, lent credence to the proposition that founders of new ventures tend to have a more internal locus of control than non-founders, although a study by Hull, Bosley, and Udell in 1980[77] failed to confirm this relationship. Of much greater import to the present research, however, was the longitudinal study by Brockhaus[78] referred to earlier. Here, a comparison between failed versus non-failed business owners three years after they went into business showed that those who failed had a significantly higher external locus of control than those who succeeded, implying that internal locus of control may indeed be linked positively with new venture performance. However, it is noticeable in Brockhaus' presentation of statistics for this study that the difference between the standard deviations of the locus of control for the successful and unsuccessful entrepreneurs is greater than the difference in the means between the two groups. This implies that a higher proportion of unsuccessful entrepreneurs actually had *very* internal locuses of control (less than 4.23) than did successful entrepreneurs. In others words, although Brockhaus' study shows that, in general, internal locus of control is associated with being a successful entrepreneur, there may be a point above which additional internal locus of control becomes destructive. Again, this implies non-linearity in the relationship between a characteristic of the entrepreneur and new venture performance.

More recently, Begley and Boyd[79] found that internal locus of control in entrepreneurs is strongly and negatively associated with liquidity of new ventures, indicating that different aspects of NVP may be affected by locus of control in quite different fashions.

Thus there is modest support for a connection between locus of control of the entrepreneur and performance of a new venture, but the nature and strength of the relationship is very much in doubt.

Other Psychological Characteristics

Other psychological characteristics of the entrepreneur have been studied such as tolerance for ambiguity, personality type, and personal values. One of the first major studies of entrepreneurs involving personal values was done by Hornaday and Aboud in 1971.[80] They concluded that need for achievement, independence, effectiveness of leadership, and low need for support were characteristics of successful entrepreneurs as opposed to the general population at large, but they did not attempt to connect these characteristics with new venture performance. Komives[81] basically confirmed these results and added low conformity, high aesthetic and theoretical values, and low religious values but again attempted no linkage with new venture performance. Gasse, in two related studies[82,83] used a modified version of Rokeach's (1960) Dogmatism Scale to conclude that open-mindedness of the entrepreneur is associated with a managerial, scientific, and rational orientation which is related to growth and innovation, and is more effective in specific industrial environments, but again the linkages here with new venture performance are tenuous.

Begley and Boyd[84], in their study of founders (entrepreneurs) versus non-founders (non-entrepreneurs), concluded that Friedman and Roseman's (1974) Type A personality was not correlated with entrepreneurship, but that tolerance for ambiguity was, albeit again not with any practical significance. Moreover, tolerance for ambiguity among entrepreneurs was another non-linear predictor of ROA much as risk-taking had been. It was associated with rising ROA up to a point, and then beyond that point was a predictor of declining ROA.

Thus there has been little conclusive empirical research linking psychological characteristics with new venture performance. The majority of studies concerning entrepreneurial characteristics have attempted to use these characteristics to differentiate between entrepreneurs and various non-entrepreneurial populations. Among those studies which have attempted to link new venture performance with entrepreneurial characteristics, remarkably little of statistical significance has been found and usually even this is of little practical significance in explaining performance variance.

Previous Studies Linking the Experience Characteristics of the Entrepreneur to New Venture Performance

Just as the psychological characteristics of the entrepreneur have been studied in an attempt to differentiate the population of existent entrepreneurs from the general population at large, so have experience characteristics. However, with experience, there has been more additional work attempting to link these characteristics directly with new venture performance, though much of this work is also inconclusive.

Managerial Experience

Smith,[85] in a study using data from Collins and Moore,[86] reported greater success among entrepreneurs who had the skills and orientations of managers rather than those of artisans. The composition of his sample, however, prevented positive support of his proposition.[87] Hoad and Rosko,[88] argued that management experience, even in an unrelated business, is important to new venture success. However, their own data failed to indicate any relationship between new venture performance and years of experience as a business owner-manager. Roure,[89] in a study of thirty-six high-growth, high-tech ventures found that new venture performance was positively related to both high growth experience of the entrepreneur and experience of the entrepreneur in a similar position, but again the results of neither were statistically significant.

Managerial Experience in the Line of Business

According to Buchele,[90] one of "the three main mistakes made in starting new firms" is that "the key persons do not have rounded managerial experience in the particular line of business." Hoad and Rosko[91] found that new venture success was positively related to experience as an owner or manager in a similar business, but the relation was not statistically significant. Sandberg[92] also found the same phenomena as Hoad and Rosko, but again without statistical significance.

Startup Experience

In 1986, MacMillan[93] wrote that there is a "technology" of entrepreneurship which may be learned through repeated entrepreneurial experience. Lamont[94] confirmed the value of previous startup experience to new venture performance in his study of 24 technology-based ventures, but with no statistical analysis on this very small sample.

Education

Collins and Moore[95] reported that the proportion of college graduates among business executives was higher than that among manufacturing entrepreneurs, although the proportion of college graduates among these entrepreneurs was three times that of the surrounding population. Brockhaus and Nord[96] confirmed these results. Hoad and Rosko[97] found that there were higher rates of both success and failure among educated entrepreneurs while uneducated entrepreneurs had higher rates of marginal ventures. Roberts[98] found that high-performing entrepreneurs typically had masters degrees whereas lower performers typically had doctorates.

Overall, research attempting to link the experience of the entrepreneur with new venture performance has been inconclusive, at least from the point of view of showing statistical significance.

Previous Studies Linking the Demographic Characteristics of the Entrepreneur to New Venture Performance

Age, longevity of residency, and foreign birth of entrepreneurs have all been studied with regard to discriminating entrepreneurs from the general population. Brockhaus and Nord[99] found that the mean period of residence in a local area was both considerably greater and statistically significant for entrepreneurs as opposed to managers. Little else of importance has been found regarding these variables as discriminators, and very little work has related them to new venture performance.

The Possibility of Other Characteristics of the Entrepreneur Being Linked to New Venture Performance

Given the rather limited success previous research has had in linking new venture performance to the personality, experience, and demographic characteristics of the entrepreneur, the question remains as to whether such a linkage can be made and, if so, why previous research has not been successful at establishing that link. Certainly, one question for speculation is whether other important characteristics of the entrepreneur have been overlooked.

One characteristic variable that has not been researched is intelligence or ability to learn. Many hints that such research could be valuable lie in the economic literature.[100] [101] [102] [103] Further, Drucker[104] states that entrepreneurship is a practice which may be "learned". Timmons[105] suggests that one of the major current controversies in the field is whether entrepreneurs are born versus whether entrepreneurial behavior may be learned, and, if so, whether it is a discrete or iterative learning process. MacMillan[106] states that entrepreneurship is a "technology" which may be learned. If entrepreneurship can indeed be learned, then intelligence, or some proxy for it such as SAT scores,[107] is likely to be linked to economic performance. Yet, in spite of such conceptual foundations, empirical studies connecting entrepreneurial intelligence to new venture performance have yet to be conducted.

Still another hint that some other important characteristics may not yet have been addressed is provided by MacMillan et al.[108] This was the first large-sample study to address the specific criteria which venture capitalists use in making their decisions regarding financing of new ventures. The study found seven criteria involving characteristics of the entrepreneur which were important to the venture capitalists. These criteria were: capability of sustained intense effort; articulation in discussing the venture; attention to detail; demonstrated past leadership ability; familiarity with target market; ability to evaluate and react to risk well; and track record relevant to the venture. The first four of these criteria have not been found to have been discussed in the research literature linking characteristics of the entrepreneur to new venture performance. It is noteworthy that these characteristics may be formulated as traits, skills, and/or behaviors. More attention will be paid to each of these areas as this literature review progresses.

The Possibility of Behavioral Characteristics of the Entrepreneur Being Linked to New Venture Performance

Several works of theory in the entrepreneurial literature provide clues that past attempts to link entrepreneurial characteristics with venture performance may have focused on the wrong *type* of independent variables. Stevenson and Gumpert[109] suggest that thought patterns governing entrepreneurial behavior may be grouped into five continua with the two extremes of each continuum representing "entrepreneurial" versus its antithesis: "administrative" thinking. They define "entrepreneurial" in terms of Schumpeter's[110] concept, that it is a way of thinking and behaving, and not just behavior directly involved with new organization creation. Their five continua are: strategic orientation; commitment to seize opportunities; commitment of resources; control of resources; and management structure. It may well be that, if Stevenson and Gumpert[111] are right, failure to operationalize and study the propensity of entrepreneurs to engage in various *behaviors* (instead of concentrating on *traits*) may lie at the root of past failures to establish the characteristic-performance linkage.

Another indication that behavioral variables should have been researched is provided by Drucker.[112] He lists five entrepreneurial behaviors or thought patterns which he believes are critical to successful new venture management. These five are: the need for [correct] market focus; financial foresight; building a top management team; defining the entrepreneur's personal role; and seeking outside advice. Again, it may be that failure to operationalize and study the propensity of entrepreneurs to engage in these behaviors is related to past failures to establish the characteristic-performance linkage.

Gartner[113] goes so far as to define entrepreneurship itself as a set of behaviors rather than a person, and believes that one is an entrepreneur only in so far as one participates in those behaviors. Thus, in this view, the characteristics of an entrepreneur *must* be behaviors and *only* behaviors.

The concept of studying behaviors instead of personality traits will be further discussed during the following literature reviews pertaining to the strategy implementation literature and to the psychological literature.

Possible Contingency of the Characteristic-Performance Link

Another facet of the characteristics of the entrepreneur which may have been overlooked in previous research is that the nature of their linkage to new venture performance may not be universal, but may instead be contingent upon the existence of contextual criteria. Timmons[114] lends credence to this position by stating that "the wide range in the nature of the businesses and the entrepreneurs who have started them make generalizations about their characteristics at best risky, and at worst, somewhat misleading." Miller,[115] defining entrepreneurship as the process by which organizations renew themselves and their markets by pioneering, innovation, and risk-taking, found not only that entrepreneurship is a function of the organizational structure, the strategy of the firm, and the characteristics of the entrepreneur, but also that the nature of that relationship is contingent upon the type of the firm involved. Sandberg and Hofer[116] state that the interactive effects of industry structure, strategy, and the characteristics of the entrepreneur have a far greater impact on new venture performance than any of those variables in isolation. Gartner,[117] defining entrepreneurs as those who start new organizations, recommends studying the entrepreneur in terms of those activities undertaken to enable the organization to come into existence. Given that different organizations are created with different actions, such behavioral views would also lead to contingency theory.

A more detailed explication of contingency criteria will be forthcoming during the literature review of the strategy implementation literature.

Teams as Contributing to Entrepreneurial Characteristics

Another notable paucity of research linking entrepreneurial characteristics with new venture performance involves the concept of entrepreneurial teams. MacMillan et. al.[118] found that 42% of the venture capitalists they studied felt that a balanced management team was essential to the successful functioning of new ventures and that such a team could make up for certain shortcomings in the characteristics of the lead entrepreneur if that entrepreneur had enough leadership strength. Maidique[119] stated that the results of an as yet unpublished study in which he was involved revealed that "prior joint experience of the founding team" was a key success factor in high-tech ventures. Stuart and Abetti,[120,121] in their study of those factors determining "initial success" of start-up ventures, used entrepreneurial team balance as one of their independent variables, although they were frustrated in that effort by low reliability. Roure[122] found significant portions of performance variance among high tech new ventures explained by prior joint experience of the entrepreneurial team.

Possible Non-Linearity of the Characteristic-Performance Relationship

Yet another area where there has been a paucity of research involving the characteristic-performance link is that of non-linearity of the characteristic-performance relationship. As mentioned above, the study by Begley and Boyd[123] is one of the first to begin bridging this gap. Their research found that risk-taking and tolerance for ambiguity of the entrepreneurship both had curvilinear relationships with venture ROA. In addition, Brockhaus'[124] study reveals strong indications that the locus of control relationship with performance may be non-linear. If such non-linearity is common in characteristic-performance relationships, then the bulk of the past studies into those relationships may have been inconclusive precisely because they assumed linearity.

Synopsis of the Entrepreneurship Literature

Thus, although there is good reason to believe that at least some characteristics of the entrepreneur effect new venture performance, previous research into personality, experience, demographic and other characteristics of the entrepreneur have failed to establish such a link. The foregoing search of the entrepreneurship literature, however, has provided hints that this may have been due to at least the five reasons outlined below:
   1. Failure to investigate all of the relevant characteristics.
   2. Investigation of personality traits rather than of behavior,s.
   3. Failure to consider contingency relations.
   4. Failure to investigate entrepreneurial teams.
   5. Failure to consider non-linear relationships.

The existence of these five reasons suggests that the effect of characteristics of the entrepreneur upon new venture performance have

Model Development

not been thoroughly explored to date despite an extensive empirical literature, and that there is thus little evidence against a model of new venture performance which includes the effects of the characteristics of the entrepreneur. This fact, taken together with the economic literature on entrepreneurship which suggests that the entrepreneur personally performs a unique business function, tends to support the work of Sandberg and others who make the case that indeed new venture performance is a function of the characteristic of the entrepreneur as well as of the structure of the industry in which the venture competes, and its business strategy [NVP=f(E,IS,S)].

Thus, Sandberg's[125] model (see Figure 2-1) will be accepted as the foundation for building a conceptual, structural model of the effects of characteristics of the entrepreneur upon new venture performance in an attempt to answer the research questions which have been posed in this thesis.

As ideas relevant to the development of this model are explored during the subsequent literature review, the model itself will be developed and changed as an aid to understanding and integrating the impact of that literature.

IMPORTANT DIRECTIONS SUGGESTED BY THE STRATEGY IMPLEMENTATION LITERATURE ON MATCHING MANAGERS TO JOBS

The failure of the entrepreneurship literature to consider contingency relations and behavioral variables, as well as the controversy in that literature as to which, if any, attribute variables should be considered important entrepreneurial characteristics, strongly suggests relations between this entrepreneurship literature and the literature of strategy implementation which seeks to match managers to managerial situations. This strategy implementation literature has in many ways paralleled that entrepreneurship literature, and yet no attempt has been made to date to integrate these two. The following attempt to do so casts light upon several of the problems postulated above to be causing failure of the entrepreneur-performance link.

Review of the Strategy Implementation LIiterature on Matching Managers to Jobs

As least as early as 1974[126], scholars in the field of strategic management had been postulating contingency linkages between general managerial characteristics and business performance. The moderator of

FIGURE 2 - 1

SANDBERG'S BASIC NVP MODEL

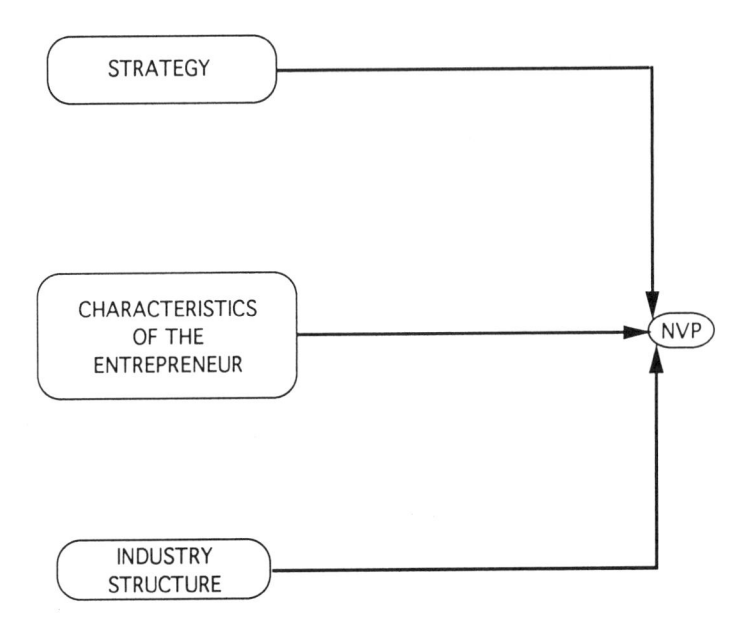

Model Development

these linkages has been seen by this literature as strategy, which has been generally based upon industry life cycles. Wright[127] believed that general managers should be selected for their *behavioral* characteristics contingent upon the stage of the product life cycle of their businesses' major product. He also believed that managers fairly consistently displayed sets of characteristic behaviors which differentiated them one from the other. He delimited these managerial archetypes as "critical administrator", "opportunistic milker", etc.

Following in Wright's footsteps, Wissema et al.,[128] Business Week,[129] and Tichy et al.[130] all developed behavioral managerial archetypes which they recommended should be selected for general managerships contingent upon SBU (strategic business unit) level strategies which they defined as "Build", "Hold", "Sell", etc. (what Hofer & Schendel, 1978,[131] would define as financial substrategies). Leontiades,[132] in developing a somewhat more sophisticated matching model, borrowed his manager prototypes from Eastlack & McDonald,[133] and utilized both strategy and structure at the business level, and strategy and management style at the corporate level, as matching contingencies.

Miles and Snow,[134] on the other hand, took a slightly different tack. They developed strategy archetypes for businesses and used these as contingencies to select managers on the basis of their functional knowledge or expertise. The Strategic Planning Institute (1981) turned also to financial substrategies as contingencies but recommended selecting managers based on age, functional background, and industry and organizational experience. Porter,[135] recommended using generic strategies as contingencies and selecting managers based on skills.

Gupta,[136] in a review of the literature, set forth twenty-three propositions linking effectiveness to six managerial characteristics: organizational familiarly, industry experience, functional background, willingness to take risks, self versus other directedness, and interpersonal orientation. In these propositions, the links between characteristics and effectiveness were contingent upon financial substrategy and organizational level: corporate versus SBU.

In summary, the above scholars set the conceptual precedent that general managers should be selected on the basis of behavioral, attribute, or knowledge characteristics, but that the choice should be contingent upon strategy.

Unfortunately, there has been a near absence of empirical work in the strategy implementation literature to support these concepts. However, in 1984, Gupta and Govindarajan[137] used data from 53 SBUs of eight Fortune 500 diversified firms to test three hypotheses relating characteristics of the general managers of these SBUs to SBU performance. They found support for the notions that general manager experience, willingness to take risks, and tolerance for ambiguity are all positively related to SBU effectiveness and that the character of the relationship is contingent upon SBU financial substrategy. However, the ability of these variables to explain practically significant variance in SBU performance was very limited.

The Szilagyi - Schweiger Model

In 1984, Szilagyi and Schweiger,[138] in an attempt to consolidate and further the manager-matching literature, published what would seem to stand today as the most comprehensive and sophisticated model for matching managers to jobs. Their model uses three "matching criteria": knowledge skills, integrative skills, and administrative skills, which are in turn based upon Katz's[139] skills framework, Kotter's[140] managerial research, Steward's[141] three elements of managerial jobs, and Mintzberg's[142] ten managerial roles. Their matching criteria are used to match job requirements to managerial "skills and behaviors". In other words, job requirements pertaining to knowledge acquisition, use, and dissemination are matched with knowledge "skills and behaviors", etc. Job requirements are in turn largely determined by strategy while the need for managerial skills and behaviors are largely determined by personal attributes although both are contingent upon organizational power, structure, and culture. In addition, the matching criteria are subject to subordination at any given time to any overriding organizational priorities which might exist.

This model not only serves to integrate the manager-matching literature but also serves to explicate several other points of importance to this research. First, it establishes as matching criteria a simple skills typology (knowledge, integrative and administrative skills) which would be of importance in any managerial situation, including the managerial situation of entrepreneurship. Second, it points out that each of these skill areas has sub-skills contained under their "umbrella", a fact of considerable importance to the potential operationalization of this typology. Third, it points out that the requirements of the situation (job requirements) must match with these sub-skills to enhance performance. Fourth, it shows that the requirements of the situation derive from the firm's strategy and other contextual elements. Fifth, it indicates that the skills a manager possesses and the behaviors in which he engages are derived from his attributes together with other contextual elements.

Model Development

A Synthesis of the Relevant Strategy Implementation Lliterature with the Entrepreneurship Literature

The strategy implementation literature clearly indicates that performance in carrying out, or implementing, formulated strategy will affect performance of the firm.[143][144][145][146] This is also true, of course, for new ventures as well.[147] That this "implementation performance" is largely performance on the part of the entrepreneur (or the entrepreneurial team, as more recently formulated by Stuart and Abetti,[148] and Roure[149]) is what Sandberg[150] would mean by the "E" in his model given that strategy and industry had already been formulated. Thus, given the context of the research posed by this thesis, we may draw the literature-supported modification of Sandberg's model of new venture performance shown in Figure 2-2.

IMPORTANT DIRECTIONS SUGGESTED BY THE PSYCHOLOGY, PSYCHOLOGICAL TESTING, AND RELATED LITERATURE

The foregoing literature reviews have been instructive in the attempt to understand some of the reasons why the research questions of this study have not yet been answered despite nearly thirty years of empirical research. If, however, an attempt is to be made to remedy the shortcomings found in that research, many other questions still remain to be answered. If the wrong personality attributes have been investigated, where might one seek a typology of personality traits from which to choose new attributes to investigate? Why have the personality traits previously investigated shown so little explained variance when some of them, such as locus of control, would seem to possess such high face validity? What are skills and how are they measured? If behavioral variables are important to performance, how might such behavior be anticipated before the fact? The key to these and other related questions, if they exist at all, must lie within the literatures of psychology and psychological testing.

Personality Triats and their Effect on Behavior and Individual Performance

The Distinction between Behavior and Performance

Behavior is a specific *observable* action[151] or set of actions on the part of an individual which leads to individual performance, given a

FIGURE 2-2
SANDBERG'S MODEL AUGMENTED BY SZILAGYI-SCHWEIGER MODEL

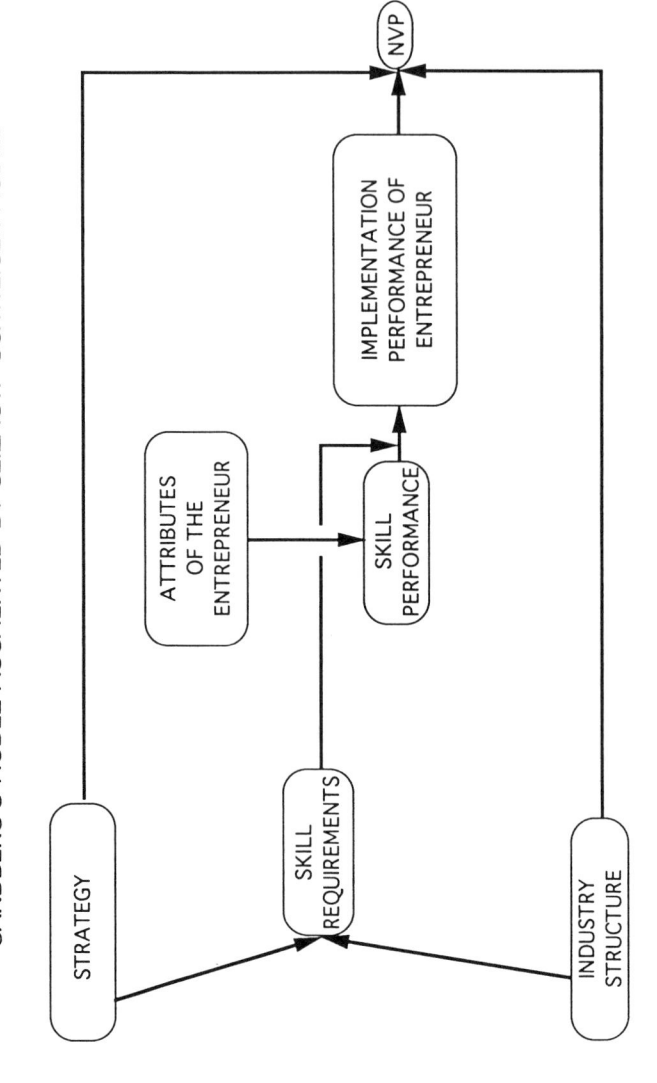

specific context. Performance, on the other hand, is the result of behavior within a specific context. A behavior may be modified as the result of improving a skill; whether this modified behavior will lead to better performance depends partly upon whether and to what extent that particular behavior is required by the situational context in question. Since behavior is viewed as a causal determinant of performance, variables which affect behavior will also necessarily affect performance caused by that behavior. Personality traits affect behavior[152][153] and thus are causal determinants of performance in our model (Figure 2-2).

Selecting Personality Traits for Study

Empirical research in entrepreneurship has addressed many different personality traits such as locus of control, need for achievement, and tolerance for ambiguity. Apparently, however, no one in managerial research has attempted to obtain a universe of such traits and then select appropriate traits for research from that universe.

A review of the psychological literature, on personality traits shows such an approach to be entirely feasible. In 1936, Allport and Odbert compiled a list of over 18,000 trait terms.[154] However, Cattell[155][156] reduced these to first twenty, and then to sixteen traits using cluster and factor analysis. Numerous trait typologies have been published since then, apparently ranging in size from about fifteen[157] to forty-six.[158] Further, many of these trait typologies are translatable one into another by changing factor loadings.[159]

A review of one modern trait typology[160] shows at least four traits which have apparently not been investigated by entrepreneurial researchers, yet which may possess face validity for future studies of entrepreneurial behavior and thus entrepreneurial performance. These are the traits of: activity, excitement seeking, impulsivity, and blunter-monitor.

Activity involves the expenditure of energy in any and all instrumental behaviors, an instrumental behavior being one which has an impact on the environment (as opposed to the inner self).[161] This trait has two major aspects, one being rapidity of pace and the other being high intensity of response.[162]

Excitement seeking contains elements of seeking change, unusual stimuli, and new environments.[163]

Impulsivity implies a lack of the "breaks" of inhibitory control applied to the "metaphorical engine" of achievement, activity, and excitement seeking.[164][165] As such, it may well have a non-linear relation to successful performance.

Blunter-monitor concerns cognitive coping strategies used by people when confronted by threats. Blunting is the avoidance of information whereas monitoring is the opposite (or seeking of complete information).[166]

The Stability of Personality Traits

Another important question for the study of the relationship of personality traits to behavior and thus individual performance involves the issues of their stability and reliability. Personality traits must be reliable in test-retest situations and perhaps over long periods of time as well if they are to be useful predictors of performance.

There has been debate among psychologists over the test-retest reliability of personality trait measures, although the consensus seems to have evolved in favor of longitudinal stability as well as reliability:[167] [168] [169]

> "One of the classic debates in psychology concerns the stability of personality. With rare exception, studies that have correlated objective behavior on two occasions have obtained coefficients below .30... The issue can be resolved by recognizing that most single items of behavior have a high component of error measurement and a narrow range of generality...It is normally not possible to predict single instances of behavior, but...it is possible to predict behavior averaged over a sample of situations and/or occasions."[170]

Also of some import as regards personality traits, and the study of entrepreneurship is this:

> "The degree of aggregation [of behaviors] that is required [to produce test-retest reliability in trait measures] varies inversely with the degree to which events are ego-involving..."[171]

To the extent that most entrepreneurial situations are ego-involving, Epstein would expect less need for aggregation of behaviors to stabilize the relationship between them and personality traits.

The work of Anderson[172] on locus of control and coping behaviors of business owner-managers whose businesses had been destroyed by a flood following Hurricane Agnes in Pennsylvania in June of 1972 is a useful example supporting the longitudinal stability of personality traits.[173][174][175] With a sample of 64 owner-managers, Anderson[176] found that mean *change* in locus of control over a two-year period was only 0.41 on a scale of 1 to 23, while each of the four subgroups composing this sample had mean changes in locus of control ranging from .01 to 1.58. Although Anderson does not report the standard deviation nor variance of locus of control for his sample, Rotter (1966, whose scale Anderson used) reported standard deviations of 3.88 and 4.06 for two locus of control samples of around 600 each and split-half and test-retest reliabilities ranging from .65 to .70. Anderson's locus of control change numbers show remarkable stability over a two and one-half year period involving extreme emotional upheaval which might have been assumed to change the locus of control of the owner-managers. The work of Epstein, Anderson, and others thus suggests that personality traits are quite stable.

The Causal Relation between Personality Traits and Performances

Given that additional personality traits are available for investigation, the question still remains as to why such traits as locus of control have not shown more explained new venture performance, particularly since such traits are seen to display reliability and longitudinal stability.

In the context of personnel selection, measures of individual differences in personality traits have consistently demonstrated low validity for almost all occupational groups.[177] Hollenbeck and Whitener[178] have suggested that the reason this is so is because such traits are moderated and mediated by other variables. In particular, they have modeled personality traits as being distally causal to job performance, being mediated by motivation and moderated by ability. They drew this idea from Maier[179][180] who was not explicit in his definition of motivation, but who regarded motivation as being a determinant of behavior per unit time. Motivation is likewise often defined as that which causes, channels, and sustains behavior.[181] In line with these uses and definitions of "motivation", the term "behavioral propensity" will be substituted for future clarity. Hollenbeck and Whitener's model is thus altered as in Figure 2-3 below.

This suggestion lends credence to the Szilagyi - Schweiger model which shows personality traits as well as other variables as leading to behaviors. It also would explain why empirical research attempting to link personality traits of entrepreneurs to new venture performance has

FIGURE 2 - 3

HOLLENBECK - WHITENER MODEL

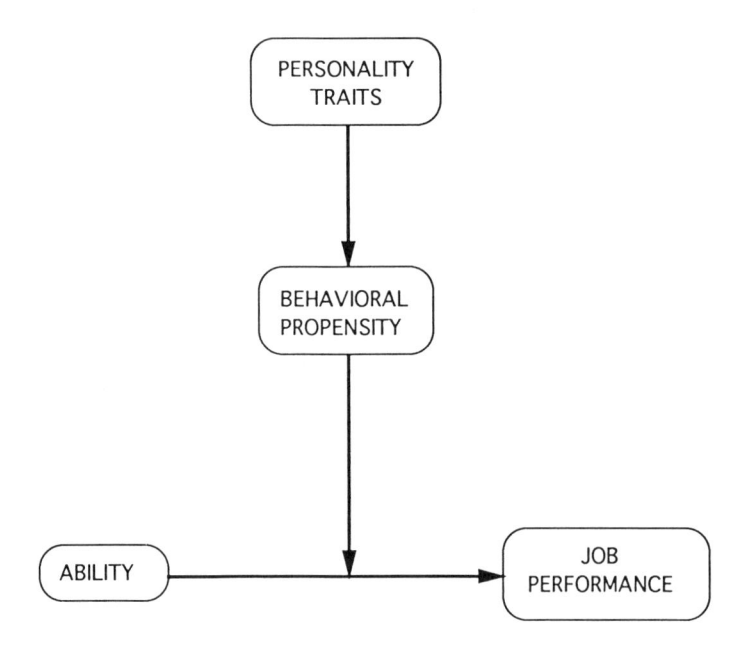

Model Development

shown such disappointing results. For example, if the moderating influence of ability on behavioral propensity were positive and multiplicative as is likely the case,[182] the effect of personality traits on job performance would be nearly zero under conditions of low skill, even if the correlations between traits and behavioral propensity, and between behavioral propensity and performance were both high. In fact, even at high levels of ability, if the correlation between traits and behavioral propensity, and between behavioral propensity and performance were both .67, traits would still only explain 20% of the variance in performance with this model.

We may now use the above literature review to modify our model to that shown in Figure 2-4.

Other Variables Affecting Behavioral Propensity

Given the Hollenbeck-Whitener model with behavioral propensity mediating the effect of personality traits upon performance, the question arises as to what other variables drive this propensity in addition to personality traits.

The Causal Relationship between Self-efficacy and Behavioral Propensity

Albert Bandura of Stanford University is one of the foremost advocates of the role of self-efficacy in motivating performance:

> Knowledge, transformational operations, and component skills are necessary but insufficient for accomplished performances. Indeed, people often do not behave optimally, even though they know full well what to do. This is because self-referent thought also mediates the relationship between knowledge and action.[183]

> In applying skills, strong self-efficaciousness intensifies and sustains the effort needed for optimal performance, which is difficult to realize if one is beleaguered by self-doubts.[184]

FIGURE 2 - 4

PREVIOUS MODEL WITH ADDITION OF HOLLENBECK - WHITENER

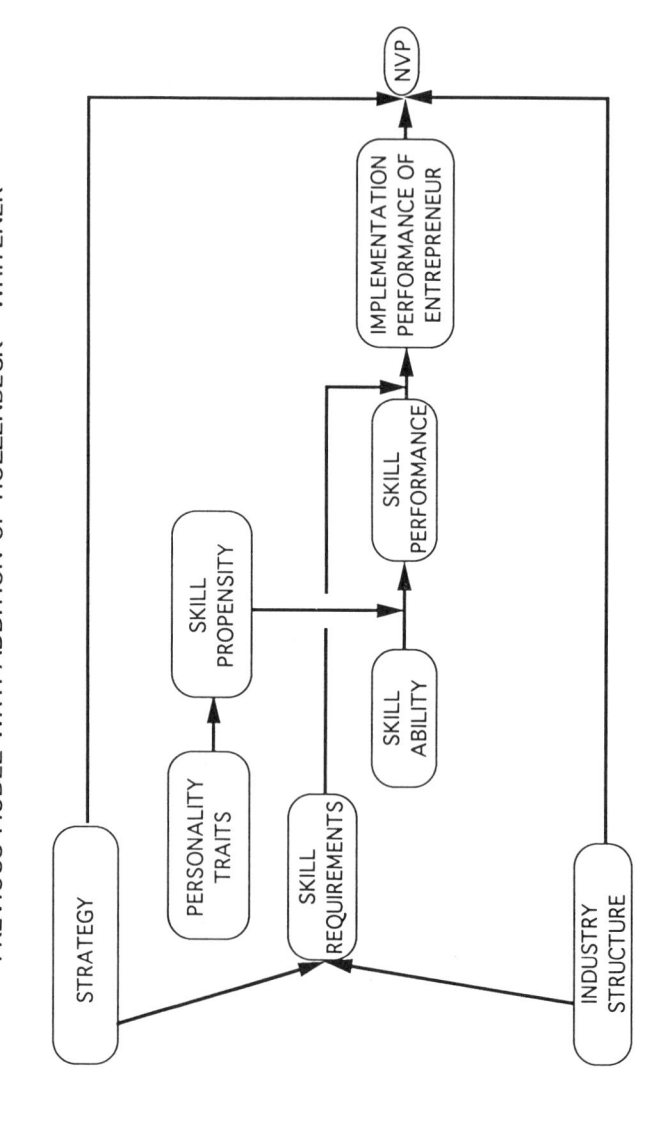

There is also good reason to believe that self-efficaciousness in regard to a skill depends partially on the extent of possession of the skill:

> Enactive attainments provide the most influential source of efficacy information because it can be based on authentic mastery experiences. Successes heighten perceived self-efficacy; repeated failures lower it, especially if failures occur early in the course of events and do not reflect lack of effort or adverse external circumstances.[185]

The Causal Relationship between Values and Behavioral Propensity

There is also good reason to believe that values held by persons affect their propensity to perform various behaviors. Hambrick, in a discussion of the importance of values to management considerations writes:

> Values affect an executive's contributions...in three ways. First, values cause executives to prefer certain behaviors and outcomes over others. Second, they affect the way in which the person searches and filters data used in decision making. Third, values affect the person's receptivity to any incentives and norms.....[186]

These beliefs are in turn supported by other psychological as well as management literature.[187][188]

Based upon this literature, we may now modify our model to that shown in Figure 2-5.

The Relationship Between Behavioral Propensity, skills, and Performance

The above literature review has established that values, self-efficacy, and personality traits are among the determinants of propensity to behave, and that behavior leads to performance given a specific context. Further, it may be recalled that the Szilagyi - Schweiger model used a skills typology as criteria with which to match situational requirements to the specific skills and behaviors of the manager.

FIGURE 2 - 5

PREVIOUS MODEL WITH ADDITION OF BANDURA AND HAMBRICK

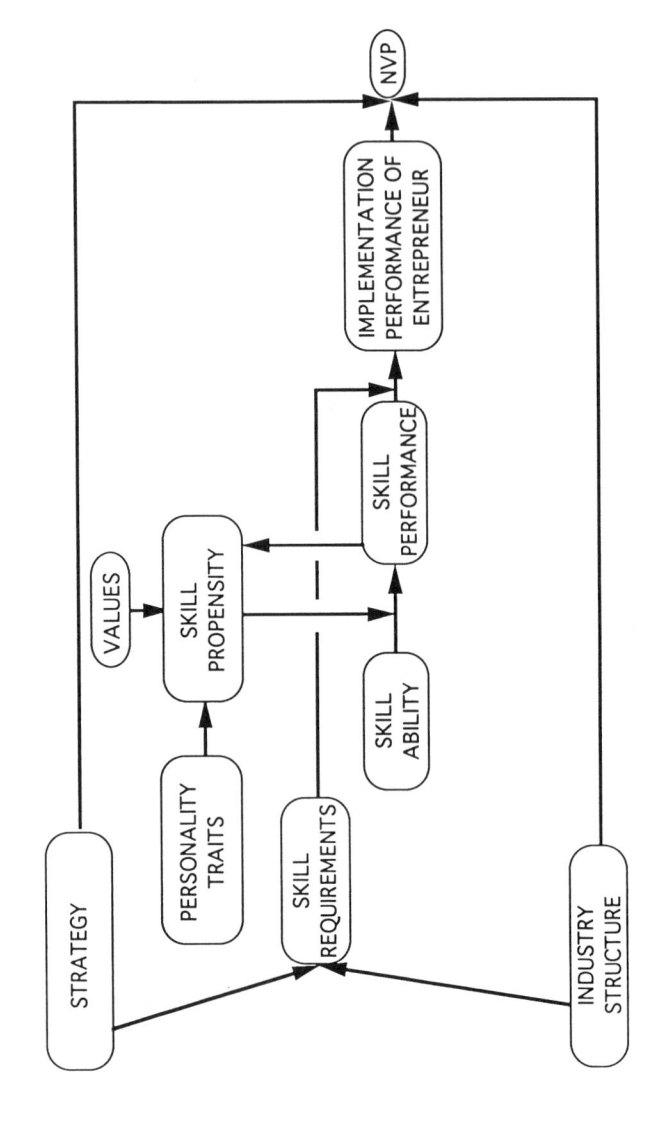

Model Development 43

The industrial psychologist Maier[189] has defined abilities as being of two kinds: (1) aptitudes (abilities as they develop without training); and achievements (abilities which contain the modifications that are induced by training or practice). Achievement in this context means proficiency, a synonym for skill.[190] This study will refer to Maier's first ability as an aptitude and his second ability as a skill. In these terms, Maier[191] presents the following equation:

$$\text{skill} = \text{Aptitude} \times \text{Training}$$

He further presents a discussion which leads to the following relationship:[192]

$$\text{Performance} = \text{skill} \times \text{Propensity to Perform the skill}$$

These relationships are consistent with both the Hollenbeck - Whitener model and the Szilagyi - Schweiger model. Given these relationships (plus the fact that the requirements for the performance of a skill will tend to call forth performance of that skill), we may now modify our model to that shown in Figure 2-6 as the "Full model":

Mental Aptitudes

It may be recalled from the literature review of the economic theories of entrepreneurship that, as regards the more modern theories, the entrepreneur is seen to be a manager, and that the aptitudes and skills peculiar to the entrepreneur qua entrepreneur are mental aptitudes and skills. Further, the Szilagyi - Schweiger model and the literature utilized in constructing that model[193,194,195,196] all imply that the aptitudes and skills of managers are also mental aptitudes and skills. Therefore, to deal with the skills of the entrepreneur we must deal with mental skills and thus mental aptitudes.

Introduction to Intelligence

The field of intelligence is that branch of psychology which deals with mental aptitudes. Accounts of intelligence are of two basic kinds: explicit theories and implicit theories.[197] Explicit theories are based upon objective test data collected from the performance of tasks presumed to measure intelligence. Implicit theories of intelligence are based on people's conceptions of what intelligence is, and in this sense need to be "discovered" rather than "formulated." Both types of theory are needed, and in fact explicit theories may be seen as formalizations of

FIGURE 2 - 6

FULL MODEL

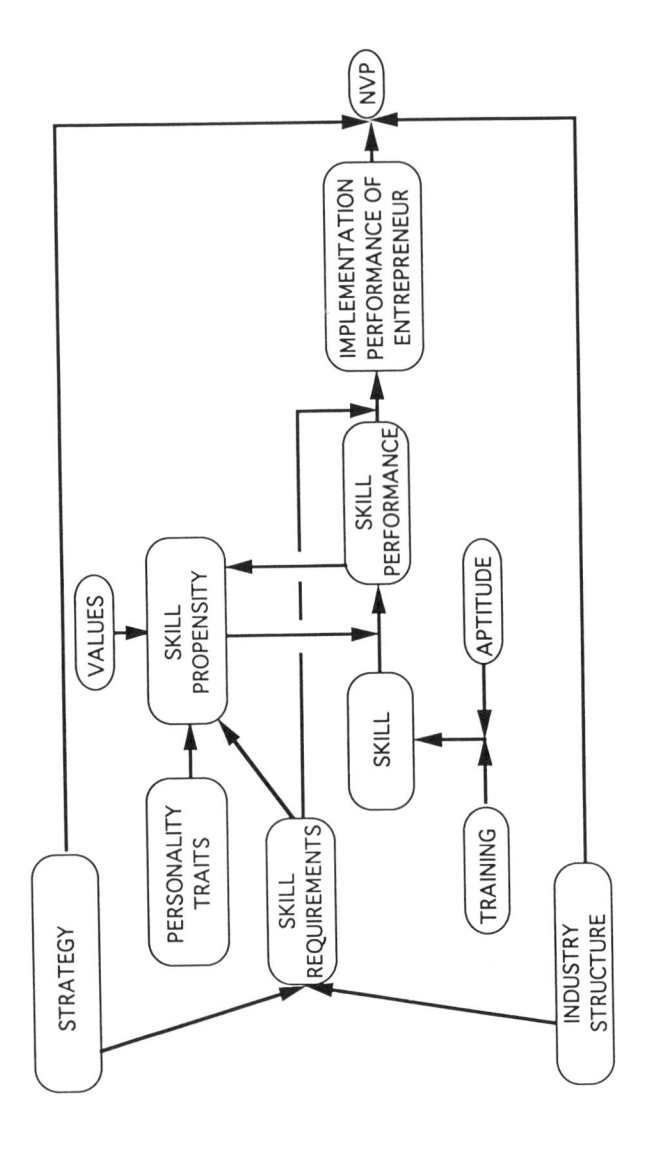

experts' implicit theories.[198] The types of intelligence theories dealt with in psychology are usually explicit theories, but are "kept on track" by implicit theories. Explicit theories of human intelligence in psychology are further broken into two broad types: differential (or psychometric) theories and cognitive (or information-processing) theories.[199] The differential theories attempt to understand intelligence in terms of a set of underlying aptitudes identified through factor analysis of test results. Examples of this type theory are the works of Spearman,[200] Thurstone,[201] and Guilford.[202] The cognitive theories attempt to understand intelligence in terms of the mental processes that take place during cognitive task performance, analyzing mental functioning much as if the brain were a type of computer. This is done by measuring the speed and accuracy of hypothesized mental processes as well as studying the mental strategies used during processing. Examples of this type research are the works of Hunt,[203] Jensen,[204] and Sternberg.[205]

Differential Theories

The earliest differential theorist was Spearman, the "father of factor analysis".[206] Spearman[207] proposed that intelligence comprises two kinds of factors, a general factor and specific factors. The aptitude represented by the general factor, g, affects performance on all intellectual tasks while the specific factors each affect performance only on each specific task.

Thurstone[208] invented multiple factor analysis and, in 1938,[209] applied it to intelligence to derive seven primary mental aptitudes: verbal comprehension, verbal fluency, number, spatial visualization, memory, reasoning, and perceptual speed. Later, in 1941, Cattell reconciled the views of Thurstone and Spearman by showing that Spearman's "g" was essentially a second-order factor influencing all seven of Thurstone's factors.[210]

Since Thurstone, others[211,212,213,214] have proposed elaborations on Spearman's and Thurstone's models by using various hierarchical arrangements of n-order factors.[215]

Guilford however, proposed a non-hierarchical factor-theory model.[216,217] He conceived of a three-dimensional model, or cube, with the three dimensions representing mental operations, the contents operated upon, and the products of those operations. Factor theories generally specify mental structures, but not the mental processes that underlie contextually appropriate behaviors. In this regard, Guilford's theory is a distinct exception to other differential theories of intelligence.[218]

In his original presentation of the model, Guilford [219] postulated five operations, four contents and six products. Thus, there were 5x4x6=120 different factors in his model. These 120 factors were arrived at using orthogonal factor rotation.[220] [221] Later[222] the model was expanded to include 150 factors by splitting the original figural content up into visual and auditory contents. As of 1982, the existence of around 100 of these factors had been demonstrated by Guilford and his co-workers.[223] Moreover, Meeker[224] has done work relating many of these factors to the Stanford-Binet, WISC, and WPPSI intelligence tests, showing that these tests in fact incorporate many of Guilford's factors. Further, the Educational Testing Service has published a battery of intelligence tests called the ETS Kit of Factor-Referenced Cognitive Tests which include tests for many of Guilford's factors.[225]

Information-processing Theories

Information-processing (or cognitive) theories of intelligence go back at least as far as 1883 when Galton supported the importance of speed in mental functioning.[226] Later researchers complicated this view to investigate the importance of speed of choice-making when humans were exposed to simple stimuli, the "choice-reaction-time" paradigm.[227] Still later investigators have looked at speed of access to lexical information stored in long term memory, as well as the speed of various reasoning processes.[228] Essentially, investigators in this area are now seeking to understand intelligence in terms of the processes individuals use to perform problem solving of various kinds by breaking mental tasks down into their component parts and timing and analyzing these portions of the process.[229]

A Synthesis of the Differential and Information-processing Paradigms.

In 1971, Cattell[230] published a hierarchical, differential theory of intelligence that he had been developing since at least 1941 when he attempted to design "culture free" intelligence tests. This theory, while essentially differential, provided, at the same time, a bridge to the information-processing paradigm. The Cattell theory postulates two subfactors of Spearman's "g", g_f and g_c (i.e. fluid and crystallized abilities or aptitudes). Crystallized ability operates in areas where judgements have been taught systematically or experienced before. Fluid abilities, by contrast, show up in tests where the sheer perception of

Model Development

complex relations is involved to such an extent that borrowing from stored, crystallized judgmental skills brings no advantage.[231] Here was a differential theory which seemed to be modeling the brain with a computer-like analogy: crystallized abilities referring to the memory of the computer, and fluid abilities referring to its processor.

Sternberg,[232] building on the work of Cattell and many others, has attempted an outright synthesis of the differential and information-processing schools with his triarchic theory of human intelligence. Sternberg's triarchic theory is based upon a structural theory of mental abilities (or aptitudes) in which the fundamental unit of analysis is the information-processing component.[233]

Components may be classified by function and by level of generality.[234] By function there are three types of components: metacomponents which are specific realizations of control processes that may loosely be referred to as "executive" components and which determine processing strategies; performance components which are used in the execution of the task performances dictated by these strategies; and knowledge-acquisition components which are used in gaining new knowledge for processing and storage. By level of generality, each of these three types of components may occupy any of three hierarchical levels: general components are required to perform all tasks within a given task universe; class components are required to perform a proper subset of tasks that includes at least two tasks within that given universe; and specific components that are required to perform single tasks within the task subset.[235] Factors, Sternberg[236] believes, are ways of recognizing how these components cluster together:

> Factor scores are useful in summarizing performance, because rather than being bound by the constraints of the ways in which tasks and subtasks are put together (as are task and subtask scores), they are bound by the constraints of individual differences - of how components tend to cluster together in tasks and subtasks.[237]

Thus, Sternberg believes that the factors of differential theories are the result of the structuring of components:

> [While] factors do not occupy a central position in the present [componential] theory, as they do in

most differential theories, ... they are nevertheless important, indicating as they do constellations of components that tend to co-occur in the tasks we use to measure mental abilities.[238]

Sternberg thus points out that there are many similarities between his componential theory and Guilford's structure-of-intellect theory, with the main difference being that his (Sternberg's) theory is hierarchical while Guilford's is cubic and thus non-hierarchical.[239] However, it should be noted that Guilford's tests usually load significantly on more than one of his (Guilford's) factors, a clear indication that Guilford's tests may in fact be measuring Sternberg's hierarchical components.[240][241]

THE FURTHER DEVELOPMENT OF KATZ'S SKILLS TYPOLOGY AND ITS SYNTHESIS WITH GUILFORD'S STRUCTURE OF INTELLECT MODEL

Investigation of the literature-based model developed thus far (Figure 2-6) necessitates delineating mental aptitudes and skills, and linking them to each other.

Extending Katz's Skill Typology

The skill typology of Katz was used as the basis for matching requirements and skills in the Szilagyi and Schweiger model.[242] However, these three skill categories are too broad to measure accurately, to link with strategy or industry structure, or to match with specific mental aptitudes. In fact, Szilagyi and Schweiger indicate that each subsumes more specific skills under its broad umbrella. Therefore, each of these three skill areas will now be analyzed in somewhat greater depth.

Technical Skills

Katz defines technical skill as an understanding of, and proficiency in, a specific kind of activity.[243] In their model, Szilagyi and Schweiger[244] denote in essence three specific groups of activities or technical activity arenas: the specific functional arena, the business arena, and the industry arena. Based upon these ideas, a useful method of subdividing Katz' technical skill area would be as follows:

Model Development

1. *Technical product/service skill*: skill in understanding and designing or redesigning the specific products or services rendered by the business.

2. *Technical organizational skill*: skill in understanding and designing or redesigning the specific business organization in question.

3. *Technical industry skill*: skill in understanding and maneuvering in the business' industry.

Human Skills

Katz[245] defines human skills as the ability to work effectively as a group member and to build cooperative effort. Szilagyi and Schweiger[246] denote in essence in their model two kinds of human skills: those involved in dealing with the internal organization and those involved in dealing with the external environment. Based upon this idea, a useful method of subdividing Katz' human skills would be as follows:

1. *Leadership skill*: skill in motivating and positively effecting the behavior of organizational members.

2. *Networking skill*: skill involved in creating and effectively utilizing networks in the organization's environment.

Conceptual Skills

Katz[247] defines conceptual skills as involving the ability to see the enterprise as a whole. Szilagyi and Schweiger[248] term these skills administrative and include within them a variety of skills involved in understanding and controlling the enterprise as a whole, including innovative enterprise behavior. Based upon these ideas, and considering that we are dealing herein with new ventures, a useful method of subdividing Katz' conceptual skill area would be as follows:

1. *Administrative skill*: skill in comprehensive, detailed planning.

2. *Entrepreneurial skill*: skill in conceiving opportunities to profitability reallocate company resources to new endeavors.

Reviewing Guilford's Structure of Intellect Model

The extension of Katz's skills typology above was accomplished partly for the purpose of allowing elements of that typology to be matched to specific mental abilities. For a model of mental abilities rich and comprehensive enough to accomplish the purpose, one must look to Guilford,'s Structure of Intellect model.

As mentioned earlier, Guilford employs a cubic model consisting of three dimensions which purport to describe any possible mental aptitude, the three dimensions being operation, content, and product.[249] Operations are the types of mental acts performed, contents are the form or type of information operated upon, and products are the output of those operations.

Operations

In her 1969 book entitled "Structure of intellect", Mary Meeker has done an outstanding job of clarifying the terms used in the model. In her words, operations represent: "Major kinds of intellectual activities or processes; things the organism does with the raw materials of information, information being defined as 'that which the organism discriminates".[250]

Guilford has identified five major operations: cognition, memory, evaluation, convergent production, and divergent production. These have been defined by Meeker[251] as follows:

"Cognition: Immediate discovery, awareness, rediscovery, or recognition of information in various forms; comprehension or understanding."[252]

"Memory: Retention or storage, with some degree of availability, of information in the form it was committed to storage and in response to the same cues in connection with which it was learned."[253]

"Evaluation: Reaching decisions or making judgements concerning criterion satisfaction (correctness, suitability, adequacy, desirability, etc.) of information."[254]

"Convergent Production: Generation of information from given information, where the emphasis is upon achieving unique or conventionally accepted best outcomes. It is likely the given information (cue) fully determines the response."[255]

"Divergent Production: Generation of information from given information, where emphasis is upon variety and quality of output from the same source. Likely to involve what has been called transfer. This operation is most clearly involved in aptitudes of creative potential."[256]

Contents
Contents represent the broad types of information upon which these processes operate. Guilford[257] has defined five types: Visual figural (called figural), auditory figural (called auditory), symbolic, semantic, and behavioral.

Products
Products have been defined by Meeker[258] as the organization that information takes in the organism's processing of it. Of these Guilford[259] has identified six types: units, classes, relations, systems, transformations, and implications. Among these, the last two are of import to the current research.

Transformations require the redefinition or modification of the existing information into new information. This kind of ability may demand more flexibility than normal and has been found to often characterize people who have been termed creative.[260]

Implications involve the ability to foresee consequences involved in various kinds of information.

Matching Aptitudinal Elements from Guilford's Model with Elements from Katz's Extended skills Typology

Technical Product/Service Skill
The aptitude from Guilford's model which most closely matches the technical product or service design skill is that called divergent production of figural transformations (DFT). Divergent production was picked because design involves the generation of new information from existing information. Figural content was picked because both products and services are usually designed using visual and figural information. The product of transformation was picked because design requires the modification and redefinition of existing information. This factor (DFT) has been termed "adaptive flexibility",[261] which lends credibility to its choice in this instance.

Technical Organizational Skill
The aptitude from Guilford's model which matches the technical organizational skill is that called evaluation of symbolic systems (ESS). Evaluation was picked as the representative operation because organizational business skill is normally exercised through evaluation of the various functions. Symbolic content was picked because functions in business are often evaluated through the use of numbers. Systems was picked as the product because the systems aspect of the symbolic information is its most relevant form of organization when evaluation of business functions takes place. This factor (ESS), according to Guilford, relates to the soundness of conclusions.[262]

Technical Industry Skill
The aptitude from Guilford's model which matches with the technical industry skill is that called cognition of semantic implications (CMI). The operation of cognition has been picked because, in dealing within industry milieu, the processes of discovery, awareness, and comprehension seem paramount. The semantic content was picked because most information involving industries consists of the spoken or written word the product of implications was picked because the ability to see consequences involved in industry information is endemic to being skilled within an industry.

Leadership Skill
That aptitude from Guilford's model which most closely matches with the skills of leadership within the business is the evaluation of

Model Development 53

behavioral transformations (EBT). This factor was picked because leadership involves the evaluation of how behaviors can and have been transformed by actions on the part of the leader.

Networking Skill

Cognition of behavioral implications (CBI) is the aptitude most closely matched to the skill used to build networks. Cognition is the operation of choice because, as in dealing with industries, immediate awareness and comprehension is paramount. Behavior is the appropriate informational content, and implications (or the ability to foresee consequences involved in the information) is the appropriate product.

Administrative Skill

That aptitude from Guilford's model which matches with the administrative skill within the business is divergent production of semantic implications (DMI). Divergent production is the operation most involved because new information must be generated from existent information when exercising administrative or planning skills. The informational content is usually the written or spoken word, while the product is the implications of the information. Guilford[263] refers to this factor in conjunction with planning ability.

Entrepreneurial Skill

The entrepreneurial skill is essentially a facility in conceiving the opportunity to profitably reallocate company resources to new endeavors in the face of disequilibrium.[264,265] The aptitude from Guilford's model which matches best with this skill is divergent production of semantic transformations (DMT), a factor referred to by Guilford[266] as the "originality factor". The operation picked is divergent production because of its emphasis on variety and the generation of information from given information. The semantic content is appropriate because disequilibrium information is usually in the form of written and spoken words. The product of transformation is the correct one because change is what entrepreneurship is all about.

Summary

In summary, each of the skills in Katz's extended skills typology appear to be matched by one of the aptitudinal elements in Guilford's Structure of Intellect model. Returning to Maier's[267] equation: "skill = Aptitude x Training", it is evident that, if this match is indeed as strong as its face validity, then Guilford's validated tests for each aptitude should provide a causal determinant of its respective skill.

THE CURRENT RESEARCH MODEL

The elements of the full model (Figure 2-6) which will be concentrated upon in the current research are shown in Figure 2-7.

These elements have been chosen from the full model for two basic reasons. First, the above literature review has revealed skills behavior on the part of the entrepreneur to be more proximal to new venture performance than other entrepreneurial traits heretofore studied (such as personality traits or values) and therefore the skill linkages of the model are of primary interest. Second, the direct relationship of each of the skill propensities with strategy and industry structure (through the skill requirements in Figure 2-6) is also distal to NVP. Further, attempting to measure this linkage would require nearly as many path coefficients as the rest of the model combined and thus would require a much larger sample than this research warrants. Exploratory research must establish the basic validity of the overall model before attempts requiring even larger scale samples are feasible.

SUMMARY OF LITERATURE REVIEW

The above literature review has produced numerous salient points, some of the more important of which are summarized as follows:

The previous research attempting to link the characteristics of the entrepreneur with new venture performance has largely been unable to do so. The many reasons for this stem partly from a failure to systematically analyze the entrepreneur's function, and partly from failure to take advantage of the findings of other disciplines.

An analysis of the economic theories of entrepreneurship suggests both that the entrepreneur is a manager (and thus subject to the tenets of the strategy implementation literature) and that the peculiar function of the entrepreneur qua entrepreneur demands a further set of mental skills.

A look at the strategy implementation literature attempting to match managers to managerial situations suggests that managerial performance is driven by various mental skills of the manager and thatthe requirements for these skills are contingent upon the firm's strategy and environmental context.

Model Development 55

FIGURE 2 - 7
RESEARCH MODEL

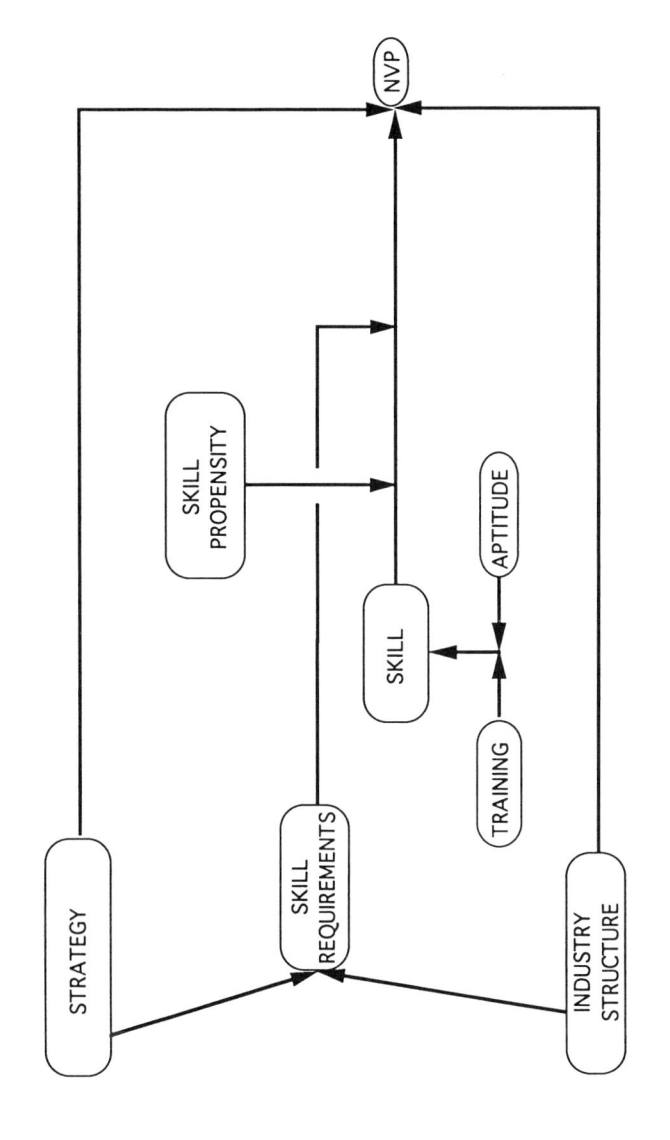

A review of the psychological and psychological testing and related literature indicates that personality traits are mediated and moderated by skills and skill behavior in their link with performance. Further, that literature possesses rich and comprehensive models capable of linking mental aptitudes to entrepreneurial skills and providing prevalidated scales for the measurement of those aptitudes.

This literature review has driven the development of a structural model of the effects of the entrepreneur upon new venture performance, and, in turn, has led to the construction of the current research model which will be fully explicated and operationalized in the next chapter.

Notes:

[1] Hoselitz, B. (1960). The early history of entrepreneurial theory. In J. Spengler & W. Allen (Eds.) *Essays in Economic Thought: Aristotle to Marshall.* pp 234-258. Chicago: Rand McNally, p. 252.

[2] Ibid, p. 235.

[3] Hébert, R. & Link, A. (1982). *The entrepreneur.* New York: Praeger Publishers.

[4] Ibid, p. 14.

[5] Martin, D.T. (1979). Alternative views of Mengerian entrepreneurship. *History of Political Economy, 11,* 271.

[6] Hoselitz, B. (1960). The early history of entrepreneurial theory. In J. Spengler & W. Allen (Eds.) *Essays in Economic Thought: Aristotle to Marshall.* pp 234-258. Chicago: Rand McNally.

[7] Hébert, R. & Link, A. (1982). *The entrepreneur.* New York: Praeger Publishers, pp. 25-27.

[8] Ibid, pp 27-29.

[9] Ibid, p. 29.

[10] Say, J.B. (1827). *A treatise on political economy* (3rd Ed). (American Edition). Philadelphia: John Grigg, p. 20.

[11] Hébert, R. & Link, A. (1982). *The entrepreneur.* New York: Praeger Publishers, p. 32.

[12] Say, J.B. (1827). *A treatise on political economy* (3rd Ed). (American Edition). Philadelphia: John Grigg, p. 100.

[13] Smith, A. (1963). *An inquiry into the nature and causes of the wealth of nations* (Vols. 1 & 2). Homewood, ILL: Richard D. Irwin.

[14]Hébert, R. & Link, A. (1982). *The entrepreneur.* New York: Praeger Publishers, pp. 36-45.
[15]Ibid, p. 45.
[16]Ibid, p. 46.
[17]Ibid, p. 58-59.
[18]Menger, C. (1950). *Principles of economics.* Translated by J. DIingwall and B.F. Hoselitz. Glencoe, IL: The Free Press, pp. 159-160.
[19]Ibid, p. 161
[20]Kirzner, I. (1979). *Perception, opportunity, and profit.* Chicago: University of Chicago Press.
[21]Schultz, T. (1980). Investment in entrepreneurial ability. *Scandinavian Journal of Economics, 82,* 437-448.
[22]Hébert, R. & Link, A. (1982). *The entrepreneur.* New York: Praeger Publishers, p. 109.
[23]Brockhaus, R.H. (1980A). Psychological and environmental factors which distinguish the successful from unsuccessful entrepreneur: A long study. *Academy of Management Proceedings.* 368-372.
[24]Brockhaus, R.H. (1980B). Risk-taking propensity of entrepreneurs. *Academy of Management Journal, 23,* 509-520.
[25]Hébert, R. & Link, A. (1982). *The entrepreneur.* New York: Praeger Publishers.
[26]Ibid, p. 66.
[27]Clark, J.B. (1907). *Essentials of economic theory.* New York: Macmillan, pp. 118-119.
[28]Hébert, R. & Link, A. (1982). *The entrepreneur.* New York: Praeger Publishers, pp. 66-67.
[29]Clark, J.B. (1907). *Essentials of economic theory.* New York: Macmillan, pp. 123-124.
[30]Knight, F.H. (1921). *Risk, uncertainty, and profit.* New York: Houghton Mifflin, p. 276.
[31]Ibid, p. 310.
[32]Von Mises, L. (1966). *Human action,* 3rd Ed. Chicago: Henry Regnery Co, p. 253.
[33]Ibid, p. 252.
[34]Schultz, T. (1980). Investment in entrepreneurial ability. *Scandinavian Journal of Economics, 82,* p. 441.

[35]Hébert, R. & Link, A. (1982). *The entrepreneur*. New York: Praeger Publishers, p. 76.
[36]Ibid, . 77.
[37]Schumpeter, J. (1934). *The theory of economic development*. Cambridge, MA: Harvard University Press, p. 75 footnote.
[38]Schumpeter, J. (1939). Business cycles. New York: McGraw-Hill, p. 62.
[39]Hébert, R. & Link, A. (1982). *The entrepreneur*. New York: Praeger Publishers, p. 78.
[40]Schumpeter, J. (1934). *The theory of economic development*. Cambridge, MA: Harvard University Press, p. 75.
[41]Hébert, R. & Link, A. (1982). *The entrepreneur*. New York: Praeger Publishers, p. 109.
[42]Ibid, pp. 90-91.
[43]Kirzner, I.M. (1985). *Discovery and the capitalist process*. Chicago: The University of Chicago Press, p. 7.
[44]Hébert, R. & Link, A. (1982). *The entrepreneur*. New York: Praeger Publishers, p. 96.
[45]Kirzner, I. (1979). *Perception, opportunity, and profit*. Chicago: University of Chicago Press, p. 7.
[46]Ibid, p. 7.
[47]Hébert, R. & Link, A. (1982). *The entrepreneur*. New York: Praeger Publishers, p. 99.
[48]Kirzner, I. (1979). *Perception, opportunity, and profit*. Chicago: University of Chicago Press, p. 104.
[49]Ibid, p. 94.
[50]Hébert, R. & Link, A. (1982). *The entrepreneur*. New York: Praeger Publishers, p. 102.
[51]Schultz, T. (1975). The value of the ability to deal with disequilibria. *Journal of Economic Literature, 13*. 827-846.
[52]Schultz, T. (1980). Investment in entrepreneurial ability. *Scandinavian Journal of Economics, 82*, 437-448.
[53]Ibid.
[54]Schultz, T. (1975). The value of the ability to deal with disequilibria. *Journal of Economic Literature, 13*. 827-846.
[55]Schultz, T. (1980). Investment in entrepreneurial ability. *Scandinavian Journal of Economics, 82*, 437-448.
[56]Ibid.

[57] Ibid, p. 446.
[58] Stevenson, H. & Gumpert, D. (1985). The heart of entrepreneurship. *Harvard Business Review, 63*(2), 85-94.
[59] Gartner, W.B. (1987). *What are we talking about when we talk about entrepreneurship?* Paper presented at the Academy of Management meeting at N.O. (in abstracts), 1-20.
[60] Schumpeter, J.A. (1935). The analysis of economic change. *Review of Economic Statistics*, (May), 2-10.
[61] Meyer, H.H., Walker, W.B., & Litwin, G.H. (1961). Motive patterns and risk perferences associated with entrepreneurship. *Journal of Abnormal and Social Psychology, 63*(3), 570-574.
[62] Brockhaus, R.H. (1980). Psychological and environmental factors which distinguish the successful from unsuccessful entrepreneur: A long study. *Academy of Management Proceedings.* 368-372.
[63] Kogan, N. & Wallace, M. (1964). *Risk Taking.* New York: Holt, Rinehart, and Winston.
[64] Brockhaus, R.H. (1980B). Risk-taking propensity of entrepreneurs. *Academy of Management Journal, 23,* 509-520.
[65] Begley, T.M. & Boyd, D.P. (1987). Psychological characteristics associated with performance in entrepreneurial firms and smaller businesses. *Journal of Business Venturing, 2*(1), 79-93.
[66] McClelland, D.C. (1961). *The achieving society.* Princeton, N.J.: Van Nostrand.
[67] McClelland, D.C. (1965). N achievement and entrepreneurship: A longitudinal study. *Journal Of Personality and Social Psychology, 1*(4), 389-392.
[68] McClelland, D.C. & Winter, D.G. (1969). *Motivating economic achievement.* New York: The Free Press.
[69] Komives, J.L. (1972). A preliminary study of the personal values of high technology entrepreneurs. In A.C. Cooper and J.L. Komives (Eds.) *Technical Entrepreneurship: A symposium.* Milwaukee, Wisconsin: The center for Venture Management. pp.231-242.
[70] Begley, T.M. & Boyd, D.P. (1987). Psychological characteristics associated with performance in entrepreneurial firms and smaller businesses. *Journal of Business Venturing, 2*(1), 79-93.
[71] Brockhaus, R.H (1982). The Psychology of the entrepreneur. In: Kent,C.A., Sexton,D.L., & Vesper,K.H. (Eds). *Encyclopedia of Entrepreneurship.* Englewood Cliffs.NJ: Prentice-Hall, 41-56.

[72] Rotter, J.B. (1966). Generalized expectations for internal versus external control of reinforcement. *Psychological Monographs: General and Aplied, 8*(1)(Whole No. 609), 1-28.

[73] Borland, C.M. (1975). *Locus of control, need for achievement and entrepreneurship.* Unpublished doctoral dissertation, The University of Texas at Austin, Austin, TX.

[74] Shapero, A. (1975). The displaced, uncomfortable entrepreneur. *Psychology Today.* (Nov.), 83-88.

[75] Brockhaus, R.H. (1980). Psychological and environmental factors which distinguish the successful from unsuccessful entrepreneur: A long study. *Academy of Management Proceedings.* 368-372.

[76] Brockhaus, R. & Nord, W. (1979). An exploration of factors affecting the entrepreneurial decision: Personal characteristics vs. environmental conditions. *Proceedings: Academy of Management.*

[77] Hull, D., Bosley, J., & Udell, G. (1980). Renewing the hunt for the heffalump: Identifying potential entrepreneurs by personality characteristics. *Journal of Small Business,18.*(1), 11-18.

[78] Brockhaus, R.H. (1980B). Risk-taking propensity of entrepreneurs. *Academy of Management Journal, 23,* 509-520.

[79] Begley, T.M. & Boyd, D.P. (1987). A Comparison of entrepreneurs and managers of small business firms. *Journal of Management, 13*(1), 99-108.

[80] Hornaday, J.A. & Aboud, J. (1971). Characteristics of successful entrepreneurs. *Personnel Psychology, 24,* 141-153.

[81] Komives, J.L. (1972). A preliminary study of the personal values of high technology entrepreneurs. In A.C. Cooper and J.L. Komives (Eds.) *Technical Entrepreneurship: A symposium.* Milwaukee, Wisconsin: The center for Venture Management. pp.231-242.

[82] Gasse, Y. (1977). *Entrepreneurial characteristics and practices: A study of the dynamics of small business organizations and their effectiveness in different environments.* Sherbrook, Québec: René Prince Imprimeur.

[83] Gasse, Y (1978). *Characteristics, functions and performance of small firm owner-managers in two industrial environments.* Unpublished doctoral dissertation, Northwestern University, Evanston,IL.

[84]Begley, T.M. & Boyd, D.P. (1987). A Comparison of entrepreneurs and managers of small business firms. *Journal of Management, 13*(1), 99-108.

[85]Smith, N.R. (1967). *The entrepreneur and his firm: The relationship between type of man and type of company.* East Lansing, MI: Bureau of Business and Economic Research, Michigan State University.

[86]Collins, O.F. & Moore, D.G. (1964). *The enterprising man.* East Lansing, MI: Michigan State University.

[87]Sandberg, W. R. 1986). *New venture performance: The role of strategy and industry structure.* Lexington, MA: D.C. Heath & Co.

[88]Hoad, W. & Rosko, P. (1964). *Management factors contributing to the sucess and failure of new small manufacturers.* Ann Arbor, Mich: Bureau of Business Research, University of Michigan.

[89]Roure, J. (1986). *Success and failure of high-growth technological ventures: The influence of prefunding factors.* Unpublished doctoral dissertation. Stanford, CA: Stanford University.

[90]Buchele, R. (1967). *Business policy in growing firms.* Scranton, PA: Chandler Publishing Company.

[91]Hoad, W. & Rosko, P. (1964). *Management factors contributing to the sucess and failure of new small manufacturers.* Ann Arbor, Mich: Bureau of Business Research, University of Michigan.

[92]Sandberg, W. R. 1986). *New venture performance: The role of strategy and industry structure.* Lexington, MA: D.C. Heath & Co.

[93]MacMillan, I.C. (1986). To really learn about entrepreneurship, let's study habitual entrepreneurs. *Journal of Business Venturing, 1*(3), 241-243.

[94]Lamont, L.M. (1972). What entrepreneurs learn from experience. *Journal of Small Business Management, 10*(July), 36-41.

[95]Collins, O.F., & Moore, D.G. (1970). *The organization makers.* New York: Meredith Corporation.

[96]Brockhaus, R. & Nord, W. (1979). An exploration of factors affecting the entrepreneurial decision: Personal characteristics vs. environmental conditions. *Proceedings: Academy of Management.*

[97]Hoad, W. & Rosko, P. (1964). *Management factors contributing to the sucess and failure of new small manufacturers.* Ann Arbor, Mich: Bureau of Business Research, University of Michigan.

[98]Roberts, E. B. (1969). Entrepreneurship and technology. In Gruber, H.W. & Marquis, D.G. (Eds.) *Factors in the transfer of technology.* Cambridge, MA: MIT Press, 219-237.

[99]Brockhaus, R. & Nord, W. (1979). An exploration of factors affecting the entrepreneurial decision: Personal characteristics vs. environmental conditions. *Proceedings: Academy of Management.*

[100]Kirzner, I. (1979). Comment: X-inefficiency, error, and the scope for entrepreneurship. In M. Rizzo (Ed.) *Time, Uncertainty, and Disequilibrium.* Lexington, MA: D.C. Heath.

[101]Kirzner, I. (1979). *Perception, opportunity, and profit.* Chicago: University of Chicago Press.

[102]Schultz, T. (1975). The value of the ability to deal with disequilibria. *Journal of Economic Literature, 13.* 827-846.

[103]Schultz, T. (1980). Investment in entrepreneurial ability. *Scandinavian Journal of Economics, 82,* 437-448.

[104]Drucker, P.F. (1985). *Innovation and entrepreneurship.* New York: Harper & Row.

[105]Timmons, J.A. (1982). New venture creation: Models and methodologies. In Kent, C.A.,Sexton,D.L., and Vesper,K.H.,(Eds). *Encyclopedia of entrepreneurship.* Englewood Cliffs, NJ: Prentice-Hall, 126-139.

[106]MacMillan, I.C. (1986). To really learn about entrepreneurship, let's study habitual entrepreneurs. *Journal of Business Venturing, 1*(3), 241-243.

[107]McClelland, D.C. (1965). N achievement and entrepreneurship: A longitudinal study. *Journal Of Personality and Social Psychology, 1*(4), 389-392.

[108]MacMillan, I., Seigel, R., & Narasimha, S. P. (1985). Criteria used by venture capitalists to evaluate new venture proposals. *Journal of Business Venturing, 1*(1), 119-128.

[109]Stevenson, H. & Gumpert, D. (1985). The heart of entrepreneurship. *Harvard Business Review, 63*(2), 85-94.

[110]Schumpeter, J. (1934). *The theory of economic development.* Cambridge, MA: Harvard University Press.

[111]Stevenson, H. & Gumpert, D. (1985). The heart of entrepreneurship. *Harvard Business Review, 63*(2), 85-94.

[112]Drucker, P.F. (1985). *Innovation and entrepreneurship.* New York: Harper & Row, pp. 189-206.

[113]Gartner, W.B. (1987). *What are we talking about when we talk about entrepreneurship?* Paper presented at the Academy of Management meeting at N.O. (in abstracts), 1-20.

[114]Timmons, J.A. (1978). Characteristics and role demands of entrepreneurship. *American Journal of Small Business, 3* (1), 5-17.

[115]Miller, D. (1983).The correlates of entrepreneurship in three types of firms. *Management Science, 29*(7), 770-791.

[116]Sandberg, W.R., & Hofer, C.W. (1987). Improving new venture performance: The role of strategy, industry structure, and the entrepreneur. *Journal of Business Venturing, 2,* 5-28.

[117]Gartner, W.B. (1987). *What are we talking about when we talk about entrepreneurship?* Paper presented at the Academy of Management meeting at N.O. (in abstracts), 1-20.

[118]MacMillan, I., Seigel, R., & Narasimha, S. P. (1985). Criteria used by venture capitalists to evaluate new venture proposals. *Journal of Business Venturing, 1*(1), 119-128.

[119]Maidque, M. (1986). Key success factors in high-technology ventures. In: Sexton, D.L. & Smilor, R.W. (EDS.). *The art and science of entrepreneurship.* Cambridge, MA: Ballinger Publishing.

[120]Stuart, R. & Abetti, P.A. (1986). Field study of Start-up ventures - part II: Predicting initial success. In: Ronstad, R., Hornaday, J.,Peterson, R., & Vesper, K. *Frontiers of entrepreneurship research.* Wellesley, MA: Babson College, 21-39.

[121]Stuart, R. & Abetti, P.A. (1987). Start-up ventures: Towards the prediction of initial success. *Journal of Business Venturing, 2,* 215-230.

[122]Roure, J. (1986). *Success and failure of high-growth technological ventures: The influence of prefunding factors.* Unpublished doctoral dissertation. Stanford, CA: Stanford University.

[123]Begley, T.M. & Boyd, D.P. (1987). Psychological characteristics associated with performance in entrepreneurial firms and smaller businesses. *Journal of Business Venturing, 2*(1), 79-93.

[124] Brockhaus, R.H. (1980A). Psychological and environmental factors which distinguish the successful from unsuccessful entrepreneur: A long study. *Academy of Management Proceedings.* 368-372.

[125] Sandberg, W. R. 1986). *New venture performance: The role of strategy and industry structure.* Lexington, MA: D.C. Heath & Co.

[126] Wright, R.V.L. (1974). *A system for manageing diversity.* Cambridge, MA: Arthur D. Little.

[127] Ibid.

[128] Wissema, J.G. Van der Pol, H.W., & Messer, H.M. (1980). Strategic management archtypes. *Strategic Management Journal,* *1*(1), 37-47.

[129] (1980.) Wanted: A manager to fit each strategy. *Business Week.* (Feb.) 166-173.

[130] Tichy, N.M., Fombrun, C.J. & Devanna, M.A. (1982). Strategic human resource management. *Sloan Management Review,23*(2) 47-61.

[131] Hofer, C.W. & Schendel, D.E. (1978). *Stategy formulation: Analytical concepts.* St. Paul: West Publishing Co.

[132] Leontiades, M. (1982). *Choosing the right manager to fit the strategy.* Journal of Business Strategy, 58-69.

[133] Eastlack, J.O. & McDonald, P.R. (1970). CEO's role in corporate growth. *Harvard Business Review,58*(3).

[134] Miles,R.E. & Snow,C.C. (1978). *Organizational strategy, structure, and process.* New York: McGraw-Hill.

[135] Porter, M.E. (1980). *Competitive Strategy.* New York: Free Press.

[136] Gupta, A.K. (1984). Contingency linkages between strategy and general manager characteristics: A conceptual examination. *Academy of Management Review, 9* (3), 399-412.

[137] Gupta, A.K. & Govindarajan, V. (1984). Business unit strategy, managerial characteristics, and business effectiveness at strategy implementation. *Academy of Management Journal, 27* (1), 25-41.

[138] Szilagyi, A.D. & Schweiger,D.M. (1984). Matching managers to strategies: A review and suggested framework. *Academy of Management Review, 9*(4), 626-637.

[139] Katz R.L.(1974). Skills of an effective administrator. *Harvard Business Review, 52*(5). 90-102.

[140] Kotter, J.P. (1982). *General managers are not generalists.* Organizational Dynamics, (Spring). 5-19.

[141] Stewart, R. (1982). A model of understanding managerial jobs and behavior. *Academy of Management Review, 7*(1), 7-13.

[142] Mintzberg, H. (1980). The nature of managerial work (2nd ed.). Chapter 7: *The future of managerial work.* Englewood Cliffs, NJ: Prentice-Hall.

[143] Wright, R.V.L. (1974). *A system for manageing diversity.* Cambridge, MA: Arthur D. Little.

[144] Leontiades, M. (1982). *Choosing the right manager to fit the strategy.* Journal of Business Strategy, 58-69.

[145] Gupta, A.K. (1984). Contingency linkages between strategy and general manager characteristics: A conceptual examination. *Academy of Management Review, 9* (3), 399-412.

[146] Pearce, J. & Robinson, R.B. (1988) *Strategic Management: Strategy formulation and implementation* (3rd ed.). Homewood, IL: Irwin.

[147] Vesper, K.H. (1980). *New Venture Strategies.* Englewood Cliffs, NJ: Prentice-Hall.

[148] Stuart, R. & Abetti, P.A. (1987). Start-up ventures: Towards the prediction of initial success. *Journal of Business Venturing, 2,* 215-230.

[149] Roure, J. (1986). *Success and failure of high-growth technological ventures: The influence of prefunding factors.* Unpublished doctoral dissertation. Stanford, CA: Stanford University.

[150] Sandberg, W. R. 1986). *New venture performance: The role of strategy and industry structure.* Lexington, MA: D.C. Heath & Co.

[151] Fishbein, M. & Ajzen, I. (1975). *Belief, attitude, intention and behavior: An introduction to theory and research.* Reading, MA: Addison-Wesley, p. 13.

[152] Epstein, S. (1979). The stability of behavior: I. On predicting most of the people much of the time. *Journal of personality & Social Psychology, 37* (7). 1097-1126.

[153] Epstein, S. (1980). The stability of behavior: II. Implications for psychological research. *American Psychologist, 35*(9), 790-806.

[154] Buss, A.H. & Finn, S.E. (1987). Classification of personality traits. *Journal of Personality and Social Psychology , 52*(2), 433-444.

[155] Cattell, R.B. (1947). Confirmation and clarification of primary personality traits. *Psychologial Bulletin, 72*, 402-421.

[156] Cattell, R.B. (1957). *Personality and motivation structure and measurement.* New York: World Book.

[157] Jackson, D. (1967). *Personality research form manual.* Goshen, NY: Research Psychologists Press.

[158] Buss, A.H. & Finn, S.E. (1987). Classification of personality traits. *Journal of Personality and Social Psychology, 52*(2), 433-444.

[159] Jackson, D. (1984). *Personality research form manual* (3rd ed.) Port Huron, MI: Research Psycologists Press.

[160] Buss, A.H. & Finn, S.E. (1987). Classification of personality traits. *Journal of Personality and Social Psychology, 52*(2), 433-444.

[161] Ibid

[162] Buss, A.H. & Plomin, R. (1984). *Temperament: Early developing personality traits.* Hillsdale, N.J.: Erlbaum.

[163] Buss, A.H. & Finn, S.E. (1987). Classification of personality traits. *Journal of Personality and Social Psychology, 52*(2), 433-444.

[164] Ibid

[165] Buss, A.H. & Plomin, R. (1984). *Temperament: Early developing personality traits.* Hillsdale, N.J.: Erlbaum.

[166] Buss, A.H. & Finn, S.E. (1987). Classification of personality traits. *Journal of Personality and Social Psychology, 52*(2), 433-444.

[167] Epstein, S. (1979). The stability of behavior: I. On predicting most of the people much of the time. *Journal of personality & Social Psychology, 37* (7). 1097-1126.

[168] Epstein, S. (1980). The stability of behavior: II. Implications for psychological research. *American Psychologist, 35*(9), 790-806.

[169] Epstein, S. & O'Brian, E.J. (1985). The person-situation debate in historical and current perspective. *Psychological Bulletin, 98*(3), 513-537.

[170] Epstein, S. (1979). The stability of behavior: I. On predicting most of the people much of the time. *Journal of personality & Social Psychology, 37* (7). 1097-1126, p. 1097.

[171] Epstein, S. (1980). The stability of behavior: II. Implications for psychological research. *American Psychologist, 35*(9), 790-806, p. 790.

[172] Anderson, C.R. (1977). Locus of control, coping behaviors, and performance in a stress setting: A longitudinal study. *Journal of Applied Psychology, 62*(4), 446-451.

[173] Ibid.

[174] Anderson, C., Hellriegel, D., & Slocum, J. (1977). Managerial response to environmentally induced stress. *Academy of Management Journal, 20*(2), 260-272.

[175] Anderson, C., & Schneier, C. (1978). Locus of control, leader behavior and leader performance among management students.*Academy of Management Journal, 21*(4), 690-698.

[176] Anderson, C.R. (1977). Locus of control, coping behaviors, and performance in a stress setting: A longitudinal study. *Journal of Applied Psychology, 62*(4), 446-451.

[177] Ghiselli, E.E. (1973). The validity of aptitude tests in personnel selection. *Personnel Psychology, 26*(4), 461-477.

[178] Hollenbeck, J. & Whitener, E., (1988). Reclaiming personality traits for personnel selection. *Journal of Management, 14* (1), 81-91.

[179] Maier, N. (1946). *Psychology in industry.* Boston: Houghton Mifflin Co.

[180] Maier, N. (1965). *Psychology in industry.* (3rd ed.). Boston: Houghton Mifflin Co.

[181] Stoner, J.A.F. & Wankel,C. (1986). *Management* (3RD Ed) Englewood Cliffs, NJ: Prentice-Hall.

[182] Maier, N. (1965). *Psychology in industry.* (3rd ed.). Boston: Houghton Mifflin Co.

[183] Bandura, A. (1982).Self-efficacy mechanism in human agency. *American Psychologist, 37*(2), 122-147, p. 122.

[184] Ibid, p. 123.

[185] Ibid, p. 126.

[186] Hambrick, D.C. (1987). The top management team: key to strategic success. *California Management Review*, (Fall) 88-108, p. 94.

[187] Fishbein, M. & Ajzen, I. (1975). *Belief, attitude, intention and behavior: An introduction to theory and research.* Reading, MA: Addison-Wesley.

[188]Guth, W.D., & Tagiuri, R. (1965). Personal values and corporate strategy. *Harvard Business Review,43*(5),123-132.

[189]Maier, N. (1965). *Psychology in industry.* (3rd ed.). Boston: Houghton Mifflin Co, p. 286.

[190]*American Heritage Dictionary*, Second College Edition, 1982.

[191]Ibid, p. 286.

[192]Ibid, pp. 479-480.

[193]Katz R.L. (1974). Skills of an effective administrator. *Harvard Business Review, 52(5).* 90-102.

[194]Mintzberg, H. (1980). The nature of managerial work (2nd ed.). Chapter 7: *The future of managerial work.* Englewood Cliffs, NJ: Prentice-Hall.

[195]Kotter, J.P. (1982). *The general managers.* New York: The Free Press.

[196]Stewart, R. (1982). A model of understanding managerial jobs and behavior. *Academy of Management Review, 7*(1), 7-13.

[197]Sternberg, R. J. (1985). *Beyond I.Q.* Cambridge, England: Cambridge University Press.

[198]Ibid.

[199]Ibid.

[200]Spearman, C. (1927). *The abilities of man.* New York: MacMillan.

[201]Thurstone, L. L. (1938). *Primary mental abilities.* Chicago: Chicago University Press.

[202]Guilford, J. P. (1967). *The nature of human intelligence.* New York: McGraw-Hill.

[203]Hunt, E. B. (1978). Mechanics of verbal ability. *Psychological Review, 85,* 109-130.

[204]Jensen, A. R. (1982). Reaction time and psychometric g. In H.J. Eysenck (Ed.) *A model for intelligence.* Berlin: Springer-Verlag.

[205]Sternberg, R.J. (1979). The nature of mental abilities. *American Psychologist, 34*(3), 214-230.

[206]Cattell, R. B. (1971). *Abilities: Their structure, growth, and action.* Boston: Houghton Mifflin.

[207]Spearman, C. (1927). *The abilities of man.* New York: MacMillan.

[208]Thurstone, L. L. (1931). Multiple factor analysis. *Psychological Review, 38,* (406-427).

[209]Thurstone, L. L. (1938). *Primary mental abilities.* Chicago: Chicago University Press.

[210] Cattell, R. B. (1971). *Abilities: Their structure, growth, and action.* Boston: Houghton Mifflin.

[211] Holzinger, K.J. (1938). Relationships between three multiple orthogonal factors and four bifactors. *Journal of Educational Psychology, 29*, 513-356.

[212] Burt, C, (1940). *The factors of the mind.* London: University of London Press.

[213] Guttman, L. (1965). A faceted definition of intelligence. In R.R. Eiferman (Ed.), *Scripta Hierosolymitana (Vol.14).* Jerusalem: Magnes Press.

[214] Vernon, P.E. (1971). *The structure of human abilities.* London: Methuen.

[215] Sternberg, R. J. (1985). *Beyond I.Q.* Cambridge, England: Cambridge University Press.

[216] Guilford, J. P. (1967). *The nature of human intelligence.* New York: McGraw-Hill.

[217] Guilford, J.P. & Hoepfner, R. (1971). *The analysis of intelligence.* New York: McGraw-Hill.

[218] Sternberg, R. J. (1985). *Beyond I.Q.* Cambridge, England: Cambridge University Press, p. 97.

[219] Guilford, J. P. (1967). *The nature of human intelligence.* New York: McGraw-Hill.

[220] Cattell, R. B. (1971). *Abilities: Their structure, growth, and action.* Boston: Houghton Mifflin, p. 28.

[221] Guilford, J.P. (1982). Cognitive psychology's ambiguities: Some suggested remedies. *Psychological Review, 89*(1), 48-59, p. 51.

[222] Guilford, J.P. (1981). Higher-order structure-of-the-intellect abilities. *Multivariate Behavioral Research, 16*(Oct), 411-435.

[223] Ibid.

[224] Meeker, M. N. (1969). *The structure of intellect.* Columbus OH: Charles E. Merrill.

[225] Ekstrom, R. B., French, J. W., & Harmon, H. H. (1979). Cognitive factors: Their identification and replication. *Multivariate Behavioral Research Monographs,* 79-82.

[226] Sternberg, R. J. (1985). *Beyond I.Q.* Cambridge, England: Cambridge University Press.

[227] Ibid, p. 11.

[228] Ibid.

[229]Ibid.
[230]Cattell, R. B. (1971). *Abilities: Their structure, growth, and action*. Boston: Houghton Mifflin.
[231]Ibid, pp. 98-99.
[232]Sternberg, R. J. (1985). *Beyond I.Q.* Cambridge, England: Cambridge University Press.
[233]Ibid, p. 228.
[234]Ibid, p. 99.
[235]Ibid, pp. 99-108.
[236]Ibid.
[237]Ibid. pp. 227-228.
[238]Ibid, p228.
[239]Ibid, p. 229.
[240]Guilford, J. P. (1967). *The nature of human intelligence*. New York: McGraw-Hill.
[241]Guilford, J.P. & Hoepfner, R. (1971). *The analysis of intelligence*. New York: McGraw-Hill.
[242]Szilagyi, A.D. & Schweiger,D.M. (1984). Matching managers to strategies: A review and suggested framework. *Academy of Management Review, 9*(4), 626-637.
[243]Katz R.L. (1974). Skills of an effective administrator. *Harvard Business Review, 52*(5). 90-102.
[244]Szilagyi, A.D. & Schweiger,D.M. (1984). Matching managers to strategies: A review and suggested framework. *Academy of Management Review, 9*(4), 626-637.
[245]Katz R.L. (1974). Skills of an effective administrator. *Harvard Business Review, 52*(5). 90-102.
[246]Szilagyi, A.D. & Schweiger,D.M. (1984). Matching managers to strategies: A review and suggested framework. *Academy of Management Review, 9*(4), 626-637.
[247]Katz R.L. (1974). Skills of an effective administrator. *Harvard Business Review, 52*(5). 90-102.
[248]Szilagyi, A.D. & Schweiger,D.M. (1984). Matching managers to strategies: A review and suggested framework. *Academy of Management Review, 9*(4), 626-637.
[249]Guilford, J.P. & Hoepfner, R. (1971). *The analysis of intelligence*. New York: McGraw-Hill.

[250] Meeker, M. N. (1969). *The structure of intellect*. Columbus OH: Charles E. Merrill, p. 13.
[251] Ibid.
[252] Ibid, p. 14.
[253] Ibid, p. 16.
[254] Ibid, p. 17.
[255] Ibid, p. 19.
[256] Ibid, p. 20.
[257] Guilford, J.P. (1982). Cognitive psychology's ambiguities: Some suggested remedies. *Psychological Review, 89*(1), 48-59.
[258] Meeker, M. N. (1969). *The structure of intellect*. Columbus OH: Charles E. Merrill.
[259] Guilford, J. P. (1967). *The nature of human intelligence*. New York: McGraw-Hill.
[260] Meeker, M. N. (1969). *The structure of intellect*. Columbus OH: Charles E. Merrill.
[261] Guilford, J. P. (1967). *The nature of human intelligence*. New York: McGraw-Hill.
[262] Ibid.
[263] Ibid.
[264] Schultz, T. (1975). The value of the ability to deal with disequilibria. *Journal of Economic Literature, 13*. 827-846.
[265] Schultz, T. (1980). Investment in entrepreneurial ability. *Scandinavian Journal of Economics, 82*, 437-448.
[266] Guilford, J. P. (1967). *The nature of human intelligence*. New York: McGraw-Hill.
[267] Maier, N. (1965). *Psychology in industry*. (3rd ed.). Boston: Houghton Mifflin Co.

Chapter Three:

Research Design

INTRODUCTION

This chapter outlines the methodology used to answer the research questions posed in the first chapter. It consists of five sections. The first section discusses the philosophy which guided selection of the research method. The second section applies the research model developed in Chapter II to the first two research questions posed in Chapter I to derive general hypotheses for the research. The third section describes the operationalization of the model through the development of empirical indicators for the unobservable constructs. The fourth section discusses the research design and the sampling frame. The fifth section outlines briefly methodology used for data analysis.

THE HOLISTIC CONSTRUAL APPROACH TO DOING RESEARCH

There are many ways of "doing science" or, as Brinberg and McGrath[1] have phrased it: "...the full research endeavor requires pursuit of multiple paths." The current research endeavor pursues what Brinberg and McGrath term "applied research using the theoretical path". The research questions have been generated in the substantive domain (the real worlds of business and academia), will lead to the generation of hypotheses by application of elements from the theoretical domain (unobservable constructs and nomological networks), and these hypotheses will be validated (or not) by application of elements (certain statistical methods) from the methodological domain[2].

One preferred method of pursuing applied research using the theoretical path is that of the holistic construal,[3,4] which will be used as a philosophic guide for the current research. This approach advocates model building prior to concept operationalization and data analysis. A basic criticism of the entrepreneurial research reviewed in Chapter 2 is the lack of such theoretical construction prior to empirical research. Researchers have attempted to link various personality traits of the entrepreneur to new venture performance without consideration of the available universe of personality traits, and without attempting to model how those traits might be mediated and/or moderated in their relationships to that performance.

Another important facet of the holistic construal for "doing science" is its explicit view of the linkages between unobservable constructs and the empirical measures or operationalizations of those constructs. In the conventional logical empiricist model of the structure of theory, empirical terms (operationalizations) give meaning to unobservable constructs, a process which Feigl[5] terms "an 'upward seepage' of meaning from the observational terms to the theoretical concepts." This view encourages the proliferation of operationalizations being used in statistical procedures without regard to their relations one to the other or their relations to past operationalizations, since, in this view, the operationalization takes philosophic priority over the concept. By contrast, the holistic construal sees operationalizations in the plane of observation as being driven by the unobservable constructs of the theoretical plane, and thus as empirical indicators (factors) of those constructs with attendant measurement error.[6] But conversely, since the very existence of those unobservable constructs is inferred as well as measured by their indicators, the constructs and their measures are put in a unique relationship, one to the other. The holistic construal thus explicitly states that *both* theoretical constructs *and* their empirical measures are necessary to give meaning to theory. It also implies that multiple indicators (operationalizations) of constructs is highly desirable whenever feasible.

DEVELOPMENT OF GENERAL HYPOTHESES FROM THE CURRENT RESEARCH MODEL

The research model developed in the Chapter II (see Figure 2-7) may now be applied to the research questions posed in Chapter I (pg. 6).

The first research question was:

1. Do characteristics of the entrepreneur have a significant impact upon new venture performance in addition to strategy and industry structure?

This research question is used to generate the following hypothesis:

> H1. skills, skill's propensities, and their interactions with strategy and industry structure will have a significant effect upon new venture performance.

The second research question was:

> 2. If so, what characteristics are important and what is their relationship with new venture performance?

This research question is used to generate the following set of hypotheses concerning the individual skills:

> H2A. The product/service design skill and skill propensity, and their interactions with strategy and industry structure will have a significant effect upon new venture performance.
>
> H2B. The technical business skill and skill propensity, and their interactions with strategy and industry structure will have a significant effect upon new venture performance.
>
> H2C. The technical industry skill and skill propensity, and their interactions with strategy and industry structure will have a significant effect upon new venture performance.
>
> H2D. The internal leadership skill and skill propensity, and their interactions with strategy and

industry structure will have a significant effect upon new venture performance.

H2E. The networking skill and skill propensity, and their interactions with strategy and industry structure will have a significant effect upon new venture performance.

H2F. The administrative skill and skill propensity, and their interactions with strategy and industry structure will have a significant effect upon new venture performance.

H2G. The entrepreneurial skill and skill propensity, and their interactions with strategy and industry structure will have a significant effect upon new venture performance.

The second research question along with the research model is also used to generate the following set of hypotheses concerning the relations between the individual skills and their attendant mental aptitude and training:

H3A. Guilford's divergent production of figural transformations, training in the product/service design area, and their interaction will have a significant effect upon the product/service design skill.

H3B. Guilford's evaluation of symbolic systems, training in the technical business area, and their interaction will have a significant effect upon the technical business skill.

H3C. Guilford's cognition of semantic implications, training in the technical industry area, and their interaction will have a significant effect upon the technical industry skill.

H3D. Guilford's evaluations of behavioral transformations, training in the leadership area, and their interaction will have a significant effect upon the leadership skill.

H3E. Guilford's cognition of behavioral implications, training in the networking area, and their interaction will have a significant effect upon the networking skill.

H3F. Guilford's divergent production of semantic implications, training in the administrative area, and their interaction will have a significant effect upon the administrative skill.

H3G. Guilford's divergent production of semantic transformations, training in the entrepreneurial area, and their interaction will have a significant effect upon the entrepreneurial skill.

OPERATIONALIZATION OF VARIABLES

The next step in development of this research was the operationalization of the variables.

Operationalization of Strategy

In line with Venkatraman and Grants'[7] proposal that strategy is a multidimensional construct, several constructs are used together in this research to represent strategy. Numerous studies have recently utilized multidimensional strategy constructs[8][9][10] but few have viewed strategy from the perspective of the new venture. An exception to this is the recent research conducted by.[11] This study identified a new venture strategy typology based on aggressiveness of growth orientation and breadth of strategic scope, and concluded that the strategies of parented as well as non-parented new ventures fit this generic framework. Based upon that study, it was decided to use aggressiveness of growth orientation, and breadth of strategic scope, as parts of the new venture strategy construct for this study. The balance of this multidimensional construct is represented by Vesper's[12] construct of entry wedges discussed later in this section.

Operationalization of Scope Strategy

In operationalizing the scope construct, there are three dimensions of primary importance to consider: those of geographic scope, product scope, and customer (or market) segment scope.[13] Within an industry, it is possible for any given firm to be more or less concentrated on each of these three dimensions. At the same time, these three scope dimensions are herein combined so that scope may be dealt with as a unidimensional construct. This is done by considering each of the three scope dimensions as the dimensions of a rectangular solid and thus multiplying them together to give the total relative volume of that solid (see Figure 3-1). The scope construct was measured in this research using three separate scales in the spirit of the holistic construal.

The first scale utilizes a set of three CEO-reported subjective measures of geographic, product, and customer scope measures multiplied together (see Figure 3-2).

The second scale utilizes a CEO-reported objective measure of geographic scope, a CEO-reported subjective measure of product scope, and a CEO-reported subjective measure of customer scope. These are multiplied together to obtain the second scope scale.

The third scale consists of a single-item overall CEO-reported subjective scope scale.

These three scales are then combined, using factor analysis (of all three strategy and both industry structure measures), into one combined scope measure.

Research Design 79

FIGURE 3-1

A BREADTH OF SCOPE MEASURE

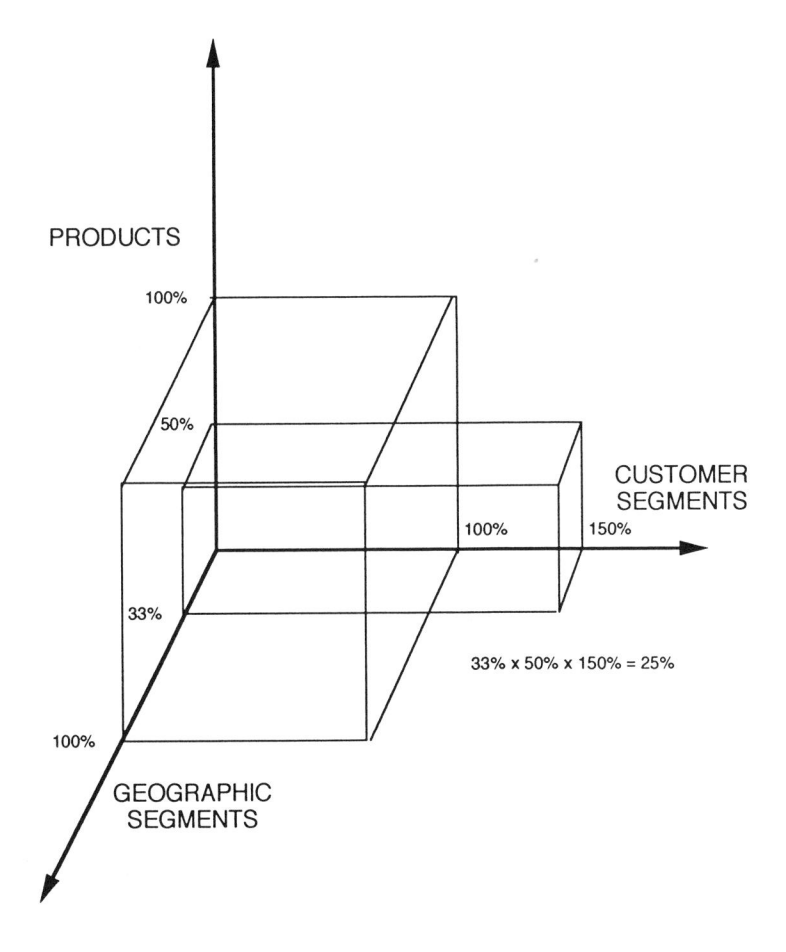

PRODUCTS

100%

50%

CUSTOMER SEGMENTS

100% 150%

33%

33% x 50% x 150% = 25%

100%

GEOGRAPHIC SEGMENTS

FIGURE 3-2

**AN EXAMPLE OF
BREADTH OF SCOPE MEASURE -
FIRST SCALE**

5). On a scale of 1 to 10 (with 1 = "extremely narrow[focused]" and
10 ="extremely wide[unfocused]"):

How wide a range of customer types do you serve? (circle one but only one):
Extremely focused < 1 2 3 4 5 6 7 8 ⑨ 10 > extremely broad or unfocused

How wide a range of geographic markets do you serve? (circle one but only one):
Extremely focused < 1 2 3 ④ 5 6 7 8 9 10 > extremely broad or unfocused

How wide a range of products/services do you provide? (circle one but only one):
Extremely focused < 1 2 3 4 5 6 ⑦ 8 9 10 > extremely broad or unfocused

$9 \times 4 \times 7 = 252$

Value of first scale = 252 for this observation

Operationalization of Aggressiveness of Growth Orientation

The construct of growth orientation is measured with three different single-item scales: a planned assets-growth scale, a planned employee-growth scale, and an overall subjective growth-orientation scale.

The planned asset-growth scale is a single-item scale derived by asking the CEO for asset levels now, and projected asset levels three years in the future. From these figures, projected average annual growth rates for assets are derived.

The planned employee-growth orientation scale is derived by asking the CEO for employment levels now, and projected employment levels three years in the future. From these figures, projected average annual growth rates for employment are derived.

The combined growth-orientation scale is a single-item CEO-administered subjective 10-point scale on overall growth-orientation with 1 being extremely conservative and 10 being extremely aggressive (see Figure 3-3)

These three scales are then combined, using factor analysis (of all three strategy and both industry structure measures), into one combined aggressiveness of growth orientation scale.

Operationalization of Entry Wedge

The above method of viewing strategy along the dimensions of both scope and aggressiveness of growth orientation has many benefits[14] and encompasses two of the three traditional generic business substrategies, competitive and financial.[15] However, from the standpoint of competitive substrategy it encompasses only one dimension, that of strategic scope, while neglecting the other major dimension of competitive advantage.[16][17] In order to remedy that neglect while continuing to focus on new venture strategies, a third strategy dimension was added: the major new venture strategy construct of Vesper[18] entitled "main competitive entry wedge". Vesper[19] defines this construct as:" ...A strategic competitive advantage for breaking into the established pattern of commercial activity". This is a measure of whether the firm is entering the market with a totally new product or service, versus entering using a near-exact replicate of the product or service of the competition with minor variations (Vesper's franchise entry will be ignored in this study).

The construct of entry wedge was measured with a single item, six-point Likert-type scale based upon CEO response. In order to reduce response bias, this scale was anchored at every point (see Figure 3-4).

FIGURE 3-3

**COMBINED GROWTH ORIENTATION
SCALE**

11). How aggressive is your orientation toward growth? (circle one but only one): Extremely conservative < 1 2 3 4 5 6 7 8 9 10 > extremely aggressive

FIGURE 3-4

ENTRY WEDGE SCALE

12). Check the one (but only one) statement which best represents your marketing strategy:

_____ "Our product or service is not at all new to the market we are serving, and prices will be our main method of competition"

_____ "Our product or service is not at all new to the market we are serving, but demand is great enough that we will have about the same prices as competition"

_____ "Our product or service is not at all new to the market we are serving, but it will be marketed or distributed with significant non-price differences from those of our competition (our prices may or may not be lower)."

_____ "Our product or service itself has aspects which are new and/or different to the market we are serving."

_____ "Nothing else like our product or service is currently being sold in the market we are serving"

_____ "Our product or service is totally new and to our knowledge has never been offered before in any market."

This scale is the only measure of entry wedge, though it was involved in the factor analysis along with the other strategy and industry measures in order to establish both factor scores and construct validity.

Operationalization of Industry Structure

Industry structure is a multi-dimensional construct.[20][21] Although research has suggested that numerous dimensions of industry structure are of importance in the determination of NVP, the focus of the operationalization of industry structure in this research is on dimensions associated with managerial and entrepreneurial characteristics important to NVP. Two dimensions that have received major emphasis in the literature as important determinants of required managerial and entrepreneurial characteristics: industry life cycle and industry product differentiation.

Operationalization of Industry Life Cycle

In line with the strategic implementation literature which has recommended matching managers to stage of the product or industry life cycle,[22][23][24] the stage of industry life cycle will be used as one dimension of industry structure in this study. Porter,[25] recognizes the importance of industry life cycle as a key industry structure dimension while also acknowledging the difficulty of knowing the exact stage of the industry life cycle or even its shape. Therefore, two proxy questions for industry life cycle were asked which together take into account both the direction of the change in sales and whether that change is accelerating or is decelerating. Two single-item scales are used, one to measure the rate of sales growth and one to measure the change in that growth rate (see Figure 3-5). These measures are then combined (see Figure 3-6) to determine the imputed stage of industry growth.

This scale is the only measure of stage of industry growth, though it was involved in the factor analysis along with the other strategy and industry measures in order to establish both factor scores and construct validity.

Operationalization of Industry Differentiation

A second dimension used to characterize industry structure was that of relative homogeneity of products versus product differentiation within the industry. This dimension has been characterized by several management theorists as important to the type of competition which takes place within an industry[26][27][28] and thus may be expected to influence required entrepreneurial and managerial characteristics in the industry. Here, six single-item three-point fully anchored scales were

Research Design 85

FIGURE 3-5

INDUSTRY STAGE ITEMS

15). Check one (but only one) blank for each question:

    For the last three years, dollar sales in our industry have been:
    ____growing at a rate of 7% or more
    ____growing, but at a rate of less than 7%
    ____remaining steady (not growing or declining)
    ____declining

    For the past three years, the rate of sales growth in our industry has been:
    ____increasing
    ____staying about the same
    ____declining

FIGURE 3-6
COMPUTATION OF STAGE OF INDUSTRY LIFE CYCLE

Changes in Sales

	7% or more per year increase	Less than 7% per year increase	Steady - no growth	Sales declining
Increasing	2	1	1	6
Steady	2.5	2.5	4	5
Declining	3	3	4	5

Changes in Sales Growth Rate

used. Each scale queries whether a facet of the extended product/service is a point of minor, significant, or major competition in the industry. The six facets of competition are uniqueness of product/service features, brand name, quality, post-sales service, personal relations with the sales personnel, and price. The first three items may be expected to indicate heterogeneity in an industry while the second three may be expected to indicate homogeneity.[29] [30] Thus the measure of heterogeneity was composed by adding the scores on the first three items and subtracting from them the scores on the last three items (See Figure 3-7).

This scale was the only measure of industry product heterogeneity, though it was involved in the factor analysis along with the other strategy and industry measures in order to establish both factor scores and construct validity.

Operationalization of Aptitudes, skills, skill Propensity, and Training

Operationalization of Skills
Each skill level was operationalized with a single-item, Likert-type ten point scale, as shown in Figure 3-8.

In addition to this self-report skill measure, a second (and confidential) "observer-report" skill measure (using the same operationalization as shown in Figure 3-8) was taken on each entrepreneur by a close colleague in the firm so as to guard against self-report bias.

Operationalization of Skill Propensity
The propensity to exercise a skill from the typology is operationalized as the percent of time which an entrepreneur spends exercising the skill in question. This is a single-item, self-report scale with the total of all seven scales adding to 100% (see Figure 3-8).

Operationalization of Aptitudes
The aptitudes from Guilford's model matching most closely each of the skills of Katz's[31] extended skills typology are measured using SI (structure of intellect) tests for each respective aptitude which had been previously validated by Guilford and his colleagues.[32] [33] For each aptitude, the SI test chosen was that which had the highest loading reported by Guilford and Hoepfner[34] on that aptitude factor among all such tests available. A compendium of these tests and their measured relationships to the aptitude in question is summarized in Figure 3-9.

FIGURE 3-7

INDUSTRY PRODUCT HETEROGENEITY ITEMS

16). In the industry in which you compete, how much competition is there on each of the following items (check one but only one blank under each question):

Uniqueness of product or service? (in features, styling, or packaging)
____ Minor competition
____ Significant competition
____ Major competition

Brand name of product or service?
____ Minor competition
____ Significant competition
____ Major competition

Quality of product or service?
____ Minor competition
____ Significant competition
____ Major competition

Other considerations? (warranty, delivery, credit, after-sales service, installation)
____ Minor competition
____ Significant competition
____ Major competition

Personal relationships between customer contact personnel and customer?
____ Minor competition
____ Significant competition
____ Major competition

Price?
____ Minor competition
____ Significant competition
____ Major competition

FIGURE 3-8
SKILLS, SKILL PROPENSITIES, AND TRAINING

17). For each of the following skills please rate your current effectiveness, give your years of experience with this type skill (since high school and including other businesses), and assess what % of your time you currently spend excercising each skill (the %s should add to 100%):

Current % of my time spent performing this skill

My skill in the detailed design of our products/services:
Not effective at all < 1 2 3 4 5 6 7 8 9 10 > extremely effective
Years of experience I have had practicing this type skill _____ %

My skill in evaluating the various functions of my organization:
Not effective at all < 1 2 3 4 5 6 7 8 9 10 > extremely effective
Years of experience I have had practicing this type skill _____ %

My skill in understanding my industry and the implications of its trends and changes:
Not effective at all < 1 2 3 4 5 6 7 8 9 10 > extremely effective
Years of experience I have had practicing this type skill _____ %

My skill in motivating and influencing the behavior of my employees:
Not effective at all < 1 2 3 4 5 6 7 8 9 10 > extremely effective
Years of experience I have had practicing this type skill _____ %

My skill in creating relations with and influencing important people outside my organization:
Not effective at all < 1 2 3 4 5 6 7 8 9 10 > extremely effective
Years of experience I have had practicing this type skill _____ %

My skill in planning and administering my business' activities:
Not effective at all < 1 2 3 4 5 6 7 8 9 10 > extremely effective
Years of experience I have had practicing this type skill _____ %

My skill in discovering opportunities to profitably change my business:
Not effective at all < 1 2 3 4 5 6 7 8 9 10 > extremely effective
Years of experience I have had practicing this type skill _____ %

FIGURE 3-9

OPERATIONALIZATION OF APTITUDES

SKILL	GUILFORD'S APTITUDE			GUILFORD'S TEST CHOSEN
	Operation	Content	Product	
Technical product/service design	Divergent Production	Figural	Transformations	Match Problems V
Technical business	Evaluation	Symbolic	Systems	Way Out Numbers
Technical industry	Cognition	Semantic	Implications	Effects
Internal leadership	Evaluation	Behavioral	Transformations	(None available - use Cartoon Predictions)
Networking	Cognition	Behavioral	Implications	Cartoon Predictions
Administrative	Divergent Production	Semantic	Implications	Planning Elaboration II
Entrepreneurial	Divergent Production	Semantic	Transformations	Consequences

The scores on each test serve as the operationalization of the aptitude it is intended to measure.

In the case of the aptitude factor "Evaluation of Behavioral Transformations" no known SI test has been developed. This being the case, the SI test "Cartoon Predictions" was used as a proxy for this factor as well as for its own factor (Cognition of Behavioral Implications). This was done for three reasons. First, Cartoon Predictions was one of the very few behavioral tests developed by Guilford and his colleagues. Second, SI tests which load on Implications factors often load on Transformation factors as well.[35] Third, this research could provide an indication as to whether Cartoon Predictions does in fact load upon Evaluation of Behavioral Transformations, a premise which Guilford and his colleagues apparently never tested.

Operationalization of Training

Training time was measured by asking each of the entrepreneurs approximately how many years since high school they had been practicing each of the skills in question (see Figure 3-8), the equivalency of "training" and "experience" being standard usage by industrial psychologists.[36] The end of high school was used as a base for two reasons. First, college has been associated with training value by previous entrepreneurial researchers.[37,38] Second, it is assumed that it would be difficult for respondents to assess childhood experience in terms of adult skills.

Operationalization of New Venture Performance

NVP was operationalized using three separate multi-item measures as befits a multi-dimensional construct.[39,40] All three scales are subjective, involving Likert-type items. The reasons for using subjective instead of objective scales are numerous. In the first place, financial figures are often very misleading for young businesses since their plans may call for several periods of losses while they build market share or develop products. Second, the performance measures in this study must be flexible enough to compare businesses across age since the sampled populations ranged from 0 to 9 years of age. Equally successful businesses at the extreme ends of this range will have very different financial pictures even when in the same industry and competing in the same fashion. Third, the performance measures involved must allow for comparisons across industries and industry types since the sample is heterogeneous by design. Forth, the subject firms in this study are closely held. The financial goals of such business can vary widely depending upon the tax status and individual goals of their owners. Fifth, financial figures from closely firms are both hard to obtain and notoriously unreliable.

The first performance measure is an index whose design is based upon the method of Gupta and Govindarajan.[41] Eight single-item goal measures (see figure 3-10) are first rated by the respondent on Likert-type scales with each scale ranging from "relatively unimportant" to "extremely important". The respondent then rates the attained performance of his firm against each of these goals on Likert-type scales with each scale ranging from "extremely dissatisfied " to "extremely satisfied". The index measure is then obtained by multiplying the importance rating of each item times its attainment rating and averaging these scores.

The second performance measure is also an index whose design is based upon the same method of Gupta and Govinjarian.[42] Sixteen single-item business success factors (see Figure 3-11) are first rated by the respondent on Likert-type scales according to their perceived importance in contributing to the success of the business with responses ranging from "relatively unimportant" to "extremely important". The respondent then rates the attained performance of his firm in each of these areas on Likert-type scales with each scale ranging from "extremely dissatisfied " to "extremely satisfied". The index measure is then obtained by multiplying the importance rating of each item times its attainment rating and averaging these scores.

The third measure is a single-item, seven-point Likert-type question anchored throughout asking the respondent to rate the performance of his business against expectations.

These three scales were then combined into one performance measure by summing their standardized scores.[43]

THE RESEARCH DESIGN

The Study

The research was quasi-experimental and conducted by use of a 10-page questionnaire (see Appendix) utilizing a multisample, cross-sectional design. Telephone follow-up was used to increase response rates. In addition, 29 of the respondents as well as 65 pre-venture volunteers were administered a timed test as described below.

FIGURE 3-10
GOAL PERFORMANCE INDEX

Goal	Level of Satisfaction with Performance against goal	×	Importance of Goal	=	Goal index
Sales growth rate	1 to 7		1 to 7		1 to 49
Market share	1 to 7		1 to 7		1 to 49
Cash flow from operations	1 to 7		1 to 7		1 to 49
Return on investments	1 to 7		1 to 7		1 to 49
Market valuation of business	1 to 7		1 to 7		1 to 49
Company stability	1 to 7		1 to 7		1 to 49
Fostering an entrepreneurial climate	1 to 7		1 to 7		1 to 49
Harvest/exit readiness	1 to 7		1 to 7		1 to 49
TOTAL GOAL INDEX					7 to 343

FIGURE 3-11
SUCCESS FACTOR PERFORMANCE INDEX

Goal	Level of Satisfaction with Performance of factor	×	Importance of Factor	=	Factor index
Development of new products/services	1 to 7		1 to 7		1 to 49
Development of new processes	1 to 7		1 to 7		1 to 49
Modification of existing products/services	1 to 7		1 to 7		1 to 49
Production of products/services	1 to 7		1 to 7		1 to 49
Distribution system and channels	1 to 7		1 to 7		1 to 49
Pricing	1 to 7		1 to 7		1 to 49
Selling	1 to 7		1 to 7		1 to 49
Advertising and promoting	1 to 7		1 to 7		1 to 49
Before sales service	1 to 7		1 to 7		1 to 49
After sales service	1 to 7		1 to 7		1 to 49
Merchandising	1 to 7		1 to 7		1 to 49
Purchasing	1 to 7		1 to 7		1 to 49
Operating efficiency	1 to 7		1 to 7		1 to 49
Finance	1 to 7		1 to 7		1 to 49
Personnel	1 to 7		1 to 7		1 to 49
General management	1 to 7		1 to 7		1 to 49
TOTAL GOAL INDEX					7 to 784

Main Sample

The main sample consisted of independent, non-franchised new ventures founded since 1980 whose current CEO is the original founder. The sample was designed around two major criteria: maximum variation and convenience. Since the model and its theoretical development were not firm nor industry specific, it was desirable to concentrate upon achieving a sample with maximal variation across those strategy types and industry environments used to operationalize the model. Only in this way could the model be fully tested and external validity enhanced. Second, since the amount of information needed from each firm was extensive and the necessary sample size for testing well over 100, it was paramount to chose a population for sampling which was easily accessible and prone to cooperate with the research.

The initial sampling population chosen was new (since 1980) manufacturing ventures in South Carolina and Georgia all of whose names, addresses, phone numbers, CEO's, founding dates, SCI codes, and other useful information were obtainable through the auspices of the respective development boards of both states. This population consisted of 547 firms, 225 of which were in South Carolina and the balance in Georgia. To this population was added another population of 82 national manufacturing firms who had cooperated in a recent new venture study at the University of South Carolina and about whom the appropriate information was known. Further, since it was undesirable to restrict the sample to manufacturing firms (even though their variance across strategies and industry situations was appropriately large), a further sample of non-manufacturing (i.e. retail and service) firms was sought on an ad hoc basis, largely from personal contacts or through faculty and students. A list of 153 businesses believed to meet the criteria of this research (firms founded since 1980 whose current CEO is the original founder) were compiled for this subsample from personal, faculty, and student contacts.

The questionnaire respondents were the CEO's themselves. Those CEO's whose questionnaire responses were usable were then contacted by phone and asked to take the timed aptitude tests described above.

Secondary (SBDC) Sample

In order to augment and enlarge the non-manufacturing sample used in this research, and to further extend the external validity of the research, the South Carolina SBDC cooperated in allowing this study to "piggy-back" an annual survey which they conduct regarding "long term clients", i.e.those clients with over 12 contact hours with the SBDC during the previous year. Questions identical to those for the main sample were inserted into the SBDC questionnaire although all of the multiple measures were not included due to space constraints. This questionnaire was similar in size and shape to the main questionnaire but was 11 pages in length. The population surveyed consisted of all long term clients (711) which they had assisted during 1988. This subsample was used independently and in conjunction with the main sample to further test the research model and add external validity to the current research.

Preventure Sample

The preventure sample was obtained for two reasons. First, it provided a much larger pool of mental test respondents than those tested from the main sample. The main sample research solicited entrepreneurs to answer a questionnaire which required approximately twenty minutes of their time and for those also agreeing to take the battery of Guilford's tests, another forty minutes of their time was consumed. Aptitude test response rates were reduced accordingly. It was therefore considered prudent to take steps to enhance reliability and validity by enlarging the size of samples in the skill reporting and testing areas. Since aspiring entrepreneurs should be more closely related to actual entrepreneurs on many dimensions than are the general population, the preventure sample was judged useful in exploring relationships between aptitude test scores and self-reported skill measures, whether skill levels could be successfully self (and/or observer) reported, and whether Guilford's Structure of Intellect model could be used to test for the aptitudes giving rise to these skills.

The second reason that the preventure sample was obtained was because the sample was believed useful in its own right to explore the relations between aspiring versus actual entrepreneurs on both skills and aptitudes.

Here again, the South Carolina SBDC was most cooperative in allowing access to their services. In this case, each month at the University of South Carolina, the SBDC conducted an evening seminar for prospective entrepreneurs throughout the midlands in South Carolina: a seminar whose subject was design and enhancement of the entrepreneur's business plans. Since, through self-selection, this group presumably shares many personality characteristics in common with active entrepreneurs, the participation of these prospective entrepreneurs was solicited to participate in the test and the skill ratings. Though the results of this subsample were used with caution, and only where reliability checks indicated their use to be appropriate, nevertheless this subsample proved to be of considerable benefit.

THE METHODOLOGY

The major methodological procedures of this study involved applying the techniques of T-tests, simple and multiple regression, and both exploratory and confirmatory factor analysis. Initially, exploratory factor analysis was used for the purposes of exploring the factor structure of the strategy and industry structure items to ensure construct validity. The factor scores from this analysis were used to represent strategy and industry structure in hypothesis testing and in other later analysis. As a check on the results of this exploratory factor analysis, confirmatory factor analysis was used to analyze the factor structure selected during the exploratory analysis.

T-tests were used to explore reliability and validity issues involving observer versus self-rated skills, and later to compare aspiring with actual entrepreneurs.

Once reliability and validity of the measures had been assured, all three sets of hypotheses were tested using multiple regression with the method of F-tests of partial determination.

In the later phases of the study, simple regression was used to derive normative propositions from interpretable regression coefficients.

Notes:

[1] Brinberg, D. & McGrath, J. (1985). Validity and the research process. Beverly Hills: Sage Publications.

[2] Ibid.

[3] Bagozzi, R.P. (1981). Evaluating structural equation models with unobserable variables and measurement error: A comment. Journal of Marketing Research, 18 (Aug), 375-381.

[4] Bagozzi, R.P. (1984). A prospectus for theory construction in marketing. Journal of Marketing, 48(Winter), 11-29.

[5] Feigl, H. (1970). The orthodox view of theories: Remarks in defense as well as critique. In M. Radnar and S. Winokur (Eds.). Minnesota studies in the philosophy of science, Vol. 4. Minneapolis: University of Minnesota Press, 3-16, p. 7.

[6] Bagozzi, R.P. (1984). A prospectus for theory construction in marketing. Journal of Marketing, 48(Winter), 11-29.

[7] Venkatraman, N. & Grant, J.H. (1986). Construct measurement in organizational strategy research: A critique and proposal. Academy of Management Review, 11(1), 71-87.

[8] Galbraith, C. & Schendel, D. (1983) An empirical analysis of strategy types. Strategic Management Journal, 4, 153-173.

[9] Dess, G.G. & Davis, P.S. (1984). Porter's (1980) generic strategies as determinants of strategic group membership and organizational performance. Academy of Management Journal, 27(3), 467-488.

[10] Robinson, R.B., & Pearce, J.A. (1985). The structure of generic strategies and their impact on business-unit performance. Academy of Managent Proceedings, San Diego, CA, 33-39.

[11] Robinson, R.B., McDougall, P., & Herron, L. (1988). Toward a new venture strategy typology. Proceedings of the Academy of Management, Aneheim Ca, 74-78.

[12] Vesper, K.H. (1980). New Venture Strategies. Englewood Cliffs, NJ: Prentice-Hall.

[13] Porter, M.E. (1980). Competitive Strategy. New York: Free Press.

[14] Robinson, R.B., McDougall, P., & Herron, L. (1988). Toward a new venture strategy typology. Proceedings of the Academy of Management, Aneheim Ca, 74-78.

[15] Hofer, C.W. & Schendel, D.E. (1978). Stategy formulation: Analytical concepts. St. Paul: West Publishing Co.

[16] Porter, M.E. (1980). Competitive Strategy. New York: Free Press.

[17] Porter, M.E. (1985). Competitive Advantage. New York: Free Press.

[18] Vesper, K.H. (1980). New Venture Strategies. Englewood Cliffs, NJ: Prentice-Hall.

[19] Ibid.

[20] Porter, M.E. (1980). Competitive Strategy. New York: Free Press.

[21] Sandberg, W. R. 1986). New venture performance: The role of strategy and industry structure. Lexington, MA: D.C. Heath & Co.

[22] Wright, R.V.L. (1974). A system for manageing diversity. Cambridge, MA: Arthur D. Little.

[23] Kerr, J.(1982). Assigning managers on the basis of the life cycle. Journal of Business Strategy, 58-65.

[24] Leontiades, M. (1982). Choosing the right manager to fit the strategy. Journal of Business Strategy, 58-69.

[25] Porter, M.E. (1980). Competitive Strategy. New York: Free Press.

[26] Ibid.

[27] Gupta, A.K. (1984). Contingency linkages between strategy and general manager characteristics: A conceptual examination. Academy of Management Review, 9 (3), 399-412.

[28] Sandberg, W. R. 1986). New venture performance: The role of strategy and industry structure. Lexington, MA: D.C. Heath & Co.

[29] Porter, M.E. (1980). Competitive Strategy. New York: Free Press.

[30] Sandberg, W. R. 1986). New venture performance: The role of strategy and industry structure. Lexington, MA: D.C. Heath & Co.

[31] Katz R.L. (1974). Skills of an effective administrator. Harvard Business Review, 52(5). 90-102.

[32] Guilford, J. P. (1967). The nature of human intelligence. New York: McGraw-Hill.

[33] Guilford, J.P. & Hoepfner, R. (1971). The analysis of intelligence. New York: McGraw-Hill.

[34] Ibid.

[35] Ibid.

[36] Maier, N. (1965). Psychology in industry. (3rd ed.). Boston: Houghton Mifflin Co.

[37] Roberts, E. B. (1969). Entrepreneurship and technology. In Gruber, H.W. & Marquis, D.G. (Eds.) Factors in the transfer of technology. Cambridge, MA: MIT Press, 219-237.

[38] Brockhaus, R. & Nord, W. (1979). An exploration of factors affecting the entrepreneurial decision: Personal characteristics vs. environmental conditions. Proceedings: Academy of Management.

[39] Gupta, A.K. (1984). Contingency linkages between strategy and general manager characteristics: A conceptual examination. Academy of Management Review, 9 (3), 399-412.

[40] Sapienza, H.J. (1989). Variations in venture capitalist-entrepreneur relations: Antecedents and consequences.Unpublished doctoral dissertation. University of Maryland.

[41] Gupta, A.K. & Govindarajan, V. (1984). Business unit strategy, managerial characteristics, and business effectiveness at strategy implementation. Academy of Management Journal, 27 (1), 25-41.

[42] Ibid.

[43] Nunnally, J.C. (1967). Psychometric theory. New York: McGraw-Hill.

Chapter Four:

Analysis and Results

INTRODUCTION

Previous chapters have outlined the purpose of this research, constructed a literature-based but previously untested model as the research's framework, and developed a methodology with which to test that model. The purpose of the current chapter is to describe the implementation of the methodology and the results thus obtained.

This chapter consists of seven sections. The first section describes the data gathering phase of the research and the characteristics of the subsamples. The second section examines reliability and validity issues in the main sample database such as internal consistency reliability and construct validity. The third section explains the use of the main sample to test the first two sets of hypotheses, those dealing with the significance of skills and skill propensities as explanations for new venture performance. The fourth section explains the use of the secondary (SBDC) sample in confirming the results of the main sample testing of the first two sets of hypotheses. The fifth section describes the testing of the third set of hypotheses, those dealing with relations between skills, aptitudes and training. The sixth explains the use of the preventure sample in confirming the third set of hypotheses. The seventh section then explores the data in light of the previous analyses in order to answer the third research question of this study, namely: "What specific normative relationships are implied between characteristics of the entrepreneur and NVP?"

DATA GATHERING

The data-gathering phase of this research took place during a six month period from April until September 1989. Several subsamples were gathered during this period as described in Chapter 3.

The Main Sample

Letters containing the main questionnaire with an attendant prepaid return envelope, an "observer" skills questionnaire (for a close business colleague) with its own confidential return envelope, and a personalized and signed cover letter explaining the project were mailed initially to the three manufacturing subsamples and the non-manufacturing subsample described in the last chapter, consisting of a combined total of 728 such packages. After several weeks, those who had not responded were phoned to increase the response rate, and a second questionnaire was then mailed to those agreeing verbally to participate in the research. When questionnaires were returned and verified to be useable for the research, a second phone call was made to solicit participation in the timed test. The test was then mailed to those agreeing to participate. The test package included a certificate for the test-taker to sign certifying that the test was timed (and by whom) and that the time limits were strictly adhered to.

The SBDC Confirmation Sample

In the case of the SBDC sample, letters containing the SBDC questionnaire with an attendant prepaid return envelope, along with a personalized and signed cover letter from the director of the SBDC were sent out to all 711 (long term 1988) clients. Subsequently, two more mailings were sent to those who had not responded in the previous mailings, and a separate phone followup was made.

The Preventure Aptitude Test Subsample

The sample of preventure volunteers who took the SI test were solicited from five different SBDC seminars. The tests were identical to those given to the entrepreneurs. In this case they were administered and timed by the researcher, but the written instructions included with each test were not supplemented by any verbal instructions, thus maintaining consistency with the entrepreneur's tests which included the same written instructions. Observer questionnaires with prepaid envelopes were also given to these volunteers after the tests with instruction to give them to an observer who knew them well, preferably a close business colleague.

The Resultant Subsamples

The response rates of the various subsamples may be seen in Figure 4-1. The only statistically significant difference in response rates between subsamples was the relatively low response rate from the Georgia manufacturers and the relatively high response rate from the ad hoc, non-manufacturers group. The Georgia manufacturers low rate can be explained by the fact that they were the only non-South Carolina subsample which had no previous connection with the University of South Carolina. The ad hoc, non-manufacturers high response rate can be explained by the fact that these firms had a personal acquaintance with someone at the University.

The SBDC impact study sample were checked using chi-square goodness-of-fit tests by sex and ethnic background (two variables unavailable from the other subsamples), as well as type of business. No significant differences were found between subgroups, indicating that this sample was demographically representative of the SBDC long term client population. The useable questionnaires in this subsample encompassed 11 manufacturing and 82 non-manufacturing firms. The reason for the relatively low ratio of usable questionnaires to responses were that many of the respondents were preventure clients who were not yet in business.

RELIABILITY ISSUES

Questionnaire Construction And Pretest

The first reliability issue deals with the face validity of the questionnaire. Following an extensive literature search and discussions with both business persons and academic experts, the questionnaire was inductively derived to accomplish its purpose as regards both clarity, face validity, and ease of response. Revision was then undertaken in a reiterative process using a panel of five academic researchers and two business persons until basic agreement was reached on all items. The questionnaire was then pretested with 38 firms and further minor revisions were made to increase face validity and decrease required respondent time.

Structure of Intellect Pretest and Test Construction

The SI test measures were pre-tested on 31 prospective entrepreneurs using guilford's original tests. There were a total of six timed tests given to each respondent. The time taken to complete the battery averaged about 70 minutes. Each of the six individual tests was composed of two parts. When the test results were analyzed, it was noted that the two parts of each test were generally quite consistent with each other and with the overall test score. This suggested that one part of each test might thus be used as a proxy for the whole, resulting in a significantly reduced time to take the test and thus increasing sample size and reducing response bias.

FIGURE 4-1
SUBSAMPLE RESPONSE RATES

	Population Surveyed	Respondents	Response Rate	Usable Questionnaires	Test Responses	Test responses as a percent of usable questionnaires
South Carolina Manufacturers	225	61	27%	50	13	26%
Georgia Manufacturers	332	46	14%	35	5	14%
National Manufacturers	82	21	25%	13	3	23%
Non-manufacturers	153	56	37%	36	12	33%
SBDC Long Term Clients	711	209	29%	93	NA	NA
SBDC Preventure Seminars	222	65	29%	65	65	100%
TOTAL	1725	458	27%	292	99	34%

* 108 of these were unusable due to being preventure

Analysis and Results

After further analysis, the first half of each test was chosen as the instrument for the remainder of the research (except for Cartoon Predictions where the last half was picked). In each case, the subtest picked was that which explained the highest amount of variance in the whole test. This method of choice was used because the six SI tests themselves had been chosen on the basis that they were the tests among all SI tests that loaded the highest on the desired SI factors. In order to maintain this high loading, it was desirable that the subtests chosen correlated maximally with the original whole tests and thus that most of the whole test variance was explained by the subtest. This explained variance averaged 87% among all six subtests.

Analysis of the split halves reliability (as measured by Cronbach's α) for each of the test halves as well as that of the whole test showed that, while some internal reliability was being sacrificed by chosing a subtest, the internal reliability of the subtest chosen was still at an acceptable level. Further, four of the six subtests chosen had superior internal consistency reliability to the subtests not used (See Figure 4-2). Reduction of the tests to subtest sizes reduced the time required for the entire test battery from 70 to 37 minutes.

Item Reliability

When multiple items are used to measure a construct, their internal consistency reliability should always be assessed.[1] The most highly regarded measure of such reliability is Cronbach's α, an estimate of the shared variance (the square of the correlation) between the sum of the standardized items and the "true" variance of the construct.[2] For purposes of the early stages of research, Nunnally,[3] suggests that $\alpha \geq .50$ is adequate.

Three of the constructs in this research have multiple measures: Scope, growth orientation, and performance. Their internal consistency reliability is shown below:

Measure	No.items	Cronbach's α	Correlation with "true score"
Scope	3	.82	.91
Growth Orientation	3	.62	79
Performance	3	.75	.87

FIGURE 4-2
SI TEST EXPLAINED VARIANCES AND RELIABILITIES

	Match Problems III	Way-Out Numbers	Pertinent Questions	Cartoon Predictions	Planning Elaboration II	Consequences (Remote)
Total test: Coefficient α	.73	.73	.79	.81	.81	.80
1st half test: Coefficient α	.68	.51	.57	.70	-	.65
1st half test: Correlation with total test score	.96	.91	.94	.83	.93	.96
1st half test: Explained Variance	.93	.82	.88	.68	.86	.93
2nd half test: Coefficient α	.36	.61	.69	.77	-	.61
2nd half test: Correlation with total test score	.33	.89	.92	.89	.91	.90
2nd half test: Explained Variance	.11	.79	.84	.79	.83	.80

Construct Validity

Construct validity is often referred to as being composed of two separate parts: convergent validity and divergent validity.[4,5] Nomological validity, a third issue in construct validity,[6] will be addressed later in this study through the hypothesis testing.

Essentially, convergent validity means having the measures of a construct correlate highly with other measures of the same construct, and divergent validity means having the measures of a construct fail to correlate highly with the measures of different, distinct constructs[7] with which they might be confused.

Given that this study has 9 measures of five separate strategy and industry structure constructs, construct validity for these items was tested first by exploratory factor analysis (both orthogonal and oblique) and then by confirmatory factor analysis. The orthogonal exploratory factor analysis was done with principal components factor analysis, with the extraction of five factors, and with varimax rotation. This is the factor analysis whose factor scores were used to opertionalize the three strategy and two industry structure measures. The results are shown in Figure 4-3.

Essentially all of the measures are well-behaved, loading largely on their own factors and only their own factors, with the sole exception of the first measure of growth orientation: the overall, subjective growth-orientation scale. Although this measure has it highest correlation with growth orientation, it also correlates significantly in a positive direction with breadth of scope and in a negative direction with industry stage. Its positive correlation with scope is consistent with Robinson, et al.[8] who found that new ventures with broad scope contained a higher proportion of firms with aggressive growth orientation than did new ventures with narrow scope. Further, its negative correlation with stage of industry growth is consistent with generally slower growth rates of firms in later industry stages.[9] This well-behaved exploratory factor analysis, which explain 80.1% of the variance in the original variables, is suggestive of both convergent and divergent validity. Further evidence of divergent validity is shown in Figure 4-4 which displays the intercorrelations between factors when this same factor matrix is subjected to orthotran/varimax factor rotation (oblique rotation). None of these factors has a higher intercorrelation with any other than .197, a good indication of divergent validity.

As a further test of the construct validity of the five strategy and industry structure constructs, confirmatory factor analysis was run on the measurement model displayed in Figure 4-5 using the LISREL VI

FIGURE 4-3

FACTOR LOADINGS FOR STRATEGY AND INDUSTRY STRUCTURE MEASURES

Factor Loadings

Measures	Scope	Growth Orient- ation	Entry Wedge	Industry Stage	Industry Product Hetero- genety
1st Scope Measure	.920	-.002	.003	-.018	-.035
2nd Scope Measure	.897	.000	-.074	-.014	-.039
3rd Scope measure	.741	-.000	-.116	-.136	-.075
1st Growth Orientation Measure	.401	.575	.035	-.349	-.079
2nd Growth Orientation Measure	-.094	.856	.011	-.065	.015
3rd Growth Orientation Measure	-.021	.800	.115	.148	-.040
Entry Wedge Measure	-.133	.115	.978	-.046	.054
Industry Stage Measure	-.089	.009	-.041	.961	-.026
Industry Product Hetero- geneity Measure	-.106	-.047	.052	-.018	.991

FIGURE 4-4

FACTOR CORRELATIONS FOR STRATEGY AND INDUSTRY STRUCTURE MEASURES - OBLIQUE FACTOR ANALYSIS

	Scope	Growth Orientation	Entry Wedge	Industry Stage	Industry Product Heterogenety
Scope	1.000				
Growth Orientation	.018	1.000			
Entry Wedge	-.144	.197	1.000		
Industry Stage	-.157	-.084	-.093	1.000	
Industry Product Heterogenety	-.124	-.075	.106	-.048	1.000

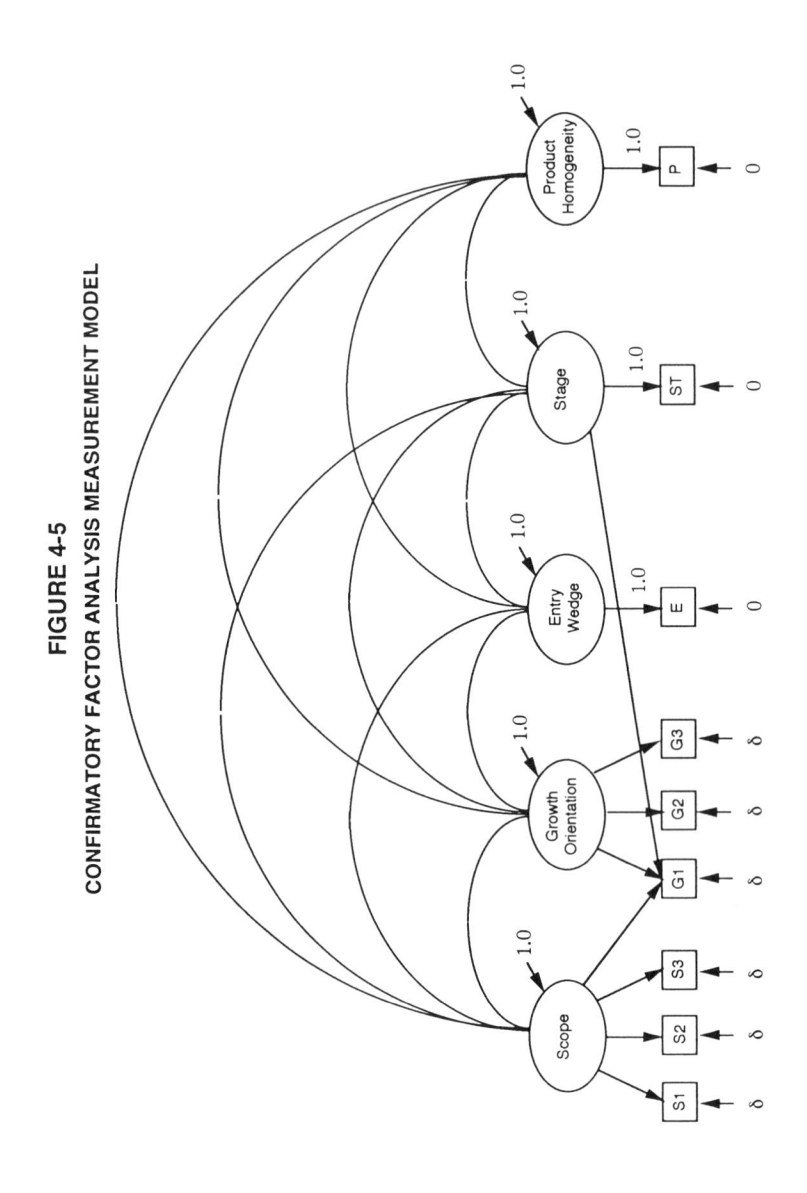

FIGURE 4-5
CONFIRMATORY FACTOR ANALYSIS MEASUREMENT MODEL

Analysis and Results

program.[10] Confirmatory factor analysis assesses the "fit" of a particular model to the actual data by comparing the results of a covariance matrix calculated from the model to the actual covariance matrix of the data.

In the current instance, the estimation method used was maximum likelihood. This estimation procedure assumes that the population sampled is distributed multivariate normally and that the sample size is sufficiently large. However, lack of normality or lack of sufficient size[11] will bias the technique toward rejection of the model, not toward acceptance.

Using this method, when the model is correct, the appropriate test statistic for comparing the model against the alternative (that there are nine orthogonal factors all loading on each of the nine measures) is a χ^2 statistic.[12] This χ^2 statistic is the probability that both the calculated (model) and data covariance matrix were drawn from the same population. In this case χ^2 with 21 degrees of freedom was 9.33 (p≥ .986), a very good fit. The matrix of Φ correlations (the correlations between the constructs) for this analysis is displayed in Figure 4-6. None of these factors has a higher intercorrelation with any other than .232, again a good indication of divergent validity.

Likewise, a confirmatory factor analysis using LISREL was run on the measurement model for the performance measures shown in Figure 4-7.here, χ^2 with 2 degree of freedom was .05 (p≥ .975), also a very good fit.

Validity of Skills Measures

Each of the measures of the seven skills is a single-item, self-rated assessment on a Likert-type scale ranging from 1 (Not effective at all) to 10 (Extremely effective) and anchored at both ends. In order to guard against self-report bias, each respondent was asked to give an "observer" skills questionnaire to a close business colleague who was personally familiar with the skills of the respondent. This questionnaire contained the identical seven skills questions as the main questionnaire except that they were constructed in the third person. The observer was to rate the main questionnaire respondent on the seven skills in strict confidence and return them in a separate, prepaid envelope.

After the observer questionnaire results were evaluated, it was decided not to use those results for five different and specific reasons. First, contrary to the researcher's expectation, the means of the reported skills on the observer questionnaire were consistently *higher* than the self-rated skills of the main questionnaire (See Figure 4-8).This indicated a possible bias on the part the *observers*, perhaps due to the

FIGURE 4-6
FACTOR CORRELATIONS FOR STRATEGY AND INDUSTRY STRUCTURE MEASURES - CONFIRMATORY FACTOR ANALYSIS

	Scope	Growth Orientation	Entry Wedge	Industry Stage	Industry Product Heterogenety
Scope	1.000				
Growth Orientation	-.073	1.000			
Entry Wedge	-.188	.232	1.000		
Industry Stage	-.142	-.008	-.074	1.000	
Industry Product Heterogenety	-.166	-.062	.105	-.044	1.000

FIGURE 4-7

**CONFIRMATORY FACTOR ANALYSIS MEASUREMENT
MODEL - PERFORMANCE**

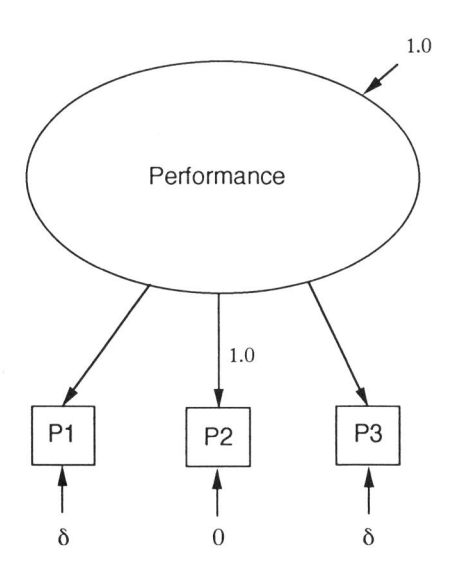

FIGURE 4-8
COMPARISONS OF SELF-REPORT WITH OBSERVER SKILL RATINGS

Skill	N	Mean	Std. Dev.	P-Value for mean difference (one tailed)
Self-report technical product/service	131	7.269	2.552	.0001
Observer technical product/service	66	8.706	1.396	
Self-report technical business	132	7.194	2.152	.0011
Observer technical business	67	8.133	1.728	
Self-report technical industry	132	7.352	2.216	.0001
Observer technical industry	67	8.809	1.411	
Self-report leadership	131	7.305	2.14	.1906
Observer leadership	67	7.599	2.404	
Self-report networking	132	6.518	2.227	.0001
Observer networking	67	8.128	1.958	
Self-report administrative	130	7.393	2.054	.0456
Observer administrative	67	7.917	2.045	
Self-report entrepreneurial	132	7.062	2.063	.0010
Observer entrepreneurial	67	8.006	1.906	

fact that they were nearly all employees of the persons they rated (their relationship to the person rated was included on the observer questionnaire). Second, the standard deviation of the observer ratings were (in all cases save one) smaller than that of the self-rated skills. This suggests, since the means of the observer skills were so close to the maximum value of 10, that the observer skills suffered from restriction of range. Third, when comparing the observer ratings to the self-ratings, coefficient α was below .5 for five of the seven skills (with the other two being .57 and .67 respectively), suggesting that the reliability of measures combining the observer and self-ratings would be below that acceptable even in exploratory research[13] and suggesting that the measures might not refer to the same construct. Fourth, the observer ratings suffered from a lack of nomological validity compared to the self-ratings. It will be seen in section five that the self-rated skills display theoretically predictable relations with aptitude and training. The observer rated skills showed none of these nomological relations whatsoever. Fifth, The number of usable observer questionnaires returned was only 51% of the number of usable main questionnaires returned.

On the other hand the validity of the self-skill rating measures is enhanced by several of the aforementioned reasons in reverse. There is indication that self-report bias is less than that of observer reported bias, and there is less restriction of range than for observer reported measures. In addition, as will be seen in section five of this chapter, the self-report skills display nomological validity in relation to aptitudes and training, as theory clearly holds they should.[14]

TEST OF HYPOTHESES H1 THROUGH H2G

The testing of the hypotheses concerning the connection of skills and skills propensities (and their interactions with strategy, and industry) with new venture performance was conducted using multivariate regression analysis.

Test of the Main Hypothesis: H1

> H1. skills, skill's propensities, and their interactions with strategy and industry structure will have a significant effect upon new venture performance.

In Chapters 2 & 3 above, it was suggested that a skill *times* the propensity to use that skill equals performance of that skill. Further, it was suggested that the effect upon new venture performance of performing a skill is contingent upon (and thus interacts with) strategy and industry structure. The nature of the second interaction (that between skill performance, and strategy and industry structure) has not been specified heretofore, and there are numerous forms which the nature of an interaction might take.[15][16] For purposes of this research, the nature of the second interaction will now be specified as multiplicative. In the multiplicative model, one assumes that effectiveness is most likely when two factors are both present but less likely when either is absent;[17] and this is the type of interaction that the literature implies between skills and strategy and industry structure.[18][19]

Using the above forms of interactions and observing the following definitions:

skills	$= R_i$
Propensities	$= T_i$
Strategy and Industry Structure	$= S_j$
New Venture Performance	$= P$

then the main equation for the current research model becomes:

$$P = \Sigma \beta_{R_i} R_i + \Sigma \beta_{T_i} T_i + \Sigma \beta_{S_j} S_j + \Sigma \beta_{R_i T_i} R_i T_i + \Sigma \beta_{R_i S_j} R_i S_j + \Sigma \beta_{T_i S_j} T_i S_j + \Sigma \beta_{R_i T_i S_j} R_i T_i S_j + \beta_0$$

There is, however, a problem using this model to test H1. The equation contains 132 terms because there are:

Variable type	Number of subtypes
$\beta_{R_i} R_i$	7
$\beta_{T_i} T_i$	7
$\beta_{S_j} S_j$	5
$\beta_{R_i T_i} R_i T_i$	7
$\beta_{R_i S_j} R_i S_j$	35
$\beta_{T_i S_j} T_i S_j$	35
$\beta_{R_i T_i S_j} R_i T_i S_j$	35
β_0	1

Analysis and Results

Since this is almost equal to the total number of usable responses in the main questionnaire (n=134) without even adjusting for any missing data, testing this model would be out of the question with the current data. Further, use of factor analysis to decrease the number of variables would be inadequate in this situation since the factors of R_iT_i cannot be constructed by multiplying factors of R_i times factors of T_i because of the necessary pairing of T_i with R_i (a T_i refers to its R_i, a factor of T would not necessarily refer to a factor of R), and since S_j has been originally constructed of orthogonal factors. In addition, factor analysis would cut down on the amount of variance available among the original variables.

One way around the problem of too many terms is to simply look at only those terms which are of maximal interest. In so doing, though, there is a problem with interpreting scaling transformations in regression equations which use multiplicative interactions.[20] As Schmidt[21] points out, the sizes of correlations between interactions and the variables upon which they are regressed are *not* invariant to linear transformations of the elements which make up the interaction. Since the scales used in this research are not ratio and are thus subject to arbitrary linear transformation, the *simple* correlations between their multiplicative interactions and new venture performance are somewhat arbitrary (though not without an "upper bound" as will be seen). However, as Cohen[22] points out, the *semi-partial* correlations between interactions and dependent variables *are* invariant to linear transformations of the elements which make up the interaction. He also points out that the multiple coefficient of determination (R^2) of the interaction *and* its constituent elements is also invariant to linear transformations of those elements, therefore placing an "upper bound" on the size of the simple correlation between the interaction term and the dependent variable despite any linear transformation. The "upper bound" on the size of the simple correlation between the multiplicative term and its dependent variable is the R^2 of the interaction *and* its constituent elements. Thus, in order to test the significance of a multiplicative interaction in a regression equation while being sure that its apparent significance is not due to transformation of its constituent elements, one must test its coefficient of partial determination given the constituent terms already in the equation.[23,24]

In light of the foregoing, hypothesis H1 may be tested considering only the following terms:

Variable type	Number of subtypes
$\beta_{R_iT_iS_j}R_iT_iS_j$	35
$\beta_{R_iT_i}R_iT_i$	7
$\beta_{S_j}S_j$	5
β_0	1

If the terms $\beta_{R_iT_iS_j}R_iT_iS_j$ and $\beta_{R_iT_i}R_iT_i$ have a significant coefficient of partial determination given $\beta_{S_j}S_j$ already in the equation, then the null should be rejected. If the null is *not* rejected, it may yet be possible to find other combinations of skill, propensity, strategy and industry terms which would reject it. However, if it *is* rejected, then H1 *must* be accepted. The reason that the terms $\beta_{R_i}R_i$ and $\beta_{T_i}T_i$ need not necessarily be brought into the test, even though they are in turn the constituents of $\beta_{R_iT_i}R_iT_i$, is that the simple correlation between $\beta_{R_iT_i}R_iT_i$ and performance has an "upper bound" (determined by $\beta_{R_i}R_i$ and $\beta_{T_i}T_i$ alone) and cannot have its explained variance inflated at the expense of any strategy or ndustry structure term by virtue of any linear transformation.

Given the test equation:

$$P = \Sigma \beta_{S_j}S_j + \Sigma \beta_{R_iT_i}R_iT_i + \Sigma \beta_{R_iT_iS_j}R_iT_iS_j + \beta_0$$

H1 is tested in two steps, the preliminary step with all of the Σ $\beta_{R_iT_iS_j}R_iT_iS_j$ terms involved and the final step with a "best regression" subset of $\Sigma \beta_{R_iT_iS_j}R_iT_iS_j$.

For purposes of this study, hypothesis testing will consider rejection of the null at three levels, $\alpha = .10$, $\alpha = .05$, and $\alpha = .01$.

The preliminary step is shown in Figure 4-9. In this case, the null is rejected at the $\alpha = .10$ level with $p \leq .074$. It should be pointed out that this equation has 40 degrees of freedom, which mitigate against an overly "tight" fit.

The final step is shown in Figure 4-10. with the "best regression subset" being arrived at by backwards stepwise regression from the full equation used in the preliminary step. Here the null is rejected at the $\alpha = .01$ level with $p \leq .0001$, this time with 60 degrees of freedom. Thus H1 should be accepted with very strong support. According to Cohen and Cohen,[25] adjusted R^2 (R^2 adjusted for the number of regression coefficients) is a realistic estimate of population variance accounted for, particularly when many predictors are used in a regression equation. It

Analysis and Results

FIGURE 4-9

HYPOTHESIS H1 - MAIN HYPOTHESIS

PRELIMINARY STEP

Base equation:	DF	SS	R^2	Adj. R^2	P-value
Regression	5	35.7	.08	.023	.2295
Residual	82	415.4			
Total	87	451.1			

Full equation:					
Regression	47	298.3	.66	.263	.0513
Residual	40	152.8			
Total	87	451.1			

$$F_{42,40} = \frac{415.4 - 152.8}{42} \div \frac{152.8}{40}$$

$$= 1.64$$

$p \leq .074$

FIGURE 4-10

HYPOTHESIS H1 -
MAIN HYPOTHESIS

FINAL STEP
(BEST PREDICTOR SUBSET)

Base equation:	DF	SS	R^2	Adj. R^2	P-value
Regression	5	35.7	.08	.023	.2295
Residual	82	415.4			
Total	87	451.1			

Full equation:

	DF	SS	R^2	Adj. R^2	P-value
Regression	27	274.7	.61	.433	.0001
Residual	60	176.4			
Total	87	451.1			

$$F_{22,60} = \frac{415.4 - 176.4}{22} \div \frac{176.4}{60}$$

$$= 3.70$$

$p \leq .0001$

Analysis and Results

should be noted here that the adjusted R^2 for the main hypothesis equation under the best subset method is .433 while the adjusted R^2 for the "base" equation (that using strategy and industry structure only) is .023. Further, when the best predictor subset among the terms in the base equation (strategy and industry structure terms) is found, it has an adjusted R^2 of .034. This suggests that the ability of skills (plus skill propensities, and their interactions with strategy and industry structure) to explain variance in the population is at least 40% (.433-.034).

Tests of Secondary Hypotheses: H2A Through H2G

> H2A. The product/service design skill and skill propensity, and their interactions with strategy and industry structure will have a significant effect upon new venture performance.

H2B	The same for the technical business skill
H2C	The same for the technical industry skill
H2D	The same for the internal leadership skill
H2E	The same for the networking skill skill
H2F	The same for the administrative skill
H2G	The same for the entrepreneurial skill

In the testing of these hypotheses, less terms are necessary in the regression equations so that the following variables may be used in full for each equation for method one:

Variable type	Number of subtypes
$\beta_{R_i} R_i$	1
$\beta_{T_i} T_i$	1
$\beta_{S_j} S_j$	5
$\beta_{R_i T_i} R_i T_i$	1
$\beta_{R_i S_j} R_i S_j$	5
$\beta_{T_i S_j} T_i S_j$	5
$\beta_{R_i T_i S_j} R_i T_i S_j$	5
β_0	1

The preliminary step for hypothesis H2A (for the technical product/service skill) is shown in Figure 4-11. In this case, the null is

FIGURE 4-11

HYPOTHESIS H2A -
THE TECHNICAL
PRODUCT/SERVICE SKILL

PRELIMINARY STEP

Base equation:	DF	SS	R^2	Adj. R^2	P-value
Regression	5	35.7	.08	.023	.2295
Residual	82	415.4			
Total	87	451.1			

Full equation:	DF	SS	R^2	Adj. R^2	P-value
Regression	23	136.0	.30	.051	.2767
Residual	64	315.0			
Total	87	451.1			

$$F_{18,64} = \frac{415.4 - 315.0}{18} \div \frac{315.0}{64}$$

$$= 1.13$$

$p \leq .12$

Analysis and Results

not rejected at the $\alpha = .10$ level with $p \leq .12$. It will be noted that the second regression has 24 calculated variables with n=88 and thus 64 degrees of freedom.

The final step is shown in Figure 4-12 with the "best regression subset" being arrived at by backwards stepwise regression. Here the null is rejected at the $\alpha = .10$ level with $p \leq .09$ this time with 71 degrees of freedom (df). Thus H2A (for the technical product/service skill) should be accepted with moderate support.

The preliminary step for hypothesis H2B (for the technical business skill) is shown in Figure 4-13. In this case, the null is rejected at the $\alpha = .05$ level with $p \leq \sim .02$ (df=64) even in this preliminary step due to the strength of the relationship.

The final step for hypothesis H2B is shown in Figure 4-14 with the "best regression subset" being arrived at by backwards stepwise regression. Here the null is rejected at the $\alpha = .01$ level $p \leq .001$ (df=72). Thus H2B (for the technical business skill) should be accepted with very strong support.

The preliminary step for hypothesis H2C (concerning the technical industry skill) is shown in Figure 4-15. In this case, the null would not be rejected with $p \leq \sim .35$ (n=88, df=64). The final step for hypothesis H2C is shown in Figure 4-16 with the "best regression subset" being arrived at by backwards stepwise regression. Here the null is rejected at the $\alpha = .05$ level with $p \leq .02$ (n=88, df=74). Thus H2C (concerning the technical industry skill) should be accepted with strong support.

The preliminary step for hypothesis H2D (concerning the leadership skill) is shown in Figure 4-17. In this case, the null would not be rejected with $p \leq \sim .30$.

The final step for hypothesis H2D is shown in Figure 4-18 with the "best regression subset" being arrived at by backwards stepwise regression as before. Here the null is rejected at the $\alpha = .10$ level with $p \leq .08$ level (df=71). Thus H2D (for the leadership skill) should be accepted with moderate support. The preliminary step for hypothesis H2E (for the networking skill) is shown in Figure 4-19. In this case, the null is not rejected with $p \leq .60$.

The final step for hypothesis H2E is shown in Figure 4-20. Here the null is rejected at the $\alpha = .05$ level with $p \leq .04$, (df=76). Thus H2C (for the networking skill) should be accepted with strong support.

The preliminary step for hypothesis H2F (for the administrative skill) is shown in Figure 4-21. In this case, the null would not be rejected with $p \leq \sim .11$.

FIGURE 4-12

HYPOTHESIS H2A - THE TECHNICAL PRODUCT/SERVICE SKILL

FINAL STEP
(BEST PREDICTOR SUBSET)

Base equation:	DF	SS	R^2	Adj. R^2	P-value
Regression	5	35.7	.08	.023	.2295
Residual	82	415.4			
Total	87	451.1			

Full equation:

Regression	16	127.1	.28	.120	.0584
Residual	71	324.0			
Total	87	451.1			

$$F_{11,71} = \frac{415.4 - 324.0}{11} \div \frac{324.0}{71}$$

$$= 1.82$$

$p \le .09$

Analysis and Results 125

FIGURE 4-13

HYPOTHESIS H2B - THE TECHNICAL BUSINESS SKILL

PRELIMINARY STEP

Base equation:	DF	SS	R^2	Adj. R^2	P-value
Regression	5	35.7	.08	.023	.2295
Residual	82	415.4			
Total	87	451.1			

Full equation:	DF	SS	R^2	Adj. R^2	P-value
Regression	23	182.9	.41	.192	.0233
Residual	64	268.2			
Total	87	451.1			

$$F_{18,64} = \frac{415.4 - 268.4}{18} \div \frac{268.4}{64}$$

$$= 1.95$$

$p \leq .02$

FIGURE 4-14

HYPOTHESIS H2B - THE TECHNICAL BUSINESS SKILL

FINAL STEP
(BEST PREDICTOR SUBSET)

Base equation:

	DF	SS	R^2	Adj. R^2	P-value
Regression	5	35.7	.08	.023	.2295
Residual	82	415.4			
Total	87	451.1			

Full equation:

	DF	SS	R^2	Adj. R^2	P-value
Regression	15	175.8	.39	.263	.0007
Residual	72	275.3			
Total	87	451.1			

$$F_{10,72} = \frac{415.4 - 275.3}{10} \div \frac{275.3}{75}$$

$$= 3.66$$

$p \leq .001$

Analysis and Results 127

FIGURE 4-15

HYPOTHESIS H2C - THE TECHNICAL INDUSTRY SKILL

PRELIMINARY STEP

Base equation:	DF	SS	R^2	Adj. R^2	P-value
Regression	5	35.7	.08	.023	.2295
Residual	82	415.4			
Total	87	451.1			

Full equation:

	DF	SS	R^2	Adj. R^2	P-value
Regression	23	131.5	.29	.037	.3262
Residual	64	319.5			
Total	87	451.1			

$$F_{18,64} = \frac{415.4 - 319.5}{18} \div \frac{319.5}{64}$$

$$= 1.07$$

$p \le$ N.S.

FIGURE 4-16

HYPOTHESIS H2C - THE TECHNICAL INDUSTRY SKILL

FINAL STEP
(BEST PREDICTOR SUBSET)

Base equation:	DF	SS	R^2	Adj. R^2	P-value
Regression	5	35.7	.08	.023	.2295
Residual	82	415.4			
Total	87	451.1			

Full equation:

	DF	SS	R^2	Adj. R^2	P-value
Regression	13	122.9	.27	.145	.0217
Residual	74	328.2			
Total	87	451.1			

$$F_{8,74} = \frac{415.4 - 328.2}{8} \div \frac{328.2}{74}$$

$$= 2.46$$

$p \leq .02$

FIGURE 4-17

HYPOTHESIS H2D - THE INTERNAL LEADERSHIP SKILL

PRELIMINARY STEP

Base equation:	DF	SS	R^2	Adj. R^2	P-value
Regression	5	35.7	.08	.023	.2295
Residual	82	415.4			
Total	87	451.1			

Full equation:					
Regression	23	140.1	.31	.063	.2359
Residual	64	310.9			
Total	87	451.1			

$$F_{18,64} = \frac{415.4 - 310.9}{18} \div \frac{310.9}{64}$$

$$= 1.20$$

$p \leq$ N.S.

FIGURE 4-18

HYPOTHESIS H2D -
THE INTERNAL LEADERSHIP SKILL

FINAL STEP
(BEST PREDICTOR SUBSET)

Base equation:	DF	SS	R^2	Adj. R^2	P-value
Regression	5	35.7	.08	.023	.2295
Residual	82	415.4			
Total	87	451.1			

Full equation:

	DF	SS	R^2	Adj. R^2	P-value
Regression	16	129.2	.29	.126	.0510
Residual	71	321.8			
Total	87	451.1			

$$F_{11,71} = \frac{415.4 - 321.8}{11} \div \frac{321.8}{71}$$

$$= 1.88$$

$p \leq .08$

Analysis and Results

FIGURE 4-19

HYPOTHESIS H2E - THE NETWORKING SKILL

PRELIMINARY STEP

Base equation:	DF	SS	R^2	Adj. R^2	P-value
Regression	5	35.7	.08	.023	.2295
Residual	82	415.4			
Total	87	451.1			

Full equation:	DF	SS	R^2	Adj. R^2	P-value
Regression	23	114.7	.25	.000	.5393
Residual	62	336.4			
Total	87	451.1			

$$F_{18,64} = \frac{415.4 - 336.4}{18} \div \frac{336.4}{64}$$

$$= .83$$

$p \leq$ N.S.

FIGURE 4-20

HYPOTHESIS H2E -
THE NETWORKING SKILL

FINAL STEP
(BEST PREDICTOR SUBSET)

Base equation:	DF	SS	R^2	Adj. R^2	P-value
Regression	5	35.7	.08	.023	.2295
Residual	82	415.4			
Total	87	451.1			

Full equation:

	DF	SS	R^2	Adj. R^2	P-value
Regression	11	103.1	.23	.117	.0350
Residual	76	348.0			
Total	87	451.1			

$$F_{6,76} = \frac{415.4 - 348.0}{6} \div \frac{348.0}{76}$$

$$= 2.45$$

$p \le .04$

Analysis and Results

FIGURE 4-21

HYPOTHESIS H2F -
THE ADMINISTRATIVE SKILL

PRELIMINARY STEP

Base equation:	DF	SS	R^2	Adj. R^2	P-value
Regression	5	35.7	.08	.023	.2295
Residual	82	415.4			
Total	87	451.1			

Full equation:	DF	SS	R^2	Adj. R^2	P-value
Regression	23	158.4	.35	.118	.1017
Residual	64	292.7			
Total	87	451.1			

$$F_{18,64} = \frac{415.4 - 292.7}{18} \div \frac{292.7}{64}$$

$$= 1.49$$

$p \leq .11$

The final step for hypothesis H2F is shown in Figure 4-22. Here the null is rejected at the $\alpha = .01$ level with $p \leq .002$ level(df=74). Thus H2F (concerning the administrative skill) should be accepted with very strong support.

The preliminary step for hypothesis H2G (concerning the entrepreneurial skill) is shown in Figure 4-23. In this case, the relationship is so strong that the null is rejected with $p \leq .099$ even before a best subset is arrived at.

The final step for hypothesis H2G is shown in Figure 4-24. Here the null is rejected at the $\alpha = .01$ level with $p \leq .001$ (df=74). Thus H2G (concerning the entrepreneurial skill) should be accepted with very strong support.

Thus all of the hypotheses in the second group are confirmed, with significance levels ranging from $\alpha = .10$ to $\alpha = .01$. A recap is shown in Figure 4-25. Thus all of the skills investigated in this research appear to have significant impact on NVP contingent upon their propensity to be exercised and upon the surrounding context of strategy and industry structure.

THE SBDC CONFIRMATION SAMPLE

This section explains the use of the SBDC sample in confirming the results of the hypothesis testing in the previous section.

The Sample

The SBDC confirmation sample was different from the main sample in two important regards. First, it was drawn through an SBDC questionnaire and therefore consisted of firms which had previously sought assistance from the South Carolina SBDC. Second, the types of firms comprising the SBDC sample differed from those comprising the main sample as follows:

Type Firm:	Number in SBDC sample	Number in Main Sample
Manufacturing	1	95
Construction	6	1
Retail	2	62

Analysis and Results

Wholesale	6	4
Service	37	27
Other	4	5
Missing Data	3	-
TOTAL	93	134

The ways in which the SBDC confirmation sample differed from the main sample are important to this study. The purpose of the SBDC sample was to confirm the results of the main sample as regards hypotheses H1 through H2G. Therefore, the greater the differences between sample characteristics, the greater the generalizability of any resulting confirmation.

Item Reliability

Items included on the SBDC questionnaire were identical with those contained in the main questionnaire with the exception that space considerations eliminated some of the scales that had been used in the multiple measures of scope, growth orientation, and performance. For comparison with the main sample, the item reliabilities of these three measures for the SBDC sample are shown below:

Measure	No.items	Cronbach's α	Correlation with "true score"
Scope	2	.76	87
Growth Orientation	1	-	-
Performance	3	.73	.85

Construct Validity

As was done for the main sample, construct validity (for the six items above) was tested first by exploratory factor analysis and then by confirmatory factor analysis. The exploratory factor analysis was done with principal components factor analysis, with the extraction of five factors and with varimax rotation. This is the factor analysis whose factor scores were used to opertionalize the three strategy and two

FIGURE 4-22

**HYPOTHESIS H2F -
THE ADMINISTRATIVE SKILL**

**FINAL STEP
(BEST PREDICTOR SUBSET)**

Base equation:	DF	SS	R^2	Adj. R^2	P-value
Regression	5	35.7	.08	.023	.2295
Residual	82	415.4			
Total	87	451.1			

Full equation:	DF	SS	R^2	Adj. R^2	P-value
Regression	13	152.7	.34	.222	.0019
Residual	74	298.4			
Total	87	451.1			

$$F_{8,74} = \frac{415.4 - 298.4}{8} \div \frac{298.4}{74}$$

$$= 3.63$$

$p \leq .002$

FIGURE 4-23

HYPOTHESIS H2G - THE ENTREPRENEURIAL SKILL

PRELIMINARY STEP

Base equation:	DF	SS	R^2	Adj. R^2	P-value
Regression	5	35.7	.08	.023	.2295
Residual	82	415.4			
Total	87	451.1			

Full equation:	DF	SS	R^2	Adj. R^2	P-value
Regression	23	163.9	.36	.135	.0755
Residual	64	287.2			
Total	87	451.1			

$$F_{18,64} = \frac{415.4 - 287.2}{18} \div \frac{287.2}{64}$$

$$= 1.59$$

$p \leq .099$

FIGURE 4-24

HYPOTHESIS H2G - THE ENTREPRENEURIAL SKILL

FINAL STEP
(BEST PREDICTOR SUBSET)

Base equation:	DF	SS	R^2	Adj. R^2	P-value
Regression	5	35.7	.08	.023	.2295
Residual	82	415.4			
Total	87	451.1			

Full equation:	DF	SS	R^2	Adj. R^2	P-value
Regression	13	153.5	.34	.224	.0017
Residual	74	297.6			
Total	87	451.1			

$$F_{8,74} = \frac{415.4 - 297.6}{8} \div \frac{297.6}{74}$$

$$= 3.66$$

$p \leq .001$

FIGURE 4-25
RECAP OF SECOND SET OF HYPOTHESES: THAT EACH OF THE INDIVIDUAL SKILLS IS OF IMPORTANCE

Hypothesis	α -level of confirmation	Explained variaance for best equation
2A: Technical product/service skill	.10	12.0%
2B: Technical business skill	.01	26.3%
2C: Technical industry skill	.05	14.5%
2D: Leadership skill	.10	12.6%
2E: Networking skill	.05	11.7%
2F: Administrative skill	.05	22.2%
2G: Entrepreneurial skill	.01	22.4%

industry structure measures. The results are shown in Figure 4-26. The measures are basically well-behaved, loading largely only on their own factors with the exception of the first scope measure and the growth-orientation measure. These measures load on each other's factors. As was the case with the main sample, these positive correlations between scope and growth measures are consistent with Robinson, et al.[26] who found that new ventures with broad scope contained a higher proportion of firms with aggressive growth orientation than did new ventures with narrow scope.

Evidence of divergent validity is shown in Figure 4-27 which displays the intercorrelations between factors when this same factor matrix is subjected to orthotran/varimax factor rotation (oblique rotation). None of these factors has a higher intercorrelation with any other than -.237 except for the .470 correlation between scope and growth orientation. This correlation (.470) is a direct consequence of the elimination of two of the items measuring growth orientation and one measuring scope that were on the main questionnaire.

To provide further evidence of construct validation, confirmatory factor analysis was run on the measurement model displayed in Figure 4-28 using the LISREL VI program[27] with maximum likelihood estimation. In this case χ^2 with 4 degrees of freedom was 0.26 (p≤ .992), a quite good fit. The matrix of Φ correlations for this analysis is displayed in Figure 4-29. Again, this analysis provides evidence of the construct validity for the three strategy constructs and the two industry structure constructs for the SBDC sample.

Likewise, a confirmatory factor analysis using LISREL was run on the measurement model for the performance measures shown in Figure 4-30. Here, χ^2 with 2 degrees of freedom was .000+ (p≤.999), also a very good fit.

Confirmation of Hypothesis H1

Data from the SBDC confirmation sample was used to confirm hypotheses H1 through H2G using multiple regression with F-tests for partial determination in a similar fashion to that of the main sample. However, in the case of the SBDC sample, missing data and a smaller data base (of 93) restricted the testing data base for these hypotheses to 43 observations. Since testing of hypothesis H1 required 47 variables for the main sample, it was apparent that the number of independent variables used to confirm hypothesis H1 with the SBDC data must be considerably reduced. Consequently, it was decided to use factor analysis to reduce the number of skills although this would preclude eliminating not only some of the variance of the skills variables themselves, but also any variance contributed by skills propensities or their interactions.

FIGURE 4-26

FACTOR LOADINGS FOR STRATEGY AND INDUSTRY STRUCTURE MEASURES

SBDC SAMPLE

Factor Loadings

Measures	Scope	Growth Orient- ation	Entry Wedge	Industry Stage	Industry Product Hetero- geneity
1st Scope Measure	.800	.280	.070	-.112	-.153
2nd Scope Measure	.917	.100	.019	-.033	-.023
Growth Orientation Measure	.278	.948	-.025	-.111	-.018
Entry Wedge Measure	.058	-.019	.992	-.100	.024
Industry Stage Measure	-.096	-.104	-.103	.983	-.037
Industry Product Hetero- geneity Measure	-.114	-.020	.024	-.036	.990

FIGURE 4-27
FACTOR CORRELATIONS FOR STRATEGY AND INDUSTRY STRUCTURE MEASURES - SBDC SAMPLE OBLIQUE FACTOR ANALYSIS

	Scope	Growth Orientation	Entry Wedge	Industry Stage	Industry Product Heterogeneity
Scope	1.000				
Growth Orientation	(.470)	1.000			
Entry Wedge	.102	-.102	1.000		
Industry Stage	-.194	-.237	-.213	1.000	
Industry Product Heterogeneity	-.204	-.078	.047	-.061	1.000

Analysis and Results 143

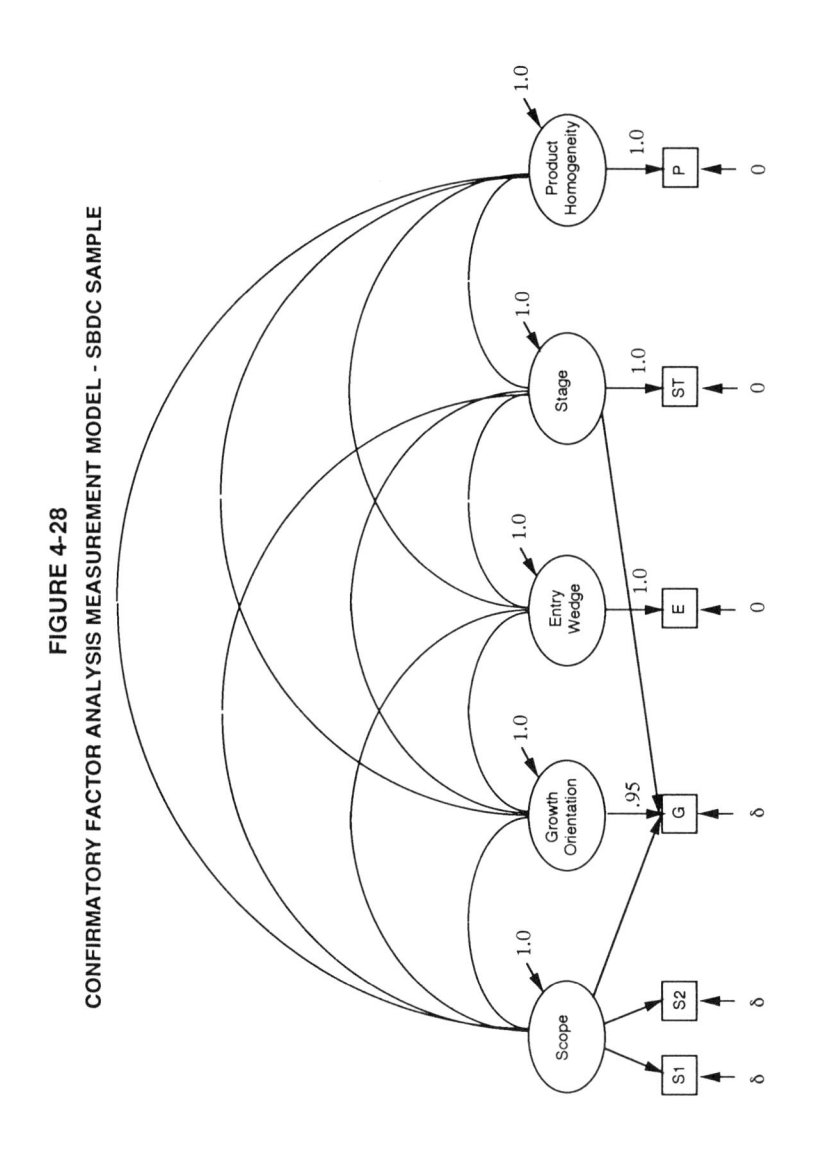

FIGURE 4-28
CONFIRMATORY FACTOR ANALYSIS MEASUREMENT MODEL - SBDC SAMPLE

FIGURE 4-29

FACTOR CORRELATIONS FOR STRATEGY AND INDUSTRY STRUCTURE MEASURES - SBDC SAMPLE CONFIRMATORY FACTOR ANALYSIS

	Scope	Growth Orientation	Entry Wedge	Industry Stage	Industry Product Heterogeneity
Scope	1.000				
Growth Orientation	.547	1.000			
Entry Wedge	.107	-.023	1.000		
Industry Stage	-.233	-.225	-.206	1.000	
Industry Product Heterogeneity	-.225	-.054	.043	-.060	1.000

FIGURE 4-30

**CONFIRMATORY FACTOR ANALYSIS MEASUREMENT
MODEL - PERFORMANCE
SBDC SAMPLE**

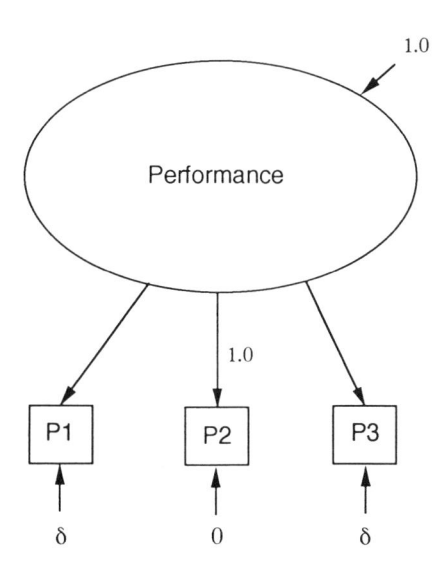

This latter was true for the simple reason that propensities to use skills bears no simple relation to propensities to use factors of skills.

Skills Factors

Exploratory factor analysis was thus run on the seven skills for the SBDC data using principal components factor analysis with varimax rotation. The three-factor solution which explains 74% of the variance is displayed in Figure 4-31. Given the pattern of factor loadings, there is considerable evidence for labeling the first factor: "internal skills"; the second factor "external skills"; and the third factor "product design skills".

For comparison, the same analysis was run on the data for the main sample and is displayed in Figure 4-32 where the three factors explain 67% of the variance.

Confirming Hypothesis H1

Hypothesis H1 was as follows:

> H1: skills, skill's propensities, and their interactions with strategy, and industry structure will have a significant effect upon new venture performance.

If the skill factors and their interactions with strategy and industry can be shown to be significant given strategy and industry structure already in the equation, the null will thus be rejected and H1 accepted. Using the above factor analysis for the SBDC sample skills and observing the following definitions:

$$\text{skills Factors} = F_i$$

$$\text{Strategy and Industry Structure} = S_j$$

$$\text{New Venture Performance} = P$$

then the main equation for the current research model becomes:

$$P = \Sigma\ \beta_{F_i} F_i + \Sigma\ \beta_{S_j} S_j + \Sigma\ \beta_{F_i S_j} F_i S_j + \beta_0$$

Analysis and Results 147

FIGURE 4-31

FACTOR LOADINGS FOR SKILLS MEASURES - SBDC SAMPLE

Factor Loadings

Skill	Factor 1	Factor 2	Factor 3
Technical product/service design	.274	.167	(.906)
Technical business	(.805)	.292	.027
Technical industry	.026	(.783)	.298
Internal leadership	(.810)	-.094	.076
Networking	.421	(.567)	.244
Administrative	(.770)	.272	.115
Entrepreneurial	.451	(.752)	-.225

FIGURE 4-32

FACTOR LOADINGS FOR SKILLS MEASURES - MAIN SAMPLE

Factor Loadings

Skill	Factor 1	Factor 2	Factor 3
Technical product/service design	.033	.098	(.939)
Technical business	(.798)	.139	.094
Technical industry	.063	(.803)	.153
Internal leadership	(.749)	-.084	-.119
Networking	.111	(.809)	-.052
Administrative	(.759)	.105	.169
Entrepreneurial	.391	(.555)	.385

Analysis and Results

H1 is tested in two steps, the preliminary step with all of the Σ $\beta_{FiSj}FiSj$ and Σ $\beta_{Fi}F_i$ terms involved, and the final step with a "best regression" subset of the Σ $\beta_{FiSj}FiSj$ and Σ $\beta_{Fi}F_i$ terms. The preliminary step for the SBDC sample is shown in Figure 4-33. In this case, the null is not rejected at the $\alpha = .10$ level with $p \le .11$. It will be noted that the second regression has 19 degrees of freedom (df), which mitigate against an overly "tight" fit.

In the second step, using the main equation with stepwise backwards to obtain a "best subsets" predictor, the null is rejected at the $\alpha = .01$ level with $p \le .01$ and df=25 (see Figure 4-34). Thus their H1 should be accepted with very strong support for the SBDC confirmation sample.

Individual Skill Factors

Having shown that the skill factors may be used to confirm hypothesis H1, it is also of interest to look at each factor individually to see if it and its interactions with strategy and industry structure is significant.

For the internal factor (factor 1) with the full set of interactions, the test is shown in Figure 4-35 where p is clearly not significant (df=31).

However, for the best predictor subset arrived at by backwards stepwise regression, the factor and its interactions is significant at the $\alpha = .10$ level with $p \le .09$ and df=36 (see Figure 4-36).

For the external factor (factor 2) with the full set of interactions, the test shown in Figure 4-37 shows the predictor set not significant at the $\alpha = .10$ level with $p \le .11$ and df=31.

However, for the best predictor subset arrived at by backwards stepwise regression, the factor and its interactions is significant at the $\alpha = .05$ level with $p \le .09$ and df=33 (see Figure 4-38).

For the product design factor (factor 3), the full predictor set is significant at the $\alpha = .10$ level with $p \le .08$ and df=31 (see Figure 4-39).

For the best predictor subset arrived at by backwards stepwise regression, the factor and its interactions is significant at the $\alpha = .05$ level with $p \le .02$ and df=33 (see Figure 4-40).

FIGURE 4-33

SBDC

**HYPOTHESIS H1 -
MAIN HYPOTHESIS -
3 FACTOR SOULTION**

PRELIMINARY STEP

Base equation:	DF	SS	R^2	Adj. R^2	P-value
Regression	5	51.5	.22	.112	.0922
Residual	37	184.7			
Total	42	236.2			

Full equation:

Regression	23	167.9	.71	.316	.0607
Residual	19	68.3			
Total	42	236.2			

$$F_{18,19} = \frac{184.7 - 68.3}{18} \div \frac{68.3}{19}$$

$$= 1.80$$

$p \leq .11$

Analysis and Results

FIGURE 4-34
SBDC
HYPOTHESIS H1 -
MAIN HYPOTHESIS -
3 FACTOR SOLUTION

FINAL STEP
(BEST PREDICTOR SUBSET)

Base equation:	DF	SS	R^2	Adj. R^2	P-value
Regression	5	51.5	.22	.112	.0922
Residual	37	184.7			
Total	42	236.2			

Full equation:	DF	SS	R^2	Adj. R^2	P-value
Regression	17	160.7	.68	.463	.0048
Residual	25	75.5			
Total	42	236.2			

$$F_{12,25} = \frac{184.7 - 75.5}{12} \div \frac{75.5}{25}$$

$$= 3.01$$

$p \leq .01$

FIGURE 4-35

SBDC
FACTOR 1, THE INTERNAL SKILLS FACTOR

PRELIMINARY STEP

Base equation:	DF	SS	R^2	Adj. R^2	P-value
Regression	5	51.5	.22	.112	.0922
Residual	37	184.7			
Total	42	236.2			

Full equation:					
Regression	11	69.2	.29	.042	.3485
Residual	31	167.0			
Total	42	236.2			

$$F_{6,31} = \frac{184.7 - 167.0}{6} \div \frac{167.0}{31}$$

$$= .55$$

$p \le$ N.S.

FIGURE 4-36

SBDC
FACTOR 1, THE INTERNAL SKILLS FACTOR

FINAL STEP
(BEST PREDICTOR SUBSET)

Base equation:

	DF	SS	R^2	Adj. R^2	P-value
Regression	5	51.5	.22	.112	.0922
Residual	37	184.7			
Total	42	236.2			

Full equation:

	DF	SS	R^2	Adj. R^2	P-value
Regression	6	66.9	.28	.160	.0526
Residual	36	170.1			
Total	42	236.2			

$$F_{1,36} = \frac{184.7 - 170.1}{1} \div \frac{170.1}{36}$$

$$= 3.09$$

$p \leq .09$

FIGURE 4-37

SBDC
FACTOR 2, THE EXTERNAL SKILLS FACTOR

PRELIMINARY STEP

Base equation:	DF	SS	R^2	Adj. R^2	P-value
Regression	5	51.5	.22	.112	.0922
Residual	37	184.7			
Total	42	236.2			

Full equation:

Regression	11	102.5	.43	.233	.0453
Residual	31	133.7			
Total	42	236.2			

$$F_{6,31} = \frac{184.7 - 133.7}{6} \div \frac{133.7}{31}$$

$$= 1.97$$

$p \leq .11$

Analysis and Results

FIGURE 4-38

SBDC
FACTOR 2, THE EXTERNAL SKILLS FACTOR

FINAL STEP
(BEST PREDICTOR SUBSET)

Base equation:

	DF	SS	R^2	Adj. R^2	P-value
Regression	5	51.5	.22	.112	.0922
Residual	37	184.7			
Total	42	236.2			

Full equation:

	DF	SS	R^2	Adj. R^2	P-value
Regression	9	98.3	.42	.257	.0212
Residual	33	137.9			
Total	42	236.2			

$$F_{4,33} = \frac{184.7 - 137.9}{4} \div \frac{137.9}{33}$$

$$= 2.80$$

$p \leq .04$

FIGURE 4-39

SBDC
FACTOR 3, THE PRODUCT DESIGN FACTOR

PRELIMINARY STEP

Base equation:

	DF	SS	R^2	Adj. R^2	P-value
Regression	5	51.5	.22	.112	.0922
Residual	37	184.7			
Total	42	236.2			

Full equation:

	DF	SS	R^2	Adj. R^2	P-value
Regression	11	106.3	.45	.255	.0332
Residual	31	129.9			
Total	42	236.2			

$$F_{6,31} = \frac{184.7 - 129.9}{6} \div \frac{129.9}{31}$$

$$= 2.20$$

$p \leq .08$

Analysis and Results 157

FIGURE 4-40

SBDC
FACTOR 3, THE PRODUCT DESIGN FACTOR

FINAL STEP
(BEST PREDICTOR SUBSET)

Base equation:	DF	SS	R^2	Adj. R^2	P-value
Regression	5	51.5	.22	.112	.0922
Residual	37	184.7			
Total	42	236.2			

Full equation:

	DF	SS	R^2	Adj. R^2	P-value
Regression	9	101.8	.43	.276	.0154
Residual	33	134.4			
Total	42	236.2			

$$F_{4,33} = \frac{184.7 - 134.4}{4} \div \frac{134.4}{33}$$

$$= 3.09$$

$p \leq .02$

Tests of Secondary Hypotheses: H2A Through H2G

H2A. The product/service design skill and skill propensity, and their interactions with strategy and industry structure will have a significant effect upon new venture performance.

H2B	The same for the technical business skill
H2C	The same for the technical industry skill
H2D	The same for the internal leadership skill
H2E	The same for the networking skill skill
H2F	The same for the administrative skill
H2G	The same for the entrepreneurial skill

In the testing of these hypotheses for the SBDC confirmation sample, less terms are necessary in the regression equations so that the following variables will be used in full for each equation for method one, just as in the main sample test:

Variable type	Number of subtypes
$\beta_{R_i} R_i$	1
$\beta_{T_i} T_i$	1
$\beta_{S_j} S_j$	5
$\beta_{R_i T_i} R_i T_i$	1
$\beta_{R_i S_j} R_i S_j$	5
$\beta_{T_i S_j} T_i S_j$	5
$\beta_{R_i T_i S_j} R_i T_i S_j$	5
β_0	1

The preliminary step for hypothesis H2A (concerning the technical product/service design skill) is shown in Figure 4-41. In this case, the null is not rejected at the $\alpha = .10$ level with p clearly insignificant (df=11).

The final step is shown in Figure 4-42 with the "best regression subset" being arrived at by backwards stepwise regression. Here the null is rejected at the $\alpha = .10$ level with p≤ .07 and df=15. Thus H2A

FIGURE 4-41

SBDC
HYPOTHESIS H2A - THE TECHNICAL PRODUCT/SERVICE SKILL

PRELIMINARY STEP

Base equation:

	DF	SS	R^2	Adj. R^2	P-value
Regression	5	59.1	.31	.185	.0504
Residual	29	134.8			
Total	34	193.9			

Full equation:

	DF	SS	R^2	Adj. R^2	P-value
Regression	23	153.3	.79	.352	.1551
Residual	11	40.6			
Total	34	193.9			

$$F_{18,11} = \frac{134.8 - 40.6}{18} \div \frac{40.6}{11}$$

$$= 1.42$$

$p \leq$ N.S.

FIGURE 4-42
SBDC

HYPOTHESIS H2A - THE TECHNICAL PRODUCT/SERVICE SKILL

FINAL STEP
(BEST PREDICTOR SUBSET)

Base equation:	DF	SS	R^2	Adj. R^2	P-value
Regression	5	59.1	.31	.185	.0504
Residual	29	134.8			
Total	34	193.9			

Full equation:

	DF	SS	R^2	Adj. R^2	P-value
Regression	19	150.5	.77	.492	.0266
Residual	15	43.5			
Total	34	193.9			

$$F_{14,15} = \frac{134.8 - 43.5}{14} \div \frac{43.5}{15}$$

$$= 2.25$$

$p \leq .07$

Analysis and Results

(concerning the technical product/service design skill) should be accepted with moderate support for the SBDC confirmation sample.

The preliminary step for hypothesis H2B (concerning the technical business skill) is shown in Figure 4-43. In this case, p is clearly not significant at the $\alpha = .10$ level with df=11.

The final step for hypothesis H2B is shown in Figure 4-44 with the "best regression subset" being arrived at by backwards stepwise regression. Here the null is rejected at the $\alpha = .05$ level $p \leq .02$, df=15. Thus H2B (for the technical business skill) should be accepted with strong support.

The preliminary step for hypothesis H2C (for the technical industry skill) is shown in Figure 4-45. In this case, the null would not be rejected with p insignificant.

The final step for hypothesis H2C is shown in Figure 4-46 with the "best regression subset" being arrived at by backwards stepwise regression as usual. Here the null is rejected at the $\alpha = .05$ level with $p \leq .04$ and df=14. Thus H2C (concerning the technical business skill) should be accepted with strong support.

The preliminary step for hypothesis H2D (for the leadership skill) is shown in Figure 4-47. In this case, the null would not be rejected with p clearly insignificant.

The final step for hypothesis H2D is shown in Figure 4-48. Here the null is rejected at the $\alpha = .05$ level with $p \leq .04$ and df=23. Thus H2D (for the leadership skill) should be accepted with strong support.

The preliminary step for hypothesis H2E (for the networking skill) is shown in Figure 4-49. In this case, the null is not rejected with p clearly insignificant.

The final step for hypothesis H2E is shown in Figure 4-50 with the "best regression subset" being arrived at by backwards stepwise regression. Here the null is rejected at the $\alpha = .01$ level with $p \leq .005$ with df=20. Thus H2C (for the networking skill) should be accepted with very strong support.

The preliminary step for hypothesis H2F (for the administrative skill) is shown in Figure 4-51. In this case, the null would not be rejected with p insignificant.

The final step for hypothesis H2F is shown in Figure 4-52. Here the null is rejected at the $\alpha = .01$ level with $p \leq .005$ level and df=17. Thus H2F (for the administrative skill) should be accepted with very strong support. The preliminary step for hypothesis H2G (for the entrepreneurial skill) is shown in Figure 4-53. In this case, the null is not rejected with p clearly insignificant.

FIGURE 4-43

**SBDC
HYPOTHESIS H2B -
THE TECHNICAL BUSINESS
SKILL**

PRELIMINARY STEP

Base equation:	DF	SS	R^2	Adj. R^2	P-value
Regression	5	59.1	.31	.185	.0504
Residual	29	134.8			
Total	34	193.9			

Full equation:	DF	SS	R^2	Adj. R^2	P-value
Regression	23	162.3	.84	.496	.0617
Residual	11	31.6			
Total	34	193.9			

$$F_{18,11} = \frac{134.8 - 31.6}{18} \div \frac{31.6}{11}$$

$$= 2.00$$

$p \leq$ N.S.

Analysis and Results

FIGURE 4-44
SBDC
HYPOTHESIS H2B -
THE TECHNICAL BUSINESS SKILL

FINAL STEP
(BEST PREDICTOR SUBSET)

Base equation:	DF	SS	R^2	Adj. R^2	P-value
Regression	5	59.1	.31	.185	.0504
Residual	29	134.8			
Total	34	193.9			

Full equation:

	DF	SS	R^2	Adj. R^2	P-value
Regression	19	160.2	.83	.606	.0061
Residual	15	33.7			
Total	34	193.9			

$$F_{14,15} = \frac{134.8 - 33.7}{14} \div \frac{33.7}{15}$$

$$= 3.21$$

$p \leq .02$

**FIGURE 4-45
SBDC
HYPOTHESIS H2C -
THE TECHNICAL INDUSTRY
SKILL**

PRELIMINARY STEP

Base equation:

	DF	SS	R^2	Adj. R^2	P-value
Regression	5	59.1	.31	.185	.0504
Residual	29	134.8			
Total	34	193.9			

Full equation:

	DF	SS	R^2	Adj. R^2	P-value
Regression	23	158.6	.82	.438	.0937
Residual	11	35.3			
Total	34	193.9			

$$F_{18,11} = \frac{134.8 - 35.3}{18} \div \frac{35.3}{11}$$

$$= 1.72$$

$p \leq$ N.S.

Analysis and Results

FIGURE 4-46
SBDC
HYPOTHESIS H2C -
THE TECHNICAL INDUSTRY
SKILL

FINAL STEP
(BEST PREDICTOR SUBSET)

Base equation:	DF	SS	R^2	Adj. R^2	P-value
Regression	5	59.1	.31	.185	.0504
Residual	29	134.8			
Total	34	193.9			

Full equation:

	DF	SS	R^2	Adj. R^2	P-value
Regression	20	157.4	.81	.543	.0194
Residual	14	36.5			
Total	34	193.9			

$$F_{15,14} = \frac{134.8 - 36.5}{15} \div \frac{36.5}{14}$$

$$= 2.51$$

$p \leq .04$

FIGURE 4-47
SBDC
HYPOTHESIS H2D - THE INTERNAL LEADERSHIP SKILL

PRELIMINARY STEP

Base equation:	DF	SS	R^2	Adj. R^2	P-value
Regression	5	59.1	.31	.185	.0504
Residual	29	134.8			
Total	34	193.9			

Full equation:

Regression	23	126.5	.65	.000	.6051
Residual	11	67.4			
Total	34	193.9			

$$F_{18,11} = \frac{134.8 - 67.4}{18} \div \frac{67.4}{11}$$

$$= .61$$

$p \leq$ N.S.

Analysis and Results

FIGURE 4-48
SBDC
HYPOTHESIS H2D -
THE INTERNAL LEADERSHIP SKILL

FINAL STEP
(BEST PREDICTOR SUBSET)

Base equation:	DF	SS	R^2	Adj. R^2	P-value
Regression	5	59.1	.31	.185	.0504
Residual	29	134.8			
Total	34	193.9			

Full equation:

	DF	SS	R^2	Adj. R^2	P-value
Regression	11	114.6	.59	.396	.0122
Residual	23	79.3			
Total	34	193.9			

$$F_{6,23} = \frac{134.8 - 79.3}{6} \div \frac{79.3}{23}$$

$$= 2.68$$

$p \leq .04$

FIGURE 4-49

SBDC

HYPOTHESIS H2E - THE NETWORKING SKILL

PRELIMINARY STEP

Base equation:	DF	SS	R^2	Adj. R^2	P-value
Regression	5	59.1	.31	.185	.0504
Residual	29	134.8			
Total	34	193.9			

Full equation:

Regression	23	154.5	.80	.373	.1389
Residual	11	39.4			
Total	34	193.9			

$$F_{6,23} = \frac{134.8 - 39.4}{18} \div \frac{39.4}{11}$$

$$= 1.48$$

$p \leq$ N.S.

FIGURE 4-50
SBDC
HYPOTHESIS H2E -
THE NETWORKING SKILL
FINAL STEP
(BEST PREDICTOR SUBSET)

Base equation:	DF	SS	R^2	Adj. R^2	P-value
Regression	5	59.1	.31	.185	.0504
Residual	29	134.8			
Total	34	193.9			

Full equation:

	DF	SS	R^2	Adj. R^2	P-value
Regression	14	148.7	.77	.603	.0009
Residual	20	45.2			
Total	34	193.9			

$$F_{6,23} = \frac{134.8 - 45.2}{9} \div \frac{45.2}{20}$$

$$= 4.41$$

$p \leq .005$

FIGURE 4-51
SBDC

**HYPOTHESIS H2F -
THE ADMINISTRATIVE SKILL**

PRELIMINARY STEP

Base equation:	DF	SS	R^2	Adj. R^2	P-value
Regression	5	59.1	.31	.185	.0504
Residual	29	134.8			
Total	34	193.9			

Full equation:	DF	SS	R^2	Adj. R^2	P-value
Regression	23	161.8	.84	.489	.0654
Residual	11	32.1			
Total	34	193.9			

$$F_{18,11} = \frac{134.8 - 32.1}{18} \div \frac{32.1}{11}$$

$$= 1.96$$

$p \le$ N.S.

Analysis and Results 171

FIGURE 4-52
SBDC
HYPOTHESIS H2F - THE ADMINISTRATIVE SKILL

FINAL STEP
(BEST PREDICTOR SUBSET)

Base equation:	DF	SS	R^2	Adj. R^2	P-value
Regression	5	59.1	.31	.185	.0504
Residual	29	134.8			
Total	34	193.9			

Full equation:	DF	SS	R^2	Adj. R^2	P-value
Regression	17	159.1	.82	.641	.0015
Residual	17	34.8			
Total	34	193.9			

$$F_{12,17} = \frac{134.8 - 34.8}{12} \div \frac{34.8}{17}$$

$$= 4.07$$

$p \leq .005$

FIGURE 4-53
SBDC

HYPOTHESIS H2G - THE ENTREPRENEURIAL SKILL

PRELIMINARY STEP

Base equation:	DF	SS	R^2	Adj. R^2	P-value
Regression	5	59.1	.31	.185	.0504
Residual	29	134.8			
Total	34	193.9			

Full equation:

	DF	SS	R^2		P-value
Regression	23	131.1	.68	.000	.5251
Residual	11	62.8			
Total	34	193.9			

$$F_{18,11} = \frac{134.8 - 62.8}{18} \div \frac{62.8}{11}$$

$$= .70$$

p ≤ N.S.

Analysis and Results

The final step for hypothesis H2G is shown in Figure 4-54. Here the null is rejected at the $\alpha = .10$ level with $p \le .10$ and df=26. Thus H2G (concerning the entrepreneurial skill) should be accepted with moderate support.

Thus all of the hypotheses in the second group are confirmed, with significance levels ranging from $\alpha = .10$ to $\alpha = .01$. A recap is shown in Figure 4-55.

Thus *all* of the skills investigated in this research appear to have significant impact on NVP contingent upon their propensity to be exercised and upon the surrounding context of strategy and industry structure.

TESTS OF HYPOTHESES H3A THROUGH H3G

The testing of the hypotheses concerning the relations between the individual skills and their attendant mental aptitudes was also conducted using multivariate regression analysis.

> H3A. guilford's divergent production of figural transformations, training in the product/service design area, and their interaction will have a significant effect upon the product/service design skill.

H3B	Analogous for the technical business skill
H3C	Analogous for the technical industry skill
H3D	Analogous for the internal leadership skill
H3E	Analogous for the networking skill skill
H3F	Analogous for the administrative skill
H3G	Analogous for the entrepreneurial skill

These hypotheses were tested by regressing the self-rating of the skill (R_i) on training (G_i), aptitude test score (A_i), and achievement (G_iA_i, the interaction of training and aptitude). All seven possible combinations of predictors were investigated by the adjusted R^2 method (minimum mean squared error) to obtain the "best predictor subset" for each skill.[28] If any of these predictor subsets displayed statistically

FIGURE 4-54

SBDC

HYPOTHESIS H2G - THE ENTREPRENEURIAL SKILL

FINAL STEP
(BEST PREDICTOR SUBSET)

Base equation:	DF	SS	R^2	Adj. R^2	P-value
Regression	5	59.1	.31	.185	.0504
Residual	29	134.8			
Total	34	193.9			

Full equation:

Regression	8	80.4	.41	.261	.0289
Residual	26	113.8			
Total	34	193.9			

$$F_{2,27} = \frac{134.8 - 113.8}{2} \div \frac{113.8}{27}$$

$$= 2.49$$

$p \leq .10$

FIGURE 4-55

RECAP OF SECOND SET OF HYPOTHESES FOR THE SBDC CONFIRMATION SAMPLE:

Hypothesis	α-level of confirmation
2A: Technical product/service skill	.10
2B: Technical business skill	.05
2C: Technical industry skill	.05
2D: Leadership skill	.05
2E: Networking skill	.01
2F: Administrative skill	.001
2G: Entrepreneurial skill	.10

significant results for a skill, the null would be rejected for that skill. Again, hypothesis rejection was investigated at three levels: $\alpha = .10$, $\alpha = .05$, and $\alpha = .01$.

The results of the "best predictor subsets" are displayed in Figure 4-56. All seven hypotheses were confirmed, four at the $\alpha = .01$ level, two at the $\alpha = .05$ level, and one at the $\alpha = .10$ level. The amount of variance in self-skill ratings explained by these predictors ranged from 12% to 53% and four of the seven subsets contained aptitude or achievement, providing impetus for the future use of aptitude testing in determination of entrepreneurial management skills.

THE PREVENTURE CONFIRMATION SAMPLE

In this section, hypotheses H3A through H3G are applied to the preventure test sample for three reasons. First, it is of interest in its own right to apply these hypotheses to aspiring entrepreneurs. Second, confirmation of these hypotheses as regards aspiring entrepreneurs will serve to increase the external validity of the results of the confirmation for actual entrepreneurs. Third, it is of interest to conduct the analysis for purposes of comparison between actual and aspiring entrepreneurs.

Each of the skills in for the preventure test sample were tested in the same manner as were the new venture test sample: by regressing the self-rating of the skill (R_i) on training (G_i), aptitude test score (A_i), and achievement (G_iA_i, the interaction of training and aptitude). All seven possible combinations of predictors were again investigated by the adjusted R^2 method (minimum mean squared error) to obtain the "best predictor subset" for each skill.

The results of these "best predictor subsets" are displayed in Figure 4-57. When hypotheses H3A through H3G were applied to the preventure sample, all seven hypotheses were confirmed, four at the $\alpha = .01$ level and three at the $\alpha = .05$ level. The amount of variance in self-skill ratings explained by these predictors ranged from 11% to 36% and all seven of the subsets contained aptitude or achievement. It is interesting to note that aptitudes and achievements played a more important predictor role in proportion to training among preventure observations than among new venture observations.

FIGURE 4- 56

**MAIN SAMPLE
HYPOTHESES H3A THRU H3G
CONCERNING
APTITUDE, TRAINING, AND ACHIEVEMENT**

Hypothesis	Best predictor subset	R^2	Adj. R^2	P-value
H3A: Technical Product /Service	Training	.115	.082	.0719
H3B: Technical Business	Training	.211	.15	.0459
H3C: Technical Industry	Achievement & Aptitude	.455	.413	.0004
H3D: Leadership	Achievement & Training	.533	.515	.0001
H3E: Networking	Aptitude	.312	.287	.0016
H3F: Administrative	Training	.294	.268	.0024
H3G: Entrepreneurial	Achievement	.195	.166	.0164

FIGURE 4- 57

PREVENTURE TEST SAMPLE

HYPOTHESES H3A THRU H3G

CONCERNING

APTITUDE, TRAINING, AND ACHIEVEMENT

Skill	Best predictor subset	R^2	Adj. R^2	P-value
Technical Product /Service	Achievement & Training	.335	.310	.0001
Technical Business	Achievement, Aptitude, & Training	.262	.220	.0010
Technical Industry	Achievement	.254	.240	.0001
Leadership	Achievement	.111	.095	.0112
Networking	Achievement	.069	.052	.0485
Administrative	Achievement	.206	.192	.0004
Entrepreneurial	Aptitude & Training	.130	.098	.0232

DERIVATION OF SPECIFIC NORMATIVE PROPOSITIONS

In this seventh and final section of this chapter, the third research question of this study is explored:
What specific normative relationships are implied between characteristics of the entrepreneur and new venture performance?

The Importance of Contingency Relations to Prediction of NVP

In order to assess the importance of interactions (contingency relations) to the prediction of NVP, four moderated regressions were run, observing the following definitions as before:

skills	$= R_i$
Propensities	$= T_i$
Strategy and Industry Structure	$= S_j$
New Venture Performance	$= P$

The first moderated regression involved the terms $\beta_{R_iT_i}R_iT_i$, which will henceforth be referred to as "skill executions." These terms are the product of each skill with its skill propensity, and are causes of "skill performance" as shown in the full model (Figure 2-6). They are shown as direct causes of NVP in the research model (Figure 2-7) since there was no attempt to measure "skill performance" in this research. The terms $\beta_{R_iT_iS_j}R_iT_iS_j$ are the interactions of skill execution with venture context (strategy and industry structure).

The base equation used was: $P = \Sigma \beta_{S_j}S_j + \Sigma \beta_{R_iT_i}R_iT_i + \beta_0$, while the moderated equation used was the best predictor subset of: $P = \Sigma \beta_{S_j}S_j + \Sigma \beta_{R_iT_i}R_iT_i + \Sigma \beta_{R_iT_iS_j}R_iT_iS_j + \beta_0$ with all of the terms $\Sigma \beta_{S_j}S_j + \Sigma \beta_{R_iT_i}R_iT_i$ held in the equation. This best predictor subset included at least some interaction terms for each S_j as well as for each R_iT_i.

The results of this moderated regression are shown in Figure 4-58 below. The interactions are shown to be significant at $p \leq .01$ level

FIGURE 4-58

**MODERATED REGRESSION
FOR SKILL EXECUTIONS WITH
VENTURE CONTEXT**

Base equation:

	DF	SS	R^2	Adj. R^2	P-value
Regression	12	61.7	.14	.00	.4665
Residual	75	389.4			
Total	87	451.1			

Full equation:

	DF	SS	R^2	Adj. R^2	P-value
Regression	27	274.7	.61	.433	.0001
Residual	60	176.4			
Total	87	451.1			

$$F_{15,60} = \frac{389.4 - 176.4}{15} \div \frac{176.4}{60}$$

$$= 4.83$$

$p \leq .001$

Analysis and Results

with the partial coefficient of determination (difference in adjusted R^2) being over 43% and thus showing high practical significance as well. This result means that the interactions of skill executions with venture context are important to the prediction of NVP.

The second moderated regression involved investigation of the interaction of skills themselves with venture context. The base equation used was: $P = \Sigma \beta_{Sj}S_j + \Sigma \beta_{Ri}R_i + \beta_0$, while the moderated equation used was the best predictor subset of: $P = \Sigma \beta_{Sj}S_j + \Sigma \beta_{Ri}R_i + \Sigma \beta_{RiSj}RiSj + \beta_0$ with all of the terms $\Sigma \beta_{Sj}S_j + \Sigma \beta_{Ri}R_i$ held in the equation. This best predictor subset included at least some interaction terms for each Sj as well as for each R_i.

The results of this moderated regression are shown in Figure 4-59 below. The interactions are shown to be significant at $p \leq .01$ level with the partial coefficient of determination (difference in adjusted R^2) being nearly 20% and thus showing high practical significance as well. This result means that the interactions of skills with venture context are also important to the prediction of NVP. The third moderated regression involved investigation of the interaction of skill propensities with venture context. The base equation used was: $P = \Sigma \beta_{Sj}S_j + \Sigma \beta_{Ti}T_i + \beta_0$, while the moderated equation used was the best predictor subset of: $P = \Sigma \beta_{Sj}S_j + \Sigma \beta_{Ti}T_i + \Sigma \beta_{TiSj}TiSj + \beta_0$ with all of the terms $\Sigma \beta_{Sj}S_j + \Sigma \beta_{Ti}T_i$ held in the equation. This best predictor subset included at least some interaction terms for each Sj as well as for each T_i.

The results of this moderated regression are shown in Figure 4-60 below. The interactions are shown to be significant at $p \leq .05$ level with the partial coefficient of determination (difference in adjusted R^2) being 15% and thus showing practical significance as well. This result means that the interactions of skill propensities with venture context are also important to the prediction of NVP.

The fourth moderated regression involved investigation of the interaction of skill propensities with skills. The base equation used was: $P = \Sigma \beta_{Ri}R_i + \Sigma \beta_{Ti}T_i + \beta_0$, while the moderated equation used was the best predictor subset of: $P = \Sigma \beta_{Ri}R_i + \Sigma \beta_{Ti}T_i + \Sigma \beta_{RiTi}RiTi + \beta_0$ with all of the terms $\Sigma \beta_{Ri}R_i + \Sigma \beta_{Ti}T_i$ held in the equation.

The results of this moderated regression are shown in Figure 4-61 below. The interactions are shown to be significant at $p \leq .10$ level with the partial coefficient of determination (difference in adjusted R^2) being 4%. This result means that the interactions of skill propensities

FIGURE 4-59

MODERATED REGRESSION FOR SKILLS WITH VENTURE CONTEXT

Base equation:	DF	SS	R^2	Adj. R^2	P-value
Regression	12	170.2	.38	.278	.0002
Residual	75	280.8			
Total	87	451.1			

Full equation:	DF	SS	R^2	Adj. R^2	P-value
Regression	28	290.4	.64	.475	.0001
Residual	59	160.7			
Total	87	451.1			

$$F_{16,59} = \frac{280.8 - 160.7}{16} \div \frac{160.7}{59}$$

$$= 2.76$$

$p \leq .01$

FIGURE 4-60

MODERATED REGRESSION FOR SKILL PROPENSITIES WITH VENTURE CONTEXT

Base equation:	DF	SS	R^2	Adj. R^2	P-value
Regression	12	48.8	.11	.00	.6899
Residual	75	402.2			
Total	87	451.1			

Full equation:	DF	SS	R^2	Adj. R^2	P-value
Regression	25	177.7	.39	.15	.0658
Residual	62	273.4			
Total	87	451.1			

$$F_{13,62} = \frac{402.2 - 273.4}{13} \div \frac{273.4}{62}$$

$$= 2.25$$

$p \leq .05$

FIGURE 4-61

MODERATED REGRESSION FOR SKILL PROPENSITIES WITH SKILLS

Base equation:	DF	SS	R^2	Adj. R^2	P-value
Regression	14	143.4	.32	.187	.0074
Residual	73	307.7			
Total	87	451.1			

Full equation:	DF	SS	R^2	Adj. R^2	P-value
Regression	16	164.3	.36	.221	.0038
Residual	71	286.8			
Total	87	451.1			

$$F_{2,71} = \frac{307.7 - 286.8}{2} \div \frac{286.8}{71}$$

$$= 2.59$$

$p \leq .10$

with skills are of less importance than the previous interactions but still of some use in the prediction of NVP.

Regarding the Investigation of Specific Contingency Relations

Having shown above that interactions of skills, skill propensities, and venture context are important to the prediction of NVP, the natural progression of analysis would be to investigate the moderating effects of each individual interaction versus the terms composing that interaction. However, it was realized very early on that multicollinearity played a very significant part in masking these results.

For example, the separate moderated regression equations for S1R1 and S1T1 each implied that these terms had no significant effect over and above that of their constituent terms. However, when one combined moderated regression was run to determine the simultaneous effect of S1R1 and S1T1, the combined effect was shown to be highly statistically significant. This was because the effects of multicollinearity between S1R1 and S1T1 caused their combined effects to be greater than the sum of their individual effects,[29] in essence a form of interaction between the interaction terms themselves. Likewise, the effects of this collinearity caused one of the regression coefficients in the combined equation to become negative when they had both been individually positive in their separate regressions. This is because the coefficients in the combined equation represent the partial derivatives with respect to each variable, that is, the marginal change in NVP due to one independent variable when the other independent variable is held constant, an unlikely event according to this data. The presence of extreme multicollinearity at this level of analysis suggests that isolating the NVP impact of one interaction *while holding all others constant* is impractical because these interaction elements are so intertwined with one another that, in practice, changing one will change others.

Because of these findings of multicollinearity present within the interaction terms, individual moderated regression equations will not be shown since this would be a useless exercise both in terms of determining interaction importance and in terms of interpreting regression coefficients. Instead, the next subsections of this chapter will investigate all of the *simple* regressions involved. These regressions represent the multidimensional projection of the data onto one plane, and, as such, the direction of the regression coefficients are interpretable in a normative regard, all other variables being unmanipulated.

Development of Specific Normative Propositions Concerning Possession and Use of Skills

The first series of these equations (see Figure 4-62) investigated the effect upon performance of the possession of each skill taken individually and without regard to either venture context or amount of skill usage. Five of the seven skills were statistically significant: technical business, technical industry knowledge, networking, administrative, and entrepreneurial. In addition, the analysis leading to Figure 4-62 suggests that the higher the level possessed of each of the seven skills, the higher the venture performance. When possession of all seven of the skills was looked at simultaneously but still without regard to venture context or level of skill usage, skills are able to explain about 17% of venture performance (see Figure 4-63). This suggests the first normative proposition:

> P1: The possession of any one of these skills: technical business, technical industry knowledge, networking, administrative, and entrepreneurial, should enhance venture performance.

Figure 4-63 suggests that the three most important skills that can be possessed appear to be the technical industry, the entrepreneurial, and the administrative. This would imply that experience and aptitude in these three areas are important for most entrepreneurs. The technical industry skill involves the ability to integrate and understand the implications of industry changes for the firm in question. This appears to be the most important single skill predicting NVP. The entrepreneurial skill, also extremely important, involves discovering opportunities to make profitable alterations to the firm in question. Possession of this skill requires the creativity necessary to become aware of the existence of achievable opportunities both inside and outside the firm. The administrative skill involves the ability to engage in the detailed planning necessary to implementation of change.

While the above analysis concerns the effect of possession of skills without regard to skill propensity (amount of usage), the next analysis investigates the effect of skill propensity without regard to level of skill possessed. The possession of a skill and the usage of a skill (skill propensity) are two very different ideas. When a skill is possessed it means that the potential to use it is fully formed. For example, if I am skillful at leadership, I possess the skill even when I

FIGURE 4-62
SIMPLE SKILLS REGRESSIONS

Skill	R^2	Adj. R^2	P-value	Sign of slope coefficient
Technical Product/Service	.009	-.0003	.3265	Positive
Technical Business	.034	.025	.0518	Positive
Technical Industry	.155	.148	.0001	Positive
Leadership	.018	.009	.1542	Positive
Networking	.045	.036	.0242	Positive
Administrative	.052	.043	.0166	Positive
Entrepreneurial	.087	.079	.0015	Positive

FIGURE 4-63

BEST PREDICTOR SUBSET AMONG SKILLS

	DF	SS	MS	F-value	R^2	Adj. R^2	P-value
Regression	3	119.6	39.87	8.315	.189	.166	.0001
Residual	107	513.0	4.79				
Total	110	632.7					

Skills:

Technical industry

Entrepreneurial

Administrative

Analysis and Results

am eating breakfast. At that juncture, however, I may not be using the skill. skill propensity (usage), however, refers to the relative amount of time spent actually exercising a skill regardless of the level of its possession. For example, if I were to spend all of my time designing products, I would be displaying a high propensity to exercise the skill of technical product/service design even though I might be a poor designer. If possession is important with out regard to propensity, it means that level of ability is a predictor of NVP without regard to propensity. This may be because level is a predictor of propensity or because even a little propensity is effective when possession is high. If propensity is a predictor of NVP without regard to level of possession, however, it means that exercising a skill is effective even though not much skill is possessed.

None of these seven regressions (see Figure 4-64) proved to be of significance, leading to the second proposition:

> P2: Use of a skill, irrespective of its possessed level or of the context of its use, will not enhance venture performance.

Thus, the *usage* of skills without regard to level of competence or to venture context appears to be futile. This is despite the fact that *possession* of skills (see proposition P1) is important for entrepreneurs regardless of the type of venture engaged in and regardless of whether they are used extensively or sparingly. These conclusions provide an argument that effort and desire won't necessarily "win the day" without possession of the proper skills.

The next analysis (see Figure 4-65) attempted to pinpoint those skills that are particularly influential on performance when both level of possession *and* usage are high at the same time. Only one of these seven interactions was highly significant, this being the interaction of the technical industry skill with its propensity. The networking and entrepreneurial skill interactions were moderately significant, however. In addition, all of these equations showed a positive effect on performance, indicating that higher levels of possession and usage led to higher performance levels. This analysis leads to the following proposition:

> P3: Use of the technical industry knowledge skill, when high levels of that skill are possessed, will

FIGURE 4-64

SIMPLE REGRESSIONS OF SKILL PROPENSITIES

Skill Propensities	R^2	Adj. R^2	P-value
Technical Product/Service	.003	-.006	.561
Technical Business	.002	-.008	.6593
Technical Industry	.012	.003	.2612
Leadership	.004	-.006	.5263
Networking	.015	.005	.2113
Administrative	.002	-.007	.6162
Entrepreneurial	.009	-.002	.3268

Analysis and Results

FIGURE 4-65

SIMPLE REGRESSIONS OF INTERACTIONS OF SKILLS WITH SKILL PROPENSITIES

Interactions of Skill with Skill Propensity	R^2	Adj. R^2	P-value
Technical Product/Service	.002	-.009	.8851
Technical Business	.006	-.004	.4394
Technical Industry	.036	.027	.0476
Leadership	.000	-.009	.9556
Networking	.024	.015	.1045
Administrative	.001	-.009	.8037
Entrepreneurial	.024	.015	.1058

> particularly tend to enhance venture
> performance (irrespective of venture
> context).

Again, the technical industry knowledge skill appears to be particularly predictive of NVP. In this case though, the skill and the propensity are found to interact with each other. The import of this is that, while possession of this skill is important whatever the level of usage, possession of the skill in conjunction with large amounts of usage has a particularly powerful positive effect on NVP.

Development of Specific Normative Propositions Concerning Skill Interactions with Venture Context

The first three propositions concerned possession and use of skills and their interactions with each other. The next three sets of propositions concern themselves with the interaction of venture context (strategy or industry structure) and the possession and usage of the seven skills.

The fourth set of propositions attempted to pinpoint those skills whose *possession* (without regard to propensity) was particularly important given a particular strategy or industry structure context. Strategy context was operationalized as degree of scope, degree of aggressiveness of growth, and degree of newness of entry wedge. Industry structure context was operationalized as stage of industry growth and degree of industry product heterogeneity. Ten skill - strategy/industry structure interactions were statistically significant (or very close to significant) as displayed in Figure 4-66. These results suggest that when scope is broad, technical product/service, networking, and the entrepreneurial skills are key skills to possess; and when industry product heterogeneity is high, it is important to possess all seven skills. This analysis led to the following propositions:

> P4A: Possession of the technical
> product/service skill, of the
> networking skill, and of the
> entrepreneurial skill will
> particularly enhance venture
> performance when the scope of a
> new firm's strategy is broad.

FIGURE 4-66
SIMPLE REGRESSIONS OF INTERACTIONS OF SKILLS WITH STRATEGY AND INDUSTRY STRUCTURE

Interactions of Skill with Strategy and Industry structure	R^2	Adj. R^2	P-value	Sign of Slope Coefficient
Scope with Technical Product/Service Skill	.047	.037	.0368	Positive
Scope with Networking Skill	.030	.019	.0952	Positive
Scope with Entrepreneurial Skill	.029	.018	.1019	Positive
Industry Product Homogeneity with Technical Product/Service Skill	.028	.018	.1076	Positive
Industry Product Heterogeneity with Technical Business Skill	.030	.019	.0967	Positive
Industry Product Heterogeneity with Technical Industry Skill	.031	.021	.0888	Positive
Industry Product Heterogeneity with Leadership Skill	.030	.019	.0994	Positive
Industry Product Heterogeneity with Networking Skill	.029	.018	.1032	Positive
Industry Product Heterogeneity with Administrative Skill	.037	.026	.0672	Positive
Industry Product Heterogeneity with Entrepreneurial Skill	.041	.031	.0501	Positive

> P4B: The ability of all seven skills to enhance venture performance increases as industry product heterogeneity increases.

Thus two separate venture contexts are particularly important to *possession* of skills. Ventures with broad scopes call particularly for the product/service, the networking, and the entrepreneurial skill. Likewise, ventures in industries which have high product heterogeneity are particularly sensitive to the possession of all seven skills.

These findings are of considerable interest and make intuitive sense as well. It may be recalled from the discussion earlier in this chapter that scope can be broad on one or more of several dimensions: product, customer, and geographic. That technical product/service skill possession would interact with scope, therefore, seems reasonable. A broader product line would call for more product skills, for example, as would a more extensive customer base. A broader geographic base might call for more product skills or for more service delivery skills. Likewise, a broader scope of any kind would call for the possession of "external" skills such as networking and opportunity recognition (entrepreneurial) skill.

That heterogeneous product environments would particularly call for possession of all seven of the skills also seems reasonable. Such environments are often more complicated due to a greater multiplicity of available tactics and strategies, and to more turbulence. Therefore they require possession of all skills in more than usual amounts.

The next set of propositions attempted to pinpoint those skills whose *propensity* (usage) is particularly important given a particular strategy or industry structure context. Five skill propensity - strategy/industry structure interactions were significant (or very close to significant), with two having negative relationships as displayed in Figure 4-67. The three positive relationships indicated that using the technical product/service, networking, and entrepreneurial skills is potentially more beneficial in new ventures as their strategic scope increases. The two negative relationships suggest that the positive effect of the technical product/service skill and the technical business skill on NVP diminish as an industry matures. These observations led to the following propositions:

> P5A: Use of the technical product/service skill, of the networking skill, and of the

FIGURE 4-67
SIMPLE REGRESSIONS OF INTERACTIONS OF SKILL PROPENSITY WITH STRATEGY AND INDUSTRY STRUCTURE

Interactions of Skill with Strategy and Industry structure	R^2	Adj. R^2	P-value	Sign of Slope Coefficient
Scope with Technical Product/Service Skill Propensity	.062	.052	.0166	Positive
Scope with Networking Skill Propensity	.038	.028	.0619	Positive
Scope with Entrepreneurial Skill Propensity	.037	.026	.0676	Positive
Industry Stage with Technical Product/Service Skill	.058	.048	.0203	Negative
Industry Stage with Technical Business Skill	.029	.019	.1017	Negative

entrepreneurial skill will particularly enhance venture performance in contexts where scope is broad.

P5B: The less mature the industry, the more the use of the technical product/service skill will enhance venture performance.

P5C: The less mature the industry, the more the use of the technical business skill will enhance venture performance.

Thus ventures with broad scope benefit from the use of the technical product/service, the networking, and the entrepreneurial skills. Ventures in less mature industries benefit from the use of the product/service and the business skills.

These findings have intuitive appeal. Broad scope is associated with the same three skills as in proposition P4A. This time, however, the relationship is with skill usage and not skill possession. This indicates that broad strategic scope is so powerful in demanding these skills that their exercise is indicated even when their possession is relatively weak.

The association between use of the technical product/service skill and early industry development is not surprising. For instance, in less mature industries connections between particular design options and profitability are often fluid, and diffusion of design knowledge between companies is often limited. In addition, the connection between early industry development and the technical business skill is reasonable. Apparently, less mature industries with their attendant instability call for more frequent review and evaluation of the various business functions.

The last series of propositions attempted to pinpoint those skills whose possession-usage interaction is particularly important given a particular strategy or industry structure context. Six of these possession - usage -context interactions were statistically significant, two of which had negative relationships (see in Figure 4-68). The three positive relationships indicate that the skill execution (possession - usage interaction) and the environmental context complement each other. A

FIGURE 4-68
SIMPLE REGRESSIONS OF THREE-WAY INTERACTIONS OF SKILL, SKILL PROPENSITY, AND STRATEGY AND INDUSTRY STRUCTURE

Interactions of Skill with Strategy and Industry structure	R^2	Adj. R^2	P-value	Sign of Slope Coefficient
Scope with Technical Product/Service Skill Propensity	.057	.046	.0228	Positive
Scope with Networking Skill Propensity	.032	.022	.0856	Positive
Scope with Entrepreneurial Skill Propensity	.031	.02	.0949	Positive
Industry Stage with Technical Product/Service Skill	.053	.042	.0286	Negative
Industry Stage with Technical Business Skill	.031	.020	.094	Negative
Industry Product Heterogeneity with Administrative Skill	.033	.022	.0843	Positive

negative relationship, in contrast, means that the effect of the skill execution in question is enhanced by the *reverse* of the context investigated. This analysis led to the following propositions:

> P6A: The execution (high levels of possession combined with high levels of use) of the technical product/service, networking, and entrepreneurial skills will particularly enhance venture performance in contexts where scope is broad.
>
> P6B: The execution (possession *and* use) of the technical product/service skill will particularly enhance venture performance in less mature industries.
>
> P6C: The execution (possession *and* use) of the technical business skill will particularly enhance venture performance in less mature industries.
>
> P6D: The execution (possession *and* use) of the administrative skill will particularly enhance venture performance in industries with heterogeneous products.

Thus broad scope ventures suggest a particular need for execution of the technical product/service, networking, and entrepreneurial skills. Less mature industries call for execution of the technical product/service and technical business skills. Industries with heterogeneous product environments particularly demand the execution of the administrative skill.

Once again, broad scope is associated with the same three skills as in propositions P4A and P5A. Also, industry youth is again associated with the same two skills as in propositions P5B and P5C. In P6A through P6D, however, the skill interaction with context involves the *execution* of the skill (its possession - propensity interaction) and

Analysis and Results

not just its possession or its usage. In other words, the sixth set of propositions involves three-way interaction while the fourth and fifth sets involve only two-way interactions.

Proposition P6D would seem reasonable in suggesting that administrative skill (detailed planning) is particularly called for in heterogeneous product industries, likely as a result of their contextual complications. This type of industry setting is often more complicated due to a greater multiplicity of available tactics and strategies, and to more turbulence. Such conditions demand planning skills of a higher order than would simpler, more placid environments.

SUMMARY OF ANALYSIS AND RESULTS CHAPTER

In summary, Chapter IV has discussed the data gathering phase of the research as well as the reliability and validity of the database.

The first research question was investigated through the means of hypothesis H1 and answered in the affirmative. Characteristics of the entrepreneur do have a significant impact upon new venture performance in addition to strategy and industry structure.

The second research question was also investigated through not only the means of hypothesis H1 but also through hypotheses H2A through H2G. Hypothesis H1 showed that skills, skill propensities, and their interactions with strategy and industry structure are, as a set, significant predictors of new venture performance. Hypotheses H2A through H2G showed that *each* of the seven skills with its skill propensities (and their interactions with strategy and industry structure) is a significant predictor of new venture performance in its own right.

All of the above conclusions were supported independently by the confirmation sample which consisted of a different mix of firms from a different sample.

In addition, seven hypotheses (H3A through H3G) concerning the prediction of skill levels by entrepreneurs were investigated and all were accepted. Apparently all seven skills can be significantly predicted by aptitudes, training, and interactions between the two.

All of the conclusions concerning prediction of skill levels were then independently confirmed using a sample of aspiring entrepreneurs rather than actual entrepreneurs.

Next, the impact of interactions (contingencies) was investigated and found to be of great importance to the prediction of NVP.

Finally, a series of simple regressions was investigated to establish specific normative propositions for the use of entrepreneurs, venture capitalists, and other practitioners as well as to provide aid to future research in this area.

The next and final chapter will discuss the conclusions and implications to be drawn from this study as well as its limitations and suggestions for future research.

Notes:

[1] Nunnally, J.C. (1967). Psychometric theory. New York: McGraw-Hill.
[2] Ibid, p. 180.
[3] Ibid, p. 226.
[4] Cook, T.D. & Campbell, D.T. (1979). *Quasi-expermentation: Design and analysis issues for field settings.* Chicago: Rand-McNally.
[5] Widaman, K. F. (1985). Hierarchically nested covariance structure models for multitrait-multimethod data. *Applied Psychological Measurement, 9* (1), 1-26.
[6] Cronbach, L.J. & Meehl, P.E. (1955). Construct validity in psychological tests. *Psychological Bulletin,52*, 218-302.
[7] Widaman, K. F. (1985). Hierarchically nested covariance structure models for multitrait-multimethod data. *Applied Psychological Measurement, 9* (1), 1-26.
[8] Robinson, R.B., McDougall, P., & Herron, L. (1988). *Toward a new venture strategy typology.* Proceedings of the Academy of Management, Aneheim Ca, 74-78.
[9] Porter, M.E. (1980). *Competitive Strategy.* New York: Free Press.
[10] Jöreskog, K.G. & Sörbom, D. (1986). *LISREL: User's guide.* Scientific Software, Inc: Mooresville, IN.
[11] Bearden, W.O., Sharma, S., & Teel, J.E. (1982). Sample size effects on chi square and other statistics used in evaluating causal models. *Journal of Marketing Research, 19*(Nov), 425-430.
[12] Jöreskog, K.G. & Sörbom, D. (1986). *LISREL: User's guide.* Scientific Software, Inc: Mooresville, IN.
[13] Nunnally, J.C. (1967). *Psychometric theory.* New York: McGraw-Hill.
[14] Maier, N. (1965). *Psychology in industry.* (3rd ed.). Boston: Houghton Mifflin Co.
[15] Schoonhoven, C.B. (1981). Problems with contingency theory: Testing assumptions hidden within the language of

contingency theory. *Administrative Science Quarterly, 26*, 349-377.

[16]Sharma, S., Durand, R.M., & Gur-Aire, O. (1981). Identification and analysis of moderator variables. *Journal of Marketing, 18*(Aug.), 291-300.

[17]Schoonhoven, C.B. (1981). Problems with contingency theory: Testing assumptions hidden within the language of contingency theory. *Administrative Science Quarterly, 26*, 349-377.

[18]Leontiades, M. (1982). *Choosing the right manager to fit the strategy.* Journal of Business Strategy, 58-69.

[19]Gupta, A.K. (1984). Contingency linkages between strategy and general manager characteristics: A conceptual examination. *Academy of Management Review, 9* (3), 399-412.

[20]Schmidt, F.E. (1973). Implications of a measurement problem for expectancy theory research. *Organizational behavior and human performance, 10*, 243-251.

[21]Ibid.

[22]Cohen, J. (1978). Partialed products are *interactions; partialed powers are curve components. Psychological Bulletin, 85* (4), 858-866.

[23]Ibid.

[24]Neter, J., Wasserman, W., & Kutner, M. (1985). *Applied linear statistical models.* Homewood, IL: Irwin.

[25]Cohen, J. & Cohen, P. (1975). *Applied multiple regression/correlation analysis for the behavioral sciences.* New York: John Wiley & Sons.

[26]Robinson, R.B., McDougall, P., & Herron, L. (1988). *Toward a new venture strategy typology.* Proceedings of the Academy of Management, Aneheim Ca, 74-78.

[27]Jöreskog, K.G. & Sörbom, D. (1986). *LISREL: User's guide.* Scientific Software, Inc: Mooresville, IN.

[28]Neter, J., Wasserman, W., & Kutner, M. (1985). *Applied linear statistical models.* Homewood, IL: Irwin.

[29]Cohen, J. & Cohen, P. (1975). *Applied multiple regression/correlation analysis for the behavioral sciences.* New York: John Wiley & Sons.

Chapter Five:

Conclusions

INTRODUCTION

This final chapter presents and discusses results and conclusions relative to the research questions presented in Chapter 1. It also discusses implications and limitations of the current research as well as directions for future research.

Section one, "Conclusions", provides an overview and discussion of the key results derived from the analysis of Chapter 4.

Section two, "Implications", notes features of this research which may be of particular interest to entrepreneurs, venture capitalists, and academicians.

Section three, "Limitations", discusses the limitations of this research which should be borne in mind when interpreting and applying the results of this study.

Section four, "Directions for Future Research", explores possible avenues for future research suggested by this study.

CONCLUSIONS

Chapter 4 analyzed the research hypotheses which were derived from the three research questions and from the research model. These research questions were:

1. Do characteristics of the entrepreneur have a significant impact upon new venture performance (NVP) in addition to strategy and industry structure?

2. If so, what characteristics are important and what is their relationship with NVP?

3. What specific normative relationships are implied between characteristics of the entrepreneur and NVP?

Conclusions Involving Hypothesis H1

The acceptance of hypothesis H1 showed that a research model including skills, skill propensities, and their interactions with strategy and industry structure was statistically significant overall, and that it was able to account for 40% of the variance of NVP in the population (adjusted R^2). Further, this result was subsequently confirmed with the independent SBDC survey, thus enhancing its generalizability.

From these results, several meaningful conclusions may be drawn. First, entrepreneurial characteristics *are* significantly important to the prediction of NVP, on a practical as well as a statistical level. Previous studies have found entrepreneurial characteristics to be either statistically insignificant,[1] or to be statistically significant but lacking in practical significance (explained variance).[2,3] The current study's results of 40% explained variance displays both statistical and practical significance, and thus it becomes the first study to strongly confirm the "E" in Sandberg's[4] equation [NVP=f(E,IS,S)]. Further, the heterogeneous nature of the samples adds external validity to this confirmation.

Second, the confirmation of the significance of the research model bolsters the explanation (derived from Hollenbeck and Whitener[5]) that personality traits have been relatively ineffectual in explaining NVP[6,7] because they are moderated and mediated by other variables. All of the variables in the research model either mediate personality traits (skills and skill propensities) or moderate personality trait results (strategy and industry structure). Thus this research becomes one of the first known studies of Hollenbeck and Whitener's model.

Third, demonstration of the significance of the main research equation as well as the significance of the interactions using moderated regression supports the claims of theorists[8,9] who believe that the effectiveness of managerial and entrepreneurial characteristics is *contingent* upon venture context. The last section of Chapter IV further suggests that various contingency relationships may have specific

Conclusions

normative bearing on the entrepreneur. These are extremely important (and unique) empirical conclusions which will be further discussed below in the section on implications.

Fourth, the results of this study support the thesis that skills of the entrepreneur are important characteristics in the determination of NVP. skills are involved in every term of the main research equation which explains 40% of NVP. Though the importance of skills to entrepreneurship has previously received theoretical support from various sources,[10][11] virtually no empirical evidence has existed heretofore to directly support that claim. The next section of this chapter will further suggest how skills may be of normative importance to the entrepreneur.

Fifth, this study lends support to those who claim that the entrepreneur is the *most* important causal factor in the determination of NVP. Few, if any, other moderate-to-large-sample, cross-sectional studies have compared the variance in NVP explained by the entrepreneur's characteristics to that explained by strategy and industry structure, and found the former to be greater.

Conclusions Involving Hypotheses H2A through H2G

The next issue which was investigated was whether *each* of the seven skills (technical product/service, technical business, technical industry, leadership, networking, administrative, and entrepreneurial), when taken separately (within the venture context), was significantly related to NVP. The analysis of Chapter 4 showed that each skill was indeed significant. This result was also later confirmed with the independent SBDC survey, thus enhancing its generalizability.

There are several important conclusions to be derived from these results. First, each of the five conclusions derived from hypothesis H1 above are further supported.

Second, Katz'[12] typology is supported in that skills within each of his three skills groupings (technical skills, human skills, and administrative skills) are shown to be significant predictors of NVP. Few studies in strategy implementationstrategy and none in entrepreneurship have previously tested the validity of this typology.

Third, Szilagyi and Schweiger's[13] work is supported. They suggested that Katz'[14] typology could be further broken down into the seven skills that were tested herein, and each of these seven skills was shown to be a significant predictor of NVP. Again, few studies in strategy implementationstrategy and none in entrepreneurship have tested the validity of this model.

Fourth, the idea of Kirzner[15] that the entrepreneurial skill by itself is of importance is supported. This conclusion is confirmed by the acceptance and subsequent confirmation of hypothesis H2G. As far as is known, this is the first empirical test of Kirzner's conceptualization.

Conclusions Involving Hypotheses H3A through H3G

A third set of hypotheses investigated whether each of the skills of the entrepreneur could be predicted by his/her aptitude and training for that skill. The analysis reported in Chapter 4 showed that each skill was indeed predicted by a subset of aptitude, training, and the interaction between the two. This result was later confirmed with the independent sample of aspiring entrepreneurs, thus adding to its generalizability.

From these results, several important conclusions may be drawn. First, the subset of the research model which relates aptitudes and training to skills, possesses nomological validity. In other words, that portion of the model (see Figure 2-7, the arrows leading into the bottom of the skill construct) which shows training and aptitude interacting to predict skills appears to be valid. This provides confirmation for the work of Maier[16] (who suggested that skills equal the product of training and aptitude) for the first time in entrepreneurship research.

Second, it has been shown for the first time that the aptitudes predicting these entrepreneurial skills may be measured using prevalidated aptitude tests. This lends support to the work of Guilford[17] whose "Structure of Intellect" model suggests differential mental aptitudes, and whose prevalidated tests were used in this study. Therefore those interested in future study of mental aptitudes related to entrepreneurial skills need not devise and validate their own tests, but may draw upon those already available in the field of psychology.

Third, since the same predictive relations held true for the aspiring entrepreneurs as for the entrepreneurs themselves, it would appear that skill levels can be predicted *prior* to initiation of new ventures when entrepreneurs are still in the "aspiring" stages. Organizations and individuals involved in counseling or assisting "aspiring" entrepreneurs may therefore use aptitude tests and training assessments to develop skill profiles for these aspirants. Furthermore, these results suggest that it may be possible to devise "talent-context" assessment and matching of aspiring entrepreneurs to situations, as well as to develop individual remediation for skills in which aspiring or existing entrepreneurs appear deficient. These unique empirical conclusions will be discussed further in the implications section.

Conclusions Involving the Specific Normative Propositions

Although all of the conclusions discussed in this section so far bear great importance to both theory and research in the field of entrepreneurship, little of direct practical value to the entrepreneur him/herself has yet been discussed save the possibilities of entrepreneur-situation matching and remediation. The conclusions to be drawn from the specific normative propositions remedy this shortcoming.

Three conclusions can be drawn from the simple skills regressions. First, possession of any of the seven skills seems to enhance NVP to a greater or lesser degree regardless of venture context. Second, the three most important skills for entrepreneurs to possess regardless of venture context seem to be the technical industry skill, the entrepreneurial skill, and the administrative skill in that order. Third, the possession of skills not required by the specific venture context will not of itself hinder NVP. However, the use of such skills will not enhance NVP and thus may be associated with an "opportunity cost", particularly if, as the full model suggests, the possession of such skills leads to the encouragement of their use.

The conclusion to be drawn from the simple regressions of skill execution on NVP is that the most important skill to both possess *and* use is the technical industry knowledge skill regardless of venture context.

The conclusions to be drawn from the simple regressions of interaction terms which include venture context are several. First, when the scope of a firm's strategy is broad, it is particularly important to both possess and use the technical product/service design skill, the networking skill, and the entrepreneurial skill. Second, the younger the firm's industry life cycle stage, the more important it is to both possess and use the technical product/service design skill and the technical business skill. Third, an industry with a heterogeneous product environment particularly requires possession of all of the skills, but is particularly responsive to the administrative skill.

These specific normative prescriptions convey information linking skill possession, skill usage and their contextual interactions to NVP. Thus they should be of use to practicing entrepreneurs.

IMPLICATIONS

The implications of this research are far-reaching from the standpoints theory, research, and practice.

First, this study should help to bring the entrepreneur back into the focus of entrepreneurial research. Within the bounds of its limitations, and in many ways despite them, the study provides an answer to the puzzle of why previous research has failed to show that the E in Sandberg's[18] equation [NVP=f(E,IS,S)] is significant. It suggests the need to study entrepreneurial characteristics that are more closely connected to NVP in the causal chain than are personality traits, and even implies that such research can and will show that the entrepreneur is more important to the determination of NVP than are strategy and industry structure per se. It particularly supports research into skills of entrepreneurs and the further creation of entrepreneurial skill typologies and taxonomies. It also supports the efficacy of contingency models and shows that, with proper allowance for contingencies, research on entrepreneurial characteristics can and should span diverse contexts. As such, this study should open new avenues into investigations in the entrepreneurship area.

Second, this research should help lay to rest the notion that there is one and only one entrepreneurial personality.[19,20] This is not to say that personality traits are lacking in importance; quite the contrary, as shown in the "full" model in Chapter 2. However, there are so many variables both moderating and mediating personality traits that it is no surprise that a link of practical significant has never been forged between such traits and NVP. Further, realization of this should lead to additional research into personality and value trait typologies and taxonomies, thus more closely linking the field of psychology with that of entrepreneurship. Further yet, research into such classification schemes should allowance for contingencies, and should span diverse contexts. These findings should open further avenues of research in entrepreneurship.

Third, further research into entrepreneurial skills with a contingency perspective should lead to a better understanding of entrepreneurship itself. In pursuit of a definition of entrepreneurship, Gartner[21] has asked: "How can we know the dancer from the dance?" By the dance, of course, Gartner means the set of actions or behaviors which are involved in entrepreneurship. But perhaps the question can be asked as: "How can we know the dancer from the skill exercised in dancing?" For instance, can we not look for entrepreneurship in unusual environments and settings (such as large public institutions) when we find its requisite skills being exercised in those environments? May skills not eventually become central to the very definition of entrepreneurship itself?

Fourth, and of importance to both entrepreneurs and venture capitalists, is the notion implied by the second and third sets of hypotheses that both matching of entrepreneurs with situations and remediation of entrepreneurs is possible through testing, evaluation, and training. The second set of hypotheses clearly shows that all seven skills are moderated by venture context. Thus it is possible that entrepreneurs may be able to pick both industries and strategies to fit their particular mix of skills. Likewise, venture capitalists may be able to guide entrepreneurs into situations which fit their skill mix. This study should therefore lend impetus to further research into how this may be done and what instruments could best be used to accomplish these purposes.

In addition, the third set of hypotheses, those relating aptitudes and training to skills, holds out to both entrepreneurs and venture capitalists the hope not only of better future diagnosis of strengths and weaknesses, but of remediation and training as well. The implications of these ideas for entrepreneurial education are sweeping. First, venture capitalists, incubators, other financial institutions, and organizations such as the SBDC and SCORE may be able to better assess potential investments and clients by administering mental ability tests to the aspiring entrepreneurs in question. Second, making such tests available to entrepreneurs and aspiring entrepreneurs may enhance their own self-evaluation process. Third, a better understanding of the skills involved in entrepreneurship and of the mechanisms involved in their related aptitudes and training could revolutionize both the content and the methods by which we teach entrepreneurship in the classroom. Hopefully, this research study will stimulate further investigations in these directions.

Fifth, one of the major implications of this study for other academicians is that the use of more interdisciplinary endeavors by entrepreneurship researchers is strongly indicated. The current study found it necessary to turn to at least four different academic disciplines to answer the conundrum and its attendant research questions posed in chapter 1. Interdisciplinary research is often a thankless task, both making literature reviews cumbersome and adding difficulty to academic publishing. However, since the field of entrepreneurship is in its infancy and is closely connected to many different disciplines,[22] more interdisciplinary research will prove a necessity to move our field forward.

Sixth, the specific normative propositions derived in the last chapter have implications for entrepreneurs, venture capitalists, and researchers in the need for increased understanding of the environmental context of their firms and the interactions of those environments with the firm's entrepreneur. For instance, it may be possible, even in an already established firm in a given industry, to sculpt a strategy which takes advantage of specific entrepreneurial talents. Hopefully, future research will be stimulated in this area as well.

Seventh, the literature review in Chapter II pointed out five possible weaknesses in past research into entrepreneurial characteristics:

1. Failure to investigate all of the relevant characteristics.
2. Investigation of personality traits rather than of behaviors.
3. Failure to consider contingency relations.
4. Failure to investigate entrepreneurial teams.
5. Failure to consider non-linear relationships.

This study has contributed to the literature by attacking the first and third weaknesses, and reducing the second. Further progress can be expected by studies that also overcome the remaining weaknesses, as the section on future research will discuss.

Eighth, this research study has used a large number of variables as well as a multivariate approach, both typical of research in psychology but more uncommon in entrepreneurship. Future studies into the characteristics area will continue to wrestle with the problems and opportunities which these approaches create.

LIMITATIONS

The analysis of the data and the interpretation of the findings of this research are subject to several limitations.

In examining the impact of entrepreneurial characteristics on new venture performance, this research study has examined characteristics of the lead entrepreneur exclusively. It is notable that current research indicates that teams and team balance may be an important consideration in the determination of firm performance.[23][24] It is apparent that the inclusion of entire entrepreneurial teams in research on entrepreneurial characteristics would enhance predictive validity and perhaps lead to much greater practical significance.

Another potential limitation of this study is its use of single observer measures, particularly in the skill areas. Although the application of the independent aptitude tests lent a large measure of validity to these observations, it would have been preferable to obtain multiple observer measures. The attempt to do this involved the observer-rated skill measures. The failure of these observer-rated skill measures to validate the self-observed skill measures or even to share any nomological relations with either the aptitude tests or with NVP was an unanticipated result of this research. Thus the methodological issues involved in obtaining valid multiple measures or observer measures of skills may provide a challenge to future research.

The single-observer limitation on skills also extends to the performance data in this study, although this is mitigated somewhat by the use of three different measures with a relatively high combined coefficient α. Some objective data was also gathered from these same observers and correlated well with the subjective data, but was not used due to being overly restrictive on sample size. Overall, considering the difficulty of measuring and comparing the performance of new ventures of different ages in different industry settings, the limitations on performance here are probably not too severe.

Another limitation of this study was its failure to investigate failed firms. Though entrepreneurial studies on characteristics have rarely done so, such investigation would be important to the field of entrepreneurship for several reasons. First, prevention of entrepreneurial failure is most certainly a worthy goal of entrepreneurial research and such a goal can hardly succeed without the study of failure itself. Second, neglect of failed entrepreneurs in studies of entrepreneurial characteristics very likely leads to restriction of range in significant variables. Third, elimination of failed firms from samples limits the external validity of any conclusions reached.

The cross-sectional nature of the research was another possible limitation of this study. Although the purpose underlying this study was to answer the research questions, it should be kept in mind that longitudinal studies are usually richer in capturing not only performance but also the ever-changing contextual milieu.

Another possible limitation of this study was the broad range of firms included in the sample with regard to both industry and age. Although this was done purposely to enhance the external validity of the study as well as to demonstrate the power of contextual interactions to provide power in a wide range of situations, nevertheless it limits the ability of this study to speak to specific situations.

Still another limitation was the inability of this research to investigate any but a very narrow range of contextual variables and characteristics. While the contextual variables were specifically picked from the literature review in an attempt to tailor them to the usefulness of new ventures as well as to maximize their interaction with skills, there are certainly many important aspects of both strategy and industry which were not investigated. For example, such contextual variables as financial substrategies,[25] industry concentration,[26] and stamina (capability of sustained intense effort[27]) were entirely omitted. Similarly the skills typology used was a limiting factor. While the typology was derived from the literature and is theoretically all-inclusive, there are obviously other specific skills (or more narrowly defined skills) which could have been investigated.

Finally, as with most studies, sample size has been a very definite limitation. This has caused numerous difficulties and shortcomings in the study among which are an inability to interpret regression coefficients in the multiple regressions, the inability to investigate the interaction of characteristics with interactions between contextual variables, and the inability to investigate complete multiple regressions which simultaneously contain all possible terms from the research model.

DIRECTIONS FOR FUTURE RESEARCH

Directions for future research are indicated by the present study in at least five separate areas: overcoming the limitations of this research, expanding future knowledge in the skills area, studying the balance of the "full" model model left unstudied by the "research" model, expanding the full model, and addressing issues derived from this study's findings.

Overcoming Limitations of this Research

Five potentially fruitful areas for future research are indicated in the limitations section of the study.

First, one of the most fruitful potential directions is that of studying the skills of entire entrepreneurial teams and how those skills interact based on organizational structure and team experience. Roure[28] indicates that the both team completeness (defined as the percent of functional areas headed by original founders) and joint experience (the extent to which the founders had worked together previously) are significantly related to NVP (both practically and statistically). Roure's findings together with the current study's findings indicate that research could be fruitful linking the balance of skills possessed by the entrepreneurial team to NVP and moderated by the ability of organizational structure or past joint experience to coordinate skills usage.

Second, the issue of multiple observer skill ratings should be researched. Likely the problems of invalid observer ratings from employees which this study incurred could be overcome by using venture capitalists or some other peer group to rate the entrepreneur.

Third, the issue of the skills of entrepreneurs of failed firms should be investigated. No doubt it would be extremely difficult to obtain a valid sample of adequate size, but such research, if successfully implemented, could be of very large significance to our field.

Fourth, the area of alternative contextual variables could be very fruitful for future research. There are many contextual variables which remain to be considered as moderators in the effectiveness of skills usage such as industry concentration, key industry success factors, and, and low cost versus differentiation strategies.[29]

Fifth, the way in which skills on the one hand and strategy and industry structure on the other reciprocally affect each other should be investigated by way of longitudinal studies. In the current cross-sectional study, these contextual variables were taken as a given. In fact, such contextual variables are largely determined by the entrepreneur[30] and are therefore under the influence of entrepreneurial skills.

Expanding Knowledge in the skills Area

Another broad area of directions for future research is indicated by our field's lack of detailed knowledge of the composition of skill areas critical to entrepreneurship. The current study developed a skills typology based largely upon theoretical concepts drawn from the fields of strategy implementationstrategy and economics. Most of these concepts had received scant empirical attention prior to the current research. Although this research has now lent empirical support to this skills typology, our knowledge of the details behind this typology is sadly lacking. It remains to be seen what detailed skills actually make up each of the skill groupings within the typology and whether skills could be regrouped into a more effective typology. More fine-grained research on the case study and interview levels is indicated.

Studying the Balance of the "Full" Model

Another broad area for future research involves those parts of the "full" model developed in chapter 2 which were left unstudied by the "research" model investigated in this study. Little is known about how values and personality traits effect skill usages; little is also known about how proficiency in skills effects skill usage, an issue which may be of large importance in determining how entrepreneurs use and misuse their valuable time; and little is known about whether and how context causally impacts skill usages. All of these could be potentially fruitful areas for future study.

Expanding the Full Model

Yet another area for future research is that of expanding the "full model." One of the drawbacks of this model as it now stands is its failure to describe "feedback" loops (originating from the entrepreneur) for the determination and alteration of strategy and industry structure themselves. The model has taken strategy and industry structure as a given, and of course nothing could be further from the truth. If we are to ultimately obtain a fair understanding of the effects of the characteristics of the entrepreneur on NVP, it will be important in the future to study how those characteristics act to determine and alter venture contexts themselves.

Addressing Issues Derived from this Study's Findings

Another broad area for future research is addressing issues derived from the findings of this study. Many such areas have already been alluded to in the sections concerned with conclusions and limitations above, and the reader searching for ideas for future research is urged to review those sections. In particular, the reader's attention is called to that portion of the implications section where the possibility of remediation and training following tests of mental ability is discussed. This study suggests that such testing is feasible. However, further research needs to be conducted using various mental ability tests before this possibility becomes a reality.

The areas involving the specific normative propositions also require some further discussion.

First, since the normative propositions derived in this study are the results of initial, exploratory research, they need to be confirmed by future research which uses them as hypotheses.

Second, it is not clear how the normative propositions operate over contexts other than those investigated. For instance, it is a belief in the field of entrepreneurial strategy research that the interaction of strategy and industry is more important to the determination of NVP than either by itself.[31][32] However, this study investigated only simple environmental interactions, not interactions of skills with environmental interactions. For example, although heterogeneous product industries would seem to call for more of all seven skills, is this true regardless of the strategy context? Likewise, what is the effect of other contextual variables such as industry concentration or technology on the normative propositions? Would not level and type of technology have an impact on the use of the technical product/service skill which moderates the propositions involving that skill?

Third, the importance of the skills of technical industry knowledge and entrepreneurship stand out in the normative propositions as being particularly important in the determination of NVP regardless of context. This indicated importance (See Figure 4-62) calls for further research. Apparently these particular skills are pivotal to NVP and should therefore be analyzed in much greater depth. What is the role of specific industry knowledge versus the ability to learn or pick up new knowledge? Is there a peak of specific industry knowledge over the course of an individual's career in an industry such that too little such knowledge will lead to errors while too much knowledge inhibits change? What is the exact nature of the entrepreneurial ability? How much of "opportunity awareness" involves the ability to take in new facts and how much involves the ability to integrate facts already taken in?

Fourth, and most important, one conclusion stands out beyond the rest. The skill levels of entrepreneurs are very important to their success and must be investigated much more thoroughly in the future in order to enhance our understanding of the processes both of their use and of their acquisition.

It is hoped that this study will stimulate much-needed future research in entrepreneurial skills and other important entrepreneurial characteristics. The phenomenon of entrepreneurship is central to our economic life and well-being, and should be the focus of increased social-science research. Within entrepreneurship, the entrepreneur deserves nothing less.

Notes:

[1] Sandberg, W. R. 1986). *New venture performance: The role of strategy and industry structure.* Lexington, MA: D.C. Heath & Co.

[2] Brockhaus, R.H. (1980). Psychological and environmental factors which distinguish the successful from unsuccessful entrepreneur: A long study. *Academy of Management Proceedings.* 368-372.

[3] Begley, T.M. & Boyd, D.P. (1987). Psychological characteristics associated with performance in entrepreneurial firms and smaller businesses. *Journal of Business Venturing, 2*(1), 79-93.

[4] Sandberg, W. R. 1986). *New venture performance: The role of strategy and industry structure.* Lexington, MA: D.C. Heath & Co.

[5] Hollenbeck, J. & Whitener, E., (1988). Reclaiming personality traits for personnel selection. *Journal of Management, 14* (1), 81-91.

[6] Brockhaus, R.H. (1980). Psychological and environmental factors which distinguish the successful from unsuccessful entrepreneur: A long study. *Academy of Management Proceedings.* 368-372.

[7] Begley, T.M. & Boyd, D.P. (1987). Psychological characteristics associated with performance in entrepreneurial firms and smaller businesses. *Journal of Business Venturing, 2*(1), 79-93.

[8] Szilagyi, A.D. & Schweiger,D.M. (1984). Matching managers to strategies: A review and suggested framework. *Academy of Management Review, 9*(4), 626-637.

[9] Sandberg, W.R., & Hofer, C.W. (1987). Improving new venture performance: The role of strategy, industry structure, and the entrepreneur. *Journal of Business Venturing, 2*, 5-28.

[10] Szilagyi, A.D. & Schweiger,D.M. (1984). Matching managers to strategies: A review and suggested framework. *Academy of Management Review, 9*(4), 626-637.

[11] Kirzner, I.M. (1985). *Discovery and the capitalist process.* Chicago: The University of Chicago Press.

[12] Katz R.L. (1974). Skills of an effective administrator. *Harvard Business Review, 52*(5). 90-102.

[13] Szilagyi, A.D. & Schweiger,D.M. (1984). Matching managers to strategies: A review and suggested framework. *Academy of Management Review, 9*(4), 626-637.

[14] Katz R.L. (1974). Skills of an effective administrator. *Harvard Business Review, 52*(5). 90-102.

[15] Kirzner, I.M. (1985). *Discovery and the capitalist process.* Chicago: The University of Chicago Press.

[16] Maier, N. (1965). *Psychology in industry.* (3rd ed.). Boston: Houghton Mifflin Co.

[17] Guilford, J. P. (1967). *The nature of human intelligence.* New York: McGraw-Hill.

[18] Sandberg, W. R. 1986). *New venture performance: The role of strategy and industry structure.* Lexington, MA: D.C. Heath & Co.

[19] McClelland, D.C. (1965). N achievement and entrepreneurship: A longitudinal study. *Journal Of Personality and Social Psychology, 1*(4), 389-392.

[20] Zaleznik, A. & Kets de Vries, M.F.R. (1976). What makes entrepreneurs entrepreneurial? *Business and Society Review, 17*(Spring): 18-23.

[21] Gartner, W.B. (1988). "Who is an entrepreneur?" is the wrong question. *American Journal of Small Business, 12*(4), 11-32.

Conclusions

[22] Bygrave, W. D. (1989). The entrepreneurial paradigm (I): A philosophical look at its research methodologies. *Entrepreneurship: Theory and Practice, 14* (1), 7-26.

[23] Roure, J. (1986). *Success and failure of high-growth technological ventures: The influence of prefunding factors.* Unpublished doctoral dissertation. Stanford, CA: Stanford University.

[24] Stuart, R. & Abetti, P.A. (1987). Start-up ventures: Towards the prediction of initial success. *Journal of Business Venturing, 2,* 215-230.

[25] Hofer, C.W. & Schendel, D.E. (1978). *Stategy formulation: Analytical concepts.* St. Paul: West Publishing Co.

[26] Porter, M.E. (1980). *Competitive Strategy.* New York: Free Press.

[27] MacMillan, I., Seigel, R., & Narasimha, S. P. (1985). Criteria used by venture capitalists to evaluate new venture proposals. *Journal of Business Venturing, 1*(1), 119-128.

[28] Roure, J. (1986). *Success and failure of high-growth technological ventures: The influence of prefunding factors.* Unpublished doctoral dissertation. Stanford, CA: Stanford University.

[29] Porter, M.E. (1980). *Competitive Strategy.* New York: Free Press.

[30] Child, J. (1972). Organizational structure, environment, and performance: The role of strategic choice. *Sociology, 6*(1), 1-22.

[31] McDougall, P. (1987). *An analysis of new venture business level strategy, entry barriers, and new venture origin as factors explaining new venture performance.* Unpublished doctoral dissertation. Columbia, SC: University of South Caroloina.

[32] Sandberg, W.R., & Hofer, C.W. (1987). Improving new venture performance: The role of strategy, industry structure, and the entrepreneur. *Journal of Business Venturing, 2,* 5-28.

Appendix

GENERAL DATA
Your name _____ Today's date _____
Your title or position _____
Company name _____
Company address _____
_____
_____
Phone Number (including area code)_____
Is your company: a division of another company? (Y or N) _____; a franchise? (Y or N)_____
Brief description of the business your company is in (use SIC code, if known): _____
_____
_____
How many partners do you currently have active in operating the business?_____
Date company started (Month & Year) _____
Did you found or help found the company? (Y or N) _____
Your title or position when the company was founded:_____
How many partners did you have active in operating the business at the time it was founded?_____ Were they the same partners you currently have? (Y or N) _____

STRATEGY
1). Within the U.S., we attempt to serve customers from (Check one but only one):
　___ only one neighborhood
　___ more than one neighborhood but less than one city
　___ only one city
　___ more than one city but less than one county
　___ only one county
　___ more than one county but less than one state
　___ only one state
　___ more than one state but less than one region
　___ only one region (e.g. midwest or southeast)
　___ more than one region but less than the total U.S.
　___ most or all of the U.S.

2). We also export to (check one but only one):
    ___ no one
    ___ one other country
    ___ two other countries
    ___ three to five other countries
    ___ six to ten other countries
    ___ eleven or more other countries

3). The number of significant items/services on our price list (or in our store, or on our menu, etc.) is approximately _____ .

4). We concentrate on serving (check one but only one):
    ___ only one very special type of customer
    ___ two or three special types of customers
    ___ various special types of customers
    ___ numerous but not all types of customers
    ___ almost all types of customers

5). On a scale of 1 to 10 (with 1 = "extremely narrow[focused]" and 10 = "extremely wide [unfocused]"):

   How wide a range of geographic markets do you serve? (circle one but only one):
   Extremely focused ⇐ 1 2 3 4 5 6 7 8 9 10 ⇒ extremely broad or unfocused

   How wide a range of products/services do you provide? (circle one but only one):
   Extremely focused ⇐ 1 2 3 4 5 6 7 8 9 10 ⇒ extremely broad or unfocused

   How wide a range of customer types do you serve? (circle one but only one):
   Extremely focused ⇐ 1 2 3 4 5 6 7 8 9 10 ⇒ extremely broad or unfocused

6). Considering your geographic markets, your product types, and your customer types, how broad is your business overall (circle one but only one):
   Extremely focused ⇐ 1 2 3 4 5 6 7 8 9 10 ⇒ extremely broad or unfocused

Appendix

7). Since my business has been engaged in selling, my sales increases per year have averaged about (check one but only one):

___0% to 5%   ___31% to 35%   ___61% to 65%   ___91% to 95%
___6% to 10%   ___36% to 40%   ___66% to 70%   ___96% to 100%
___11% to 15%   ___41% to 45%   ___71% to 75%   ___more than double
___16% to 20%   ___46% to 50%   ___76% to 80%   ___triple
___21% to 25%   ___51% to 55%   ___81% to 85%   ___more than triple
___26% to 30%   ___56% to 60%   ___86% to 90%   ___sales have declined

8). Since my business has been engaged in selling, sales increases in my industry (per year) have averaged about (check one but only one):

___0% to 5%   ___31% to 35%   ___61% to 65%   ___91% to 95%
___6% to 10%   ___36% to 40%   ___66% to 70%   ___96% to 100%
___11% to 15%   ___41% to 45%   ___71% to 75%   ___more than double
___16% to 20%   ___46% to 50%   ___76% to 80%   ___triple
___21% to 25%   ___51% to 55%   ___81% to 85%   ___more than triple
___26% to 30%   ___56% to 60%   ___86% to 90%   ___sales have declined

9). When my company started in business, the company's total assets were_____ $
The company's total assets are now _____ $
Within 3 years, I expect the company's total assets to be _____ $

10). When my company started in business, it's total number of employees was _____
The company's total number of employees is now _____
Within 3 years, I expect the company's total number of employees to be _____

11). How aggressive is your orientation toward growth? (circle one but only one): Extremely conservative ⇐ 1 2 3 4 5 6 7 8 9 10 ⇒ extremely aggressive

12). Check the one (but only one) statement which best represents your marketing strategy:
___ "Our product or service is not at all new to the market we are serving and prices will be our main method of competition"
___ "Our product or service is not at all new to the market we are serving, but demand is great enough that we will have about the same prices as competition"
___ "Our product or service is not at all new to the market we are serving, but it will be marketed or distributed with significant non-price differences from those of our competition (our prices may or may not be lower)."
___ "Our product or service itself has aspects which are new and/or different to the market we are serving."
___ "Nothing else like our product or service is currently being sold in the market we are serving"
___ "Our product or service is totally new and to our knowledge has never been offered before in any market."

13). How important is it that you maintain a lower cost position than your competition?
Circle one but only one: Not important ⇐ 1 2 3 4 5 6 7 8 9 10 ⇒ extremely important

14). How important is it that your product/service be different from that of your competition?
Circle one but only one: Not important ⇐ 1 2 3 4 5 6 7 8 9 10 ⇒ extremely important

INDUSTRY

15). Check one(but only one) blank for each question:

For the last three years, dollar sales in our industry have been:
___ growing at a rate of 7% or more
___ growing, but at a rate of less than 7%
___ remaining steady (not growing or declining)
___ declining

For the past three years, the rate of sales growth in our industry has been:
___ increasing
___ staying about the same
___ declining

Appendix

16). In the industry in which you compete, how much competition is there on each of the following items (check one but only one blank under each question):

Uniqueness of product or service? (in features, styling, or packaging)
　　___ Minor competition
　　___ Significant competition
　　___ Major competition

Brand name of product or service?
　　___ Minor competition
　　___ Significant competition
　　___ Major competition

Quality of product or service?
　　___ Minor competition
　　___ Significant competition
　　___ Major competition

Other considerations? (warranty, delivery, credit, after-sales service, installation)
　　___ Minor competition
　　___ Significant competition
　　___ Major competition

Personal relationships between customer contact personnel and customer?
　　___ Minor competition
　　___ Significant competition
　　___ Major competition

Price?
　　___ Minor competition
　　___ Significant competition
　　___ Major competition

SKILLS

17). For each of the following skills please rate your current effectiveness, give your years of experience with this type skill (since high school and including other businesses), and assess what % of your time you currently spend excercising each skill (the %s should add to 100%):

	Current % of my time spent performing this skill
My skill in the detailed design of our products/services:	
Not effective at all ⇐ 1 2 3 4 5 6 7 8 9 10 ⇒ extremely effective	
Years of experience I have had practicing this type skill_____	_____%
My skill in evaluating the various functions of my organization:	
Not effective at all ⇐ 1 2 3 4 5 6 7 8 9 10 ⇒ extremely effective	
Years of experience I have had practicing this type skill_____	_____%
My skill in understanding my industry and the implications of its trends and changes:	
Not effective at all ⇐ 1 2 3 4 5 6 7 8 9 10 ⇒ extremely effective	
Years of experience I have had practicing this type skill_____	_____%
My skill in motivating and influencing the behavior of my employees:	
Not effective at all ⇐ 1 2 3 4 5 6 7 8 9 10 ⇒ extremely effective	
Years of experience I have had practicing this type skill_____	_____%
My skill in creating relations with and influencing important people outside my organization:	
Not effective at all ⇐ 1 2 3 4 5 6 7 8 9 10 ⇒ extremely effective	
Years of experience I have had practicing this type skill_____	_____%
My skill in planning and administering my business' activities:	
Not effective at all ⇐ 1 2 3 4 5 6 7 8 9 10 ⇒ extremely effective	
Years of experience I have had practicing this type skill_____	_____%
My skill in discovering opportunities to profitably change my business:	
Not effective at all ⇐ 1 2 3 4 5 6 7 8 9 10 ⇒ extremely effective	
Years of experience I have had practicing this type skill_____	_____%

========
TOTAL TIME............100%

Appendix 225

18). On the average, I spend _____ hours each week working on this business (include travel time only if it is productive, i.e. if it is used for one of the skill activities in question 17.

19). My energy level and the pace of my work tends to be (check one but only one):
 ___ Extremely low ___ Just slightly above normal
 ___ Fairly low ___ Somewhat high
 ___ Just slightly below normal ___ Extremely high
 ___ About normal

20). If there are characteristics about you and your personal performance which affect the performance of your company (either positively or negatively) and about which this questionnaire should have asked but didn't, please tell us briefly about them:
_____
_____
_____
_____
_____
_____

BUSINESS SUCCESS FACTORS

21). In any business situation, there are certain business functions critical to success. Several of these potentially critical functions are listed below. Please indicate to the left of each function how important you consider it to achievement of success in your business situation. Then to the right of each function, please indicate how satisfied you are with your company's performance on that function.

RELATIVELY UNIMPORTANT	EXTREMELY IMPORTANT	FUNCTION	EXTREMELY DISSATISFIED	EXTREMELY SATISFIED
1 2 3	4 5 6 7	Development of new products/services	1 2 3	4 5 6 7
1 2 3	4 5 6 7	Development of new processes	1 2 3	4 5 6 7
1 2 3	4 5 6 7	Modification of existing products/services	1 2 3	4 5 6 7
1 2 3	4 5 6 7	Production of products/services	1 2 3	4 5 6 7
1 2 3	4 5 6 7	Distribution system and channels	1 2 3	4 5 6 7
1 2 3	4 5 6 7	Pricing	1 2 3	4 5 6 7
1 2 3	4 5 6 7	Selling	1 2 3	4 5 6 7
1 2 3	4 5 6 7	Advertising and promoting	1 2 3	4 5 6 7
1 2 3	4 5 6 7	Before sales service	1 2 3	4 5 6 7
1 2 3	4 5 6 7	After sales service	1 2 3	4 5 6 7
1 2 3	4 5 6 7	Merchandising	1 2 3	4 5 6 7
1 2 3	4 5 6 7	Purchasing	1 2 3	4 5 6 7
1 2 3	4 5 6 7	Operating efficiency	1 2 3	4 5 6 7
1 2 3	4 5 6 7	Finance	1 2 3	4 5 6 7
1 2 3	4 5 6 7	Personnel	1 2 3	4 5 6 7
1 2 3	4 5 6 7	General management	1 2 3	4 5 6 7

BUSINESS PERFORMANCE

22). This question is about how important certain goals are to you and how satisfied you are with your business' attainment of these goals. Answer this question in the same fashion as you answered the last question.

RELATIVELY UNIMPORTANT	EXTREMELY IMPORTANT	GOAL	EXTREMELY DISSATISFIED	EXTREMELY SATISFIED
1 2 3	4 5 6 7	Sales growth rate...................	1 2 3	4 5 6 7
1 2 3	4 5 6 7	Market share.......................	1 2 3	4 5 6 7
1 2 3	4 5 6 7	Cash flow from operations	1 2 3	4 5 6 7
1 2 3	4 5 6 7	Return on investments...........	1 2 3	4 5 6 7
1 2 3	4 5 6 7	Market valuation of business.	1 2 3	4 5 6 7
1 2 3	4 5 6 7	Company stability...................	1 2 3	4 5 6 7
1 2 3	4 5 6 7	Fostering an entrepreneurial culture.................................	1 2 3	4 5 6 7
1 2 3	4 5 6 7	Harvest/exit readiness.............	1 2 3	4 5 6 7

23). Considering my expectations for my business over the last three years, I am (check one but only one):
____ Extremely dissatisfied with the performance of my business.
____ Pretty much dissatisfied with the performance of my business.
____ Slightly dissatisfied with the performance of my business.
____ Neither satisfied nor dissatisfied with the performance of my business.
____ Barely satisfied with the performance of my business.
____ Pretty much satisfied with the performance of my business.
____ Extremely satisfied with the performance of my business.

24). Please give the following for each of the past three years:

	1986	1987	1988
Sales	_____	_____	_____
Cost of Goods Sold	_____	_____	_____
Assets	_____	_____	_____
Interest paid	_____	_____	_____
Profits before taxes	_____	_____	_____
% Gross sales margin	_____	_____	_____

25). If there are any other comments you have about this questionnaire (things we should have asked but didn't; complaints; etc.) please enter them below:

_____
_____
_____
_____
_____
_____
_____
_____
_____
_____

Bibliography

(1980.) Wanted: A manager to fit each strategy. *Business Week.* (Feb.) 166-173.

(1981). Matching managers to a company's life cycle. *Business Week,* (Feb.23), 62.

Aaker, D.A. & Bagozzi, R.P. (1979). Unobservable variables in structural equation models with an application in industrial selling. *Journal of Marketing Research, 16*(May),147-158.

Abell, D.F. (1980). *Defining the business: The starting point of strategic planning.* Englewood Cliffs, NJ: Prentice-Hall.

Allport, G.W., & Odbert, H.S. (1936). Trait names: A psycho-lexical study. *Psychological Monographs, 47*(1).

Anderson, C.R. (1977). Locus of control, coping behaviors, and performance in a stress setting: A longitudinal study. *Journal of Applied Psychology, 62*(4), 446-451.

Anderson, J.C. & Gerbing, D.W. (1982). Some methods of rectifying measurement models to obtain unidimensional construct measurement. *Journal of Marketing Research, 19*(Nov), 453-460.

Anderson, J.C. & Gerbing, D.W. (1984). *The effect of sampling error on convergence, improper solutions, and goodness-of-fit indicies for ml confirmatory factor analysis.* University of Texas Working Paper.

Anderson, C., & Schneier, C. (1978). Locus of control, leader behavior and leader performance among management students.*Academy of Management Journal, 21*(4), 690-698.

Anderson, C.R. & Zeithaml, C.P. (1984). Stage of the product life cycle, business strategy, and business performance. *Academy of Management Journal, 27*(1), 5-24.

Anderson, C., Hellriegel, D., & Slocum, J. (1977). Managerial response to environmentally induced stress. *Academy of Management Journal, 20*(2), 260-272.

Arnold, H.J. (1982). Moderator variables: A clarification of conceptual, analytic, and psychometric issues. *Organizational Behavior and Human Performance, 29*, 143-174.

Babakus, E., Ferguson, C.E., & Jöreskog, K.G. (1987). The sensitivity of confirmatory maximum likelihood factor analysis to violations of measurement scale and distributional assumptions. *Journal of Marketing Research, 24*(May),222-228.

Bagozzi, R.P. (1977). Structural equation models in expermental research. *Journal of Marketing Research, 14*,(May), 209-226.

Bagozzi, R.P. (1978). The construct validity of the affective, behavioral, and cognitive components of attitude by analysis of covariance structures. *Multivariate Behavioral Research*, (13) 9-31.

Bagozzi, R.P. (1981). Attitudes, intensions, and behavior: A test of some key hypotheses. *Journal of Personality and Social Psychology, 41*(4), 607-627.

Bagozzi, R.P. (1981). Evaluating structural equation models with unobserable variables and measurement error: A comment. *Journal of Marketing Research, 18* (Aug), 375-381.

Bagozzi, R.P. (1983). Issues in the application of covariance structure analysis: A further comment. *Journal of Consumer Research, 9* (Mar), 449-450.

Bagozzi, R.P. (1984). A prospectus for theory construction in marketing. *Journal of Marketing, 48*(Winter), 11-29.

Bagozzi, R.P. & Phillips, L.W. (1982). Representing and testing organizational theories: A holistic construal. *Administrative Science Quarterly, 27*,459-489.

Ballenger,J.,Pos,R.,Jimerson,D.,Lake,C.,Murphy,D.,Zuckerman,M., & Cronin,C. (1983). Biochemical Correlates of personality traits in normals: An exploratory study. *Personal Individual Differences, 4*(6), 615-625.

Bandura, A. (1982).Self-efficacy mechanism in human agency. *American Psychologist, 37*(2), 122-147.

Baty, G.B. (1989). Entrepreneurship: Too much of a good thing? *MIT Management,* (Winter), 17-19.

Bearden, W.O., Sharma, S., & Teel, J.E. (1982). Sample size effects on chi square and other statistics used in evaluating causal models. *Journal of Marketing Research, 19*(Nov), 425-430.

Begley, T.M. & Boyd, D.P. (1985). Psychological characteristics associated with entrepreneurial performance. In: *Frontiers of Entrepreneurial Research*, Wellesley, MA: Babson College.146-165.

Begley, T.M. & Boyd, D.P. (1987). A Comparison of entrepreneurs and managers of small business firms. *Journal of Management, 13*(1), 99-108.

Begley, T.M. & Boyd, D.P. (1987). Psychological characteristics associated with performance in entrepreneurial firms and smaller businesses. *Journal of Business Venturing, 2*(1), 79-93.

Bentler, P.M. & Bontee, D.G. (1980). Significance tests and goodness of fit in the analysis of covariance structures. *Psychological Bulletin, 88*(3), 588-606.

Berry,W. (1984). *Nonrecursive causal models.* Beverly Hills:Sage Publications

Bettis, R., Hall,W. & Prahalad,C.K. (1978). Diversity and performance in the multibusiness firm. *National proceedings of the Amercian Institute for Decision Sciences.*

Biggadike, R. (1979) The risky business of diversification. *Harvard Business Review,*(May-June). 103-111.

Birch, D.L. (1988). The truth about start-ups. *Inc.*(Jan.), 14-15.

Bird, B. (1988). Implementing entrepreneurial ideas: The case for intention. *Academy of Management Review, 13*(3), 442-453.

Bird, B.J. (1989). *Entrepreneurial Behavior.* Glenville, IL: Scott, Foresman and Co.

Blalock, H.M. (1965). Theory buliding and the statistical concept of interaction. *American Sociological Review, 30,* 374-380.

Blalock, H.M. (1969). *Theory construction.* Prentice-Hall, Englewood Cliffs, NJ, 1-47.

Bohrnstedt, G.W. & Marwell, G. (1977). The reliability of products of two random variables. In K.F. Schuessler (Ed.) *Socialological Methodology,* 1978. San Francisco: Josey-Bass.

Borland, C.M. (1975). *Locus of control, need for achievement and entrepreneurship.* Unpublished doctoral dissertation, The University of Texas at Austin, Austin, TX.

Braden, P.L. (1977). *Technological entrepreneurship: The allocation of time and money in technology-based firms.* Ann Arbor, MI: Division of Research, The University of Michigan.

Brinberg, D. & McGrath, J. (1985). *Validity and the research process.* Beverly Hills: Sage Publications.

Brockhaus, R.H. (1980). Psychological and environmental factors which distinguish the successful from unsuccessful entrepreneur: A long study. *Academy of Management Proceedings.* 368-372.

Brockhaus, R.H. (1980). Risk-taking propensity of entrepreneurs. *Academy of Management Journal, 23,* 509-520.

Brockhaus, R.H (1982). The Psychology of the entrepreneur. In: Kent,C.A., Sexton,D.L., & Vesper,K.H. (Eds). *Encyclopedia of Entrepreneurship.* Englewood Cliffs.NJ: Prentice-Hall, 41-56.

Brockhaus, R. & Nord, W. (1979). An exploration of factors affecting the entrepreneurial decision: Personal characteristics vs. environmental conditions. *Proceedings: Academy of Management.*

Brown, W. (1910). Some expermental results in the correlation of mental abilities. *British Journal of Psychology, 3,* 296-322.

Buchele, R. (1967). *Business policy in growing firms.* Scranton, PA: Chandler Publishing Company.

Burt, C, (1940). *The factors of the mind.* London: University of London Press.

Burt, R.S. (1973). *Confirmatory factor-analytic structures and the theory construction process.* Beverly Hills: Sage Publications.

Busemeyer, J.R. & Jones, L.E. (1983). Analysis of multiplicative combination rules when the causal variables are measured with error. *Psychological Bulletin, 93* (3), 549-562.

Buss, A.H. & Finn, S.E. (1987). Classification of personality traits. *Journal of Personality and Social Psychology, 52*(2), 433-444.

Buss, A.H. & Plomin, R. (1975). *A Temperament theory of personality development.* New York: Wiley Interscience.

Buss, A.H. & Plomin, R. (1984). *Temperament: Early developing personality traits.* Hillsdale, N.J.: Erlbaum.

Bygrave, W. D. (1989). The entrepreneurial paradigm (I): A philosophical look at its research methodologies. *Entrepreneurship: Theory and Practice, 14* (1), 7-26.

Campbell, D.T. & Fiske, D.W. (1959). Convergent and discriminant validation by the multitrait-multimethod matrix. *Psychological Bulletin, 56* (2), 81-105.

Carland, J.W., Hoy, F. & Carland, J.C.(1988). ""Who is an entrepreneur?"" Is a question worth asking. *American Journal of Small Business, 12*(4), 33-39.

Carland, J.C., Hoy, F., Boulton, W.R., Carland, J.C.(1984). Differentiating entrepreneurs from small business owners: A conceptualization. *Academy of Management Review, 9*(2), 354-359.

Carsrud, A.L., Olm, K.W. & Eddy, G.G. (1986). Entrepreneurship: Research in quest of a paradigm. In D.L. Sexton & R.W. Smilor (Eds.) *The Art and Science of Entrepreneurship.* (367-378). Cambridge, MA: Ballinger Publishing.

Cattell, R.B. (1947). Confirmation and clarification of primary personality traits. *Psychologial Bulletin, 72,* 402-421.

Cattell, R.B. (1957). *Personality and motivation structure and measurement.* New York: World Book.

Cattell, R. B. (1971). *Abilities: Their structure, growth, and action.* Boston: Houghton Mifflin.

Chamberlin, E. H. (1956). *The theory of monopolistic competition.* Cambridge, MA: Harvard University Press.

Child, J. (1972). Organizational structure, environment, and performance: The role of strategic choice. *Sociology, 6*(1), 1-22.

Chow, G.C. (1960). Tests of equality between sets of coefficients in two linear regressions. *Econometrica,28* (3), 591-605.

Christensen, C., Berg,N., Salter, M., & Stevenson,H. (1985).Policy formulation and administration(9th ed). Chapter 11: *Policy Formulation and administration in the entrepreneurial firm.* Homewood, ILL: Richard D. Irwin.

Christensen, P.R. & Guilford, J.P. (1963). An expermential study of verbal fluency factors. *The British Journal of Statistical Psychology, 16*(1), 1-26.

Churchill, G.A. (1988). *Basic marketing research.* Chicago: The Dryden Press.

Churchill, N.C. & Lewis, V.L. (1983). The five stages of small business growth. *Harvard Business Review,*(May-Jun), 30-50.

Clark, J.B. (1892). Insurance and business profit. Quarterly insurance and business profit. *Quarterly Journal of Economics*, 7(Oct. 1892 - July. 1893), 40-54.

Clark, J.B. (1907). *Essentials of economic theory*. New York: Macmillan.

Clark, J.B. (1956). *The distribution of wealth*. New York: Kelly & Millman.

Cliff, N. (1983). Some cautions concerning the application of causal modeling methods. *Multivariate Behavioral Research, 18* (Jan), 115-126.

Cochran, A.B. (1981). Small business mortality rates: A review of the literature. *Journal of Small Business*, (Oct), 50-59.

Cohen, J. (1978). Partialed products are *interactions; partialed powers are curve components*. *Psychological Bulletin, 85* (4), 858-866.

Cohen, J. & Cohen, P. (1975). *Applied multiple regression/correlation analysis for the behavioral sciences*. New York: John Wiley & Sons.

Collins, B.E. (1974). Four components of the Rotter internal-external scale: Belief in a difficult world, a just world, a predictable world and a potentially responsive world. *Journal of Personality and Social Psychology, 29*(3), 381-391.

Collins, O.F. & Moore, D.G. (1964). *The enterprising man*. East Lansing, MI: Michigan State University.

Collins, O.F., & Moore, D.G. (1970). *The organization makers*. New York: Meredith Corporation.

Conley, J.J. (1985). Longitudinal stability of personality traits: A multitrait-multimethod-multioccasion analysis. *Journal of Personality and Social Psychology, 49*(5), 1266-1282.

Cook, T.D. & Campbell, D.T. (1979). *Quasi-expermentation: Design and analysis issues for field settings*. Chicago: Rand-McNally.

Cook, V.J. (1983). Marketing strategy an differential advantage. *Journal of Marketing, 47*(Spring), 68-75."

Cooper, A.C. (1979). Strategic management: New ventures and small business. In Schendel, D.E. & Hofer, C.W. (Eds.) *Strategic management*, 316-327. Boston: Little, Brown, and Co.

Cooper, A.C. & Dunkelberg, W.C., (1987). Entrepreneurial research: Old questions, new answers and methodological issues. *American Journal of Small Business, 11*(3), 11-23.

Cooper,A.C., Dunkelberg W.C., & Woo,C.Y., (1987). Patterns of survival, growth, and change - A large-scale study. *In Wyckham. R., Meredith,L., & Bush,G.(Eds). The spirit of entrepreneurship.* Burnby, BC: Simon Fraser Univ, 140-155.

Cooper, A.C., Willard,G.E. & Woo,C.Y. (1986).Strategies of high-performaning new and small firms: A reexamination of the niche concept. *Journal of Business Venturing, 1* (3), 247-260.

Cronbach, L.J. (1951). Coefficient alpha and the internal structure of tests. *Psychometrika, 16* (Sept.), 297-334

Cronbach, L.J. & Meehl, P.E. (1955). Construct validity in psychological tests. *Psychological Bulletin,52*, 218-302.

Dalrymple, D.J. & Parsons, L.J. (1986). *Marketing mamagement: Strategy and cases* (4th Ed.). New York: John Wiley & Sons.

DeNisi, A. S. & Shaw, J. B. (1977). Investigation of the uses of self-reports of abilities. *Journal of Applied Psychology, 62* (5), 641-644."

Dess, G.G. & Davis, P.S. (1984). Porter's (1980) generic strategies as determinants of strategic group membership and organizational performance. *Academy of Management Journal, 27*(3), 467-488.

Dess, G.G. & Robinson, R.B. (1984). Measuring organizational performance in the absence of objective measures: The case of the privately-held firm and congloimerate business unit. *Strategic Management Journal, 5*, 265-273.

Dickinson, R. (1981). *Business Failure Rate. American Journal of Small Business, 2* (2), 17-25.

Dickneider, W. & Kaplan, D. (1978). *Choice and change.* St.Paul: West Publishing.

Dillon, W.R. & Kumar, A. (1987). *A discussion of selected issues in covariance analsis: An amplification and reevaluation.* Unpublished paper."

Dollinger, M.J. (1984). Measuring effectiveness in entrepreneurial organizations. *International Small Business Journal, 3*(1), 11-20.

Dressler, G. (1988). *Personnel management* (4th ed.). Englewood cliffs, New Jersey.

Drucker, P.F. (1984). Our entrepreneurial economy. *Harvard Business Review*, (Jan-Feb), 59-64.

Drucker, P.F. (1985). Entrepreneurial strategies. *California Management Review, 27*,(2), 9-25.

Drucker, P.F. (1985). *Innovation and entrepreneurship.* New York: Harper & Row.

Dubini, P. (1989). Which venture capital backed entrepreneurs have the best chances of succeeding? *Journal of Business Venturing, 4*(2),123-132.

Duffy, P.B. & Stevenson, H.H. (1984). *Entrepreneurship and self-employment: Understanding the distinctions. Frontiers of Entrepreship Research.* Wellesley, MA: Babson College. 461-477.

Duncan, O.D. (1975). *Introduction to structural equation models.* New York: Academic Press.

Dunphy, S. (1988). Definitions and usage of the term "entrepreneur". *Proceedings of the ICSB/USASBE.* Boston.

Eastlack, J.O. & McDonald, P.R. (1970). CEO's role in corporate growth. *Harvard Business Review,58*(3).

Ekstrom, R. B., French, J. W., & Harmon, H. H. (1979). Cognitive factors: Their identification and replication. *Multivariate Behavioral Research Monographs*, 79-82.

Emmons, R.A. & Diener, E. (1986). An interactional approach to the study of personality and emotion. *Journal of Personality, 54*(2), 371-384.

Epstein, S. (1979). The stability of behavior: I. On predicting most of the people much of the time. *Journal of personality & Social Psychology, 37* (7). 1097-1126.

Epstein, S. (1980). The stability of behavior: II. Implications for psychological research. *American Psychologist, 35*(9), 790-806.

Epstein, S. & O'Brian, E.J. (1985). The person-situation debate in historical and current perspective. *Psychological Bulletin, 98*(3), 513-537.

Feigl, H. (1970). The orthodox view of theories: Remarks in defense as well as critique. In M. Radnar and S. Winokur (Eds.). *Minnesota studies in the philosophy of science, Vol. 4.* Minneapolis: University of Minnesota Press, 3-16.

Finn, S.E. (1986). Structural stability of the MMPI in adult males. *Journal of Consulting and Clinical Psychology, 54*(5), 703-707.

Fishbein, M. & Ajzen, I. (1975). *Belief, attitude, intention and behavior: An introduction to theory and research.* Reading, MA: Addison-Wesley.

Fisher, F.M. (1970). Tests of equality between sets of coefficients in two linear regressions: *An expository note. Econometrica,38* (3), 361-366.

Fornell, C. (1983). Issues in the application of covariance structure analysis. A comment. *Journal of Consumer Research, 9* (Mar), 443-448.

Fornell, C. & Bookstein, F.L. (1982). Two structural equation models: LISREL and PLS applied to consumer exit-voice theory. *Journal of Marketing Research, 19*(Nov), 440-452.

Fornell, C. & Larker, D.F. (1981). Evaluating structural equation models with unobservable variables and measurement error. *Journal of Marketing Research, 18*(Feb), 39-50.

Fornell, C. & Larker, D.F. (1981). Evaluating structural equation models with unobservable variables and measurement error. *Journal of Marketing Research, 18*(1), 39-50.

French, E.G. (1958). The interaction of achievement motivation and ability in problem-solving success. *Journal of Abnormal and Social Psychology, 57*, 306-309.

Galbraith, C. & Schendel, D. (1983) An empirical analysis of strategy types. *Strategic Management Journal, 4*, 153-173.

Gartner, W.B. (1983). Entry strategies in an emerging industry. *Academy of Management Meeting Proceedings,* 413-416.

Gartner, W.B. (1985). A conceptual framework for describing the phenomina of new venture performance. *Academy of management Review,10*(4), 696-706.

Gartner, W.B. (1987). *What are we talking about when we talk about entrepreneurship?* Paper presented at the Academy of Management meeting at N.O. (in abstracts), 1-20.

Gartner, W.B. (1988). "Who is an entrepreneur?" is the wrong question. *American Journal of Small Business, 12*(4), 11-32.

Gasse, Y. (1977). *Entrepreneurial characteristics and practices: A study of the dynamics of small business organizations and their effectiveness in different environments.* Sherbrook, Québec: René Prince Imprimeur.

Gasse, Y (1978). *Characteristics, functions and performance of small firm owner-managers in two industrial environments.* Unpublished doctoral dissertation, Northwestern University, Evanston,IL.

Gerbing, D.W. & Anderson, J.C. (1984). On the meaning of within-factor correlated measurement errors. *Journal of Consumer Research, 11* (Jun), 572-580.

Gerbing, D.W. & Anderson, J.C. (1988). An updated paradigm for scale development incorporating unidimensionality and its assessment. *Journal of Marketing Research, 23*(May),186-192.

Gerbing, D.W., Ahadi, S.A., & Patton, J.H. (1987). Toward a conceptualization of impulsivity: Components across the behavioral and self-report domains. *Multivariate Behavioral Research, 22* (July), 357-379.

Ghiselli, E.E. (1966). *The validity of occupational apptitude tests.* New York:Wiley

Ghiselli, E. E. (1971). *Explorations in management talent.* Pacific Palisades, CA: Goodyear Publishing.

Ghiselli, E.E. (1973). The validity of aptitude tests in personnel selection. *Personnel Physcholgy, 26*(4), 461-477.

Goldbeger, A (1964). *Econometric theory.* New York: John Wiley & Sons.

Gorman, M. & Sahlman, W.A. (1986). *What do venture capitalists do? Frontiers of Entrepreneurship Research.* Wellesley, MA: Babson College. 414-436.

Goslin, N.L. & Barge, B. (1986). Entrepreneurial qualities considered in venture capital support. *Frontiers of Entrepreneurship Research.* Wellesley, MA: Babson College.

Gottfredson, L. (1986). The g factor in employment. *Journal of Vocational Behavior, 29,* 293-296.

Gough, H.G. (1984). A managerial potential scale for the Calfornia psychological inventory. *Journal of Applied Psychology, 69,* 233-240.

Gough, H.G. (1985). A work orientation scale for the Calfornia psychological inventory. *Journal of Applied Psychology, 70*(3), 505-513.

Greenberg, H.M. & Greenberg, J. (1980). Job matching for better sales performance. *Harvard Business Review* (Sept-Oct) 128-133.

Greiner, L.E. (1972). Evolution and revolution as organizations grow. *Harvard Business Review* (July), 37-46.

Guilford, J. P. (1967). *The nature of human intelligence.* New York: McGraw-Hill.

Guilford, J.P. (1981). Higher-order structure-of-the-intellect abilities. *Multivariate Behavioral Research, 16*(Oct), 411-435.

Guilford, J.P. (1982). Cognitive psychology's ambiguities: Some suggested remedies. *Psychological Review, 89*(1), 48-59.

Guilford, J.P. (1985). The structure of intellect model. In B.B. Wolman (Ed.): *Handbook of intelligence.* New York: Wiley, 225-266.

Guilford, J.P. (1988). Some changes in the structure-of-intellect model. *Educational and Psychological Measurement, 48,* 1-4.

Guilford, J.P. & Hoepfner, R. (1971). *The analysis of intelligence.* New York: McGraw-Hill.

Guion, R. M. (1965). *Personnel testing.* New York: McGraw-Hill.

Guion, R.M. & Gibson, W.M. (1988). Personnel selection and placement. *Annual Review of Psychology, 39,* 349-374.

Gumpert, D.E. (1986). Stalking the entrepreneur. *Harvard Business Review,* (May-Jun), 32-36.

Gupta, A.K. (1984). Contingency linkages between strategy and general manager characteristics: A conceptual examination. *Academy of Management Review, 9* (3), 399-412.

Gupta, A.K. (1986). Matching managers to strategies: Point and counterpoint. *Human Resources Management, 25*(2), 215-234.

Gupta, A.K. & Govindarajan, V. (1984). Build, hold, harvest: Converting strategic intensions into reality. *Journal of Business Strategy, 4*(3) 34-47.

Gupta, A.K. & Govindarajan, V. (1984). Business unit strategy, managerial characteristics, and business effectiveness at strategy implementation. *Academy of Management Journal, 27* (1), 25-41.

Gupta, A.K. & Govindarajan, V. (1986). Resource sharing among SBUs: Strastegic antecedents and administrative implications. *Academy of Management Journal, 29* (4), 695-714.

Guth, W.D., & Tagiuri, R. (1965). Personal values and corporate strategy. *Harvard Business Review,43*(5),123-132.

Guttman, L. (1965). A faceted definition of intelligence. In R.R. Eiferman (Ed.), *Scripta Hierosolymitana (Vol.14)*. Jerusalem: Magnes Press.

Hage, J. (1972). *Techniques and problems of theory construction in sociology.* (Chapter 1: Theoretical concepts) New York: John Wiley & Sons.

Hambrick, D.C. (1987). The top management team: key to strategic success. *California Management Review*, (Fall) 88-108.

Hayduk, L.A. (1987). *Structural equation modeling with LISREL: Essentials and advances.* Baltimore: The Johns Hopkins University Press.

Hébert, R. & Link, A. (1982). *The entrepreneur.* New York: Praeger Publishers.

Heise, D.R. & Smith-Lovin, L. (1981). Impressions of goodness, powerfulness, and liveliness from discerned social events. *Social Psychology Quarterly, 44* (2), 93-106.

Herbert, T.T., & Deresky, H., (1983). Toward matching manager and strategy. *Proceedings of the Southern Management Association* (D.F.Ray, Ed.). 28-30.

Herron, L.A., McDougall, P., & Robinson, R.B. (1988, August). *Evaluating potential entrepreneurs: The role of entrepreneurial characteristics and their effect on new venture performance.* Paper presented at national meeting of Academy of Management: New Orleans, LA

Herron, L., McDougall, P., & Robinson, R.B. (1989). *The effects of Stevenson and Gumpert's modes of entrepreneurial thinking on new venture performance: An empirical comparison with Mintzberg's managerial skills, and traditionally studied entrepreneurial characteristics.* Paper presented at Academy of Management meetings, Washington, D.C.

Hoad, W. & Rosko, P. (1964). *Management factors contributing to the sucess and failure of new small manufacturers.* Ann Arbor, Mich: Bureau of Business Research, University of Michigan.

Hofer, C.W. (1975). Toward a contingency theory of business strategy. *Academy of Management Journal,* (18), 784-810.

Hofer, C.W. & Sandberg, W.R. (1987). Improving new venture performance: Some guidelines for success. *American Journal of Small Business, 12*(1), 11-25.

Hofer, C.W. & Schendel, D.E. (1978). *Stategy formulation: Analytical concepts.* St. Paul: West Publishing Co.

Hogan, J., Hogan, R., & Busch, C.M. (1984). How to measure service orientation. *Journal of Applied Psychology, 69*(1), 167-173.

Hollenbeck, J. & Whitener, E., (1988). Reclaiming personality traits for personnel selection. *Journal of Management, 14* (1), 81-91.

Hollenbeck, J. R., Brief, A. P., & Pauli, K. E. (1988). An empirical note on the interaction of personality and aptitude in personnel selection. *Journal of Management, 14* (3), 441-451.

Holzinger, K.J. (1938). Relationships between three multiple orthogonal factors and four bifactors. *Journal of Educational Psychology, 29,* 513-356.

Horn, J.L. (1968). Organizatrion of abilities and the development of intelligence. *Psychological Review, 75*(3), 242-259.

Hornaday, J.A. & Aboud, J. (1971). Characteristics of successful entrepreneurs. *Personnel Psychology, 24,* 141-153.

Hornaday, J.A & Knutzen, P. (1981). Some psychological characteristics of successfull Norwegian entrepreneurs. *Frontiers of Entrepreneurial Research*, Wellesley, MA: Babson College, 12-20.

Hoselitz, B. (1960). The early history of entrepreneurial theory. In J. Spengler & W. Allen (Eds.) *Essays in Economic Thought: Aristotle to Marshall*. pp 234-258. Chicago: Rand McNally.

Hull, D., Bosley, J., & Udell, G. (1980). Renewing the hunt for the heffalump: Identifying potential entrepreneurs by personality characteristics. Journal of Small Business,18.(1), 11-18.

Hunt, E. B. (1978). Mechanics of verbal ability. *Psychological Review*, 85, 109-130.

Hunter, J.E. & Hunter, R.F. (1984). Validity and utility of alternative predictors of job performance. *Psychological Bulletin*, 96(1), 72-98.

Hunter, J.E. (1986). Cognitive ability, cognitive attitudes, job knowledge, job performance. *Journal of Vocational Behavior*, 29, 340-362.

Jackson, D. (1967). *Personality research form manual*. Goshen, NY: Research Psychologists Press.

Jackson, D. (1984). *Personality research form manual* (3rd ed.) Port Huron, MI: Research Psycologists Press.

Jackson, D.N., Ahmed, S.A., & Heapy, N.A. (1976). Is achievement a unitary construct? *Journal of Research in Personality*, 10, 1021.

James, L.R., Mulaik, S.A., & Brett, J.M. (1982). *Causal analysis: Assumptions, models, and data*. Beverly Hills: Sage Publications.

Jenkins, A.H. (1969). *Adam Smith today*. Port Washington, NY: Kennikat.

Jensen, A. R. (1982). Reaction time and psychometric g. In H.J. Eysenck (Ed.) *A model for intelligence*. Berlin: Springer-Verlag.

Jevons, W.S. (1965). *The principles of economics and other papers.* New York: Augustus M. Kelley.

Johnston, J. (1984). *Econometric methods.* (3rd Ed.) New York: McGraw-Hill.

Johnson, N.L. & Kotz, S. (1972) *Distributions in statistics: Continuous multivariate distributions.* New York: John Wiley & Sons

Jones, G. & Butler, J. (1988). Costs, revenue and business strategy. *Academy of Management Review, 13*(2). 202-213.

Jöreskog, K.G. & Sörbom, D. (1986). *LISREL: User's guide.* Scientific Software, Inc: Mooresville, IN.

Kanbur, S.M. (1979). Of risk taking and the personal distribution of income. *Journal of Political Economy, 87*(4). 769-797.

Kanbur, S.M. (1980). A Note on risk taking, entrepreneurship, and Schumpeter. *History of Political Economy, 12*(4). 489-498.

Kaplan, R. (1987). Entrepreneurship reconsidered: The antimanagement bias. *Harvard Business Review*, (May-Jun), 84-89.

Katz, D. & Kahn, R.L. (1978). *The social psychology of organization*, 2nd Ed. New York: John Wiley.

Katz, J. & Gartner, W.B. (1986). Properties of emergent organizations. *Paper presented at the National Academy of Management: Chicago.* 1-24.

Katz, J. & Gartner, W.M. (1988). Properties of emerging organizations *The Academy of Management Review, 13*(3). 429-441.

Katz R.L. (1974). Skills of an effective administrator. *Harvard Business Review, 52*(5). 90-102.

Kementa, J. (1971). *Elements of econometrics.* New York: macMillan

Kenny, D.A. (1976). An empirical application of confirmatory factor analysis to the multitrait-multimethod matrix. *Journal of Social Psychology, 12*, 247-252.

Kerlinger, F.N. & Pedhazur, E.J. (1973). *Multiple regression in behavioral research.* New York: Holt, Rinehart and Winston, Inc. 441-450.

Kerr, J.(1982). Assigning managers on the basis of the life cycle. *Journal of Business Strategy,* 58-65.

Kets de Vries, M.F.R. (1985). The dark side of entrepreneurship. *Harvard Business Review, 63*(6), 160-167.

Kipnis, D. (1962). A noncognitive correlate of performance among lower aptitude men. *Journal of Applied Psychology, 46* (1), 76-80.

Kirzner, I.M. (1960). *The economic point of view.* Princeton: D. Van Nostrand.

Kirzner, I.M. (1973). *Competition and entrepreneurship.* Chicago: The University of Chicago Press.

Kirzner, I.M. (1979). Comment: X-inefficiency, error, and the scope for entrepreneurship. In M. Rizzo (Ed.) *Time, Uncertainty, and Disequilibrium.* Lexington, MA: D.C. Heath.

Kirzner, I.M. (1979). *Perception, opportunity, and profit.* Chicago: University of Chicago Press.

Kirzner, I.M. (1985). *Discovery and the capitalist process.* Chicago: The University of Chicago Press.

Klemp, G.O. & McClelland, D.C. (1986). What characterizes intelligent functioning among senior managers? In Sternberg, R.J. & Wayne, R.K. (Eds.) *Practical intelligence.* Cambridge, England: Cambridge University Press, 31-50.

Knight, F.H. (1921). *Risk, uncertainty, and profit.* New York: Houghton Mifflin.

Kogan, N. & Wallace, M. (1964). *Risk Taking.* New York: Holt, Rinehart, and Winston.

Kohlberg, L. (1969). Stage and sequence: The cognitive-developmental approach to socialization. In D.A. Goslin (Ed.) *Handbook of Socialiation Theory and Research.* Chicago: Rand McNally. pp. 347-380.

Komives, J.L. (1972). A preliminary study of the personal values of high technology entrepreneurs. In A.C. Cooper and J.L. Komives (Eds.) *Technical Entrepreneurship: A symposium.* Milwaukee, Wisconsin: The center for Venture Management. pp.231-242.

Kotter, J.P. (1982). *General managers are not generalists.* Organizational Dynamics, (Spring). 5-19.

Kotter, J.P. (1982). *The general managers.* New York: The Free Press.

Kuehl, C.R. & Lambing, P.A. (1987). *Small business: Planning and management.* Chicago: The Dryden Press.

Lamont, L.M. (1972). What entrepreneurs learn from experience. *Journal of Small Business Management, 10*(July), 36-41.

Lehmann, D.R. (1988). An alternative procedure for assessing covergent and discriminant validity. *Applied Psychological Measurement, 12* (4), 411-423.

Leibenstein, H. (1966). Allocative efficiency vs. x-efficiency. *American Economic Review, 54*(3), 392-415.

Leibenstein, H. (1979). The general x-efficiency paradigm and the role of the entrepreneur. In: *Time, uncertainty, and disequilibrium.* Mario Rizzo (ED.). Lexington, MA: D.C. Heath.

Leontiades, M. (1982). *Choosing the right manager to fit the strategy.* Journal of Business Strategy, 58-69.

Levine, S. & Ursin, H. (1979). *Coping and health.* New York: Plenum Press.

Liles, P.R. (1974). *New business and the entrepreneur.* Homewood, IL: Richard D. Irwin.

Liles, P.R. (1974). *Who are the entrepreneurs?* M.S.U. Business Topics,22(1), 5-14.

Long, W. (1983). The meaning of entrepreneurship. *American Journal Of Small Business*, 8(2), 47-56.

Low, M.B. & MacMillan, I.C. (1988). Entrepreneurship: Past research and future challanges. *Journal of Management, 14*(2), 139-161.

MacMillan, I.C. (1986). To really learn about entrepreneurship, let's study habitual entrepreneurs. *Journal of Business Venturing, 1*(3), 241-243.

MacMillan, I. C. & Day, D. (1987). Corporate ventures into industrial markets: Dynamics of aggressive entry. *Journal of Business Venturing, 2* (1). 29-39.

MacMillan, I.C. & Subba Narasimha, P.N. (1987). Characteristics distinguishing funded from unfunded business plans evaluated by venture capitalists. *Strategic Management Juornal, 8,* 579-585.

MacMillan, I., Seigel, R., & Narasimha, S. P. (1985). Criteria used by venture capitalists to evaluate new venture proposals. *Journal of Business Venturing, 1*(1), 119-128.

MacMillan, I.C., Zemann, L., & Subba Narasimha, P.N. (1987). Critera distinguishing successful from unsuccessful ventures in the venture screening process. *Journal of Business Venturing,* 2(2), 123-137.

Madden, T.J. & Dillon, W.R. (1982). Causal analysis and latent class models: An application to a communication hierarchy of effects model. *Journal of Marketing Research, 19*(Nov), 472-490.

Maidque, M. (1986). Key success factors in high-technology ventures. In: Sexton, D.L. & Smilor, R.W. (EDS.). *The art and science of entrepreneurship.* Cambridge, MA: Ballinger Publishing.

Maier, N. (1946). *Psychology in industry.* Boston: Houghton Mifflin Co.

Maier, N. (1965). *Psychology in industry.* (3rd ed.). Boston: Houghton Mifflin Co.

Mancuso, J. (1974). The entrepreneur's quiz. In: *The entrepreneur's handbook, Vol. 2*, Edited by J. Mancuso, Dedham, MA: Artech House, pp 235-239.

Marsh, H.W. & Hòcevar, D. (1985). Application of confirmatory factor analysis to the study of self-concept: First- and higher order factor models and their invariance across groups. *Psychological Bulletin, 93*(3),562-582.

Marsh, H.W., Balla, J.R., & McDonald, R.P. (1988). Goodness-of-fit indexes in confirmatory factor analysis: The effect of sample size. *Psychological Bulletin, 103*(3), 391-410.

Martin, D.T. (1979). Alternative views of Mengerian entrepreneurship. *History of Political Economy, 11*, 271.

McClelland, D.C. (1961). *The achieving society.* Princeton, N.J.: Van Nostrand.

McClelland, D.C. (1965). N achievement and entrepreneurship: A longitudinal study. *Journal Of Personality and Social Psychology, 1*(4), 389-392.

McClelland, D.C. & Winter, D.G. (1969). *Motivating economic achievement.* New York: The Free Press.

McCrae, R.T., Costa, P.T., & Arenberg, D. (1980). Constancy of adult personality structure in males:Longitudanal, cross-sectional and times-of-measurement analysis. *Journal Of Gerontology, 35*(6), 877-833.

McCrane, E.W., Lambert, V.A., & Lambert, C.E. (1987). Work stress, hardiness, and burnout among hospital staff nurses. *Nursing Research, 36* (6), 374-378.

McDougall, P. & Robinson, R.B. (1987). *Modeling new venture performance: An analysis of new venture strategy, industry entry barriers, and new vebture origin.* Unpublished paper.

McDougall, P. (1987). *An analysis of new venture business level strategy, entry barriers,and new venture origin as factors explaining new venture performance.* Unpublished doctoral dissertation. Columbia, SC: University of South Caroloina.

McDougall, P.P., Robinson, R.R., & Herron, L.A. (1988). *An empirical identification of effective new venture strategies in high and low growth industries.* Presented at the Annual Meeting of the National Academy of Management in Aneheim, CA.

Meeker, M. N. (1969). *The structure of intellect.* Columbus OH: Charles E. Merrill.

Menger, C. (1950). *Principles of economics.* Translated by J. Dlingwall and B.F. Hoselitz. Glencoe, IL: The Free Press.

Meyer, H.H., Walker, W.B., & Litwin, G.H. (1961). Motive patterns and risk perferences associated with entrepreneurship. *Journal of Abnormal and Social Psychology, 63*(3), 570-574.

Miles,R.E. & Snow,C.C. (1978). *Organizational strategy, structure, and process.* New York: McGraw-Hill.

Mill, J.S.(1909). *Principles of political economy: With some of their applications to social philosophy* (5th ed)(Vol.1 & 2). New York: Appleton and Co.

Miller, D. (1983).The correlates of entrepreneurship in three types of firms. *Management Science, 29*(7), 770-791.

Miller, A. & Camp, B. (1985). Exploring determinates of success in corporate ventures. *Journal of Business Venturing, 1,* 87-105.

Miller, D. & Frieson, P.H. (1980). Momentum and revolution in organizational adaptation. *Academy of Management Journal, 23*(4), 591-614.

Miller, D., Kets De Vries, M.F.R., & Toulouse, J.M. (1982). Top executive locus of control and its relationship to strategy-making, structure, and environment. *Academy of Management Journal, 25*(2), 237-253.

Mintzberg, H. (1980). The nature of managerial work (2nd ed.). Chapter 7: *The future of managerial work*. Englewood Cliffs, NJ: Prentice-Hall.

Mintzberg, H. & Waters, J. (1982). *Academy of Management Journal, 25*(3), 465-499.

Mollenkopf, W.G., (1960). Time limits and the behavior of test takers. *Educational Psychological Measurement, 20*, 223-230.

Mulaik, S.A., James, L.R., Van Alstine, J., Bennett, N., Lind, S., & Stilwell, C.D. (1989). Evaluation of goodness-of-fit indicies for structural equation models. *Psychological Bulletin, 105* (3), 430-445.

Murphy, A.E. (1986). Richard Cantillon: *Entrepreneur and economist*. Oxford: Clarendon Press.

Naisbitt, J. (1982). *Megatrends*. New York: Warner Books.

Neter, J., Wasserman, W., & Kutner, M. (1985). *Applied linear statistical models*. Homewood, IL: Irwin.

Nunnally, J.C. (1967). *Psychometric theory*. New York: McGraw-Hill.

Olson, P.D. (1985). Entrepreneurs: Opportunistic decision makers. *Journal of Small Business*, (July), 29-35.

Olson, P.D. (1985). Entrepreneurship: Process and abilities. *American Journal of Small Business, 9*(Summer), 25-31.

Pandey, J. & Tewary, N.B. (1979). Locus of control and achievement values of entrepreneurs. *Journal of Occupational Psychology, 52*(2), 107-111.

Paulin, W.L., Coffey, R.E., Spaulding, M.E. (1982). Entrepreneurship research: Methods and directions. In: Kent, C.A., Sexton, D.L., and Vesper, K.H. (Eds.), *Encyclopedia of entrepreneurship*. Englewood Cliffs, NJ: Prentice-Hall, 352-379.

Pearce, J. & Robinson, R.B. (1988) *Strategic Management: Strategy formulation and implementation* (3rd ed.). Homewood, IL: Irwin.

Pearce, J. & Robinson, R.B. (1988) *Strategic Management: Strategy formulation and implementation* (3rd ed.). Homewood, IL: Irwin.

Pedhazur, E.J. (1982). (2nd Ed.). *Multiple regression in behavioral research*. New York: CBS College Publishing.

Perry, C., Macarthur, R., Meredith, G., & Cunnington, B. (1985). Need for achievement and locus of control of Australian small business owner-managers and super-entrepreneurs. *International Small Business Journal*, 4(4), 55-64.

Peter, J.P. (1979). Reliability: A review of psychometric basics and recent marketing practices. *Journal of Marketing Research*, 16(Feb), 6-17.

Peter, J.P. (1981). Construct validity: A review of basic issues and marketing practices. *Journal of Marketing Research*, 18(MAY), 133-145.

Peterson, R. & Smith, N.R. (1986). Entrepreneurship: A culturally appropriate combination of craft and opportunity. *Frontiers In Entrepreneurial Research*. Wellesley, MA: Babson College. 1-11.

Porter, M.E. (1980). *Competitive Strategy*. New York: Free Press.

Porter, M.E. (1985). *Competitive Advantage*. New York: Free Press.

Reagan, R. (1985). Why this is an entrepreneurial age. *Journal of Business Venturing*, 1 (1), 1-4.

Reich, R.B. (1987). Entrepreneurship[reconsidered: The team as hero. *Harvard Business Review*, 65(3), 77-83.

Reynolds, P.D. (1987). New firms: Societal contribution versus survival potential. *Journal of Business Venturing*, 2(3), 231-246.

Reynolds, P.D. (1988). *Organizational births: Perspectives on the emergence of new firms*. Academy of Management Proceedings: New Orleans. 69-73.

Roberts, E. B. (1969). Entrepreneurship and technology. In Gruber, H.W. & Marquis, D.G. (Eds.) *Factors in the transfer of technology*. Cambridge, MA: MIT Press, 219-237.

Roberts, E. B. (1985). Entering new businesses: Selecting strategies for success. *Sloan Management Review* (Spring) 57-71.

Roberts, M., (1987). *An empirical search for entrepreneurship*. Unpublished paper.

Roberts, M.J., (1986). *The transition from entrepreneurial to professional management: An exploratory study*. Unpublished paper.

Robinson, R.B., & Pearce, J.A. (1985). *The structure of generic strategies and their impact on business-unit performance*. Academy of Managent Proceedings, San Diego, CA, 33-39.

Robinson,R.B. & Pearce, J.A. (1986). Product life-cycle considerations and the nature of strategic activities in entrepreneuriel firms. *Journal of Business Venturing, 1*(2), 207-225.

Robinson, R.B., McDougall, P., & Herron, L. (1988). *Toward a new venture strategy typology*. Proceedings of the Academy of Management, Aneheim Ca, 74-78.

Rock, D.A., Werts, C.E., Linn, R.L., & Joreskog, K.G. (1977). A maximum likehood solution to the errors in variables and errors in equations model. *The Journal of Multivariate Behavioral Research, 12*, (Apr.)187-197.

Romanelli, E. (1987). New venture strategies in the minicomputer industry. *California Management Review*, (Fall), 160-175.

Ronstadt, R. (1986). Exit, stage left: Why entrepreneurs end their entrepreneurial careers before retirement. *Journal of Business Venturing, 1*, 323-338.

Rotter, J.B. (1966). Generalized expectations for internal versus external control of reinforcement. *Psychological Monographs: General and Aplied, 8*(1)(Whole No. 609), 1-28.

Roure, J. (1986). *Success and failure of high-growth technological ventures: The influence of prefunding factors*. Unpublished doctoral dissertation. Stanford, CA: Stanford University.

Roure, J.B. & Keeley, R.H. (1988). *New venture performance: The effects of management characteristics, business strategy, and industry structure.* Paper presented at the nationl meeting of the Academy of Management. Aneheim, CA. (Aug).

Roure, J.B. & Keeley, R.H. (1988). *The influence of strategic choices on the success of new firms financed with venture capital.* Studies in the Management Sciences and Systems,In Press.

Rozeboom, W.W. (1956). Mediation variables in scientific theory. *Psychological Review, 63* (4), 249-264.

Runyon, K.E. (1973). Some interactions between personality variables and management styles. *Journal of Applied Psychology, 57*(3), 288-294.

Sandberg, W. R. 1986). *New venture performance: The role of strategy and industry structure.* Lexington, MA: D.C. Heath & Co.

Sandberg, W.R., & Hofer, C.W. (1987). Improving new venture performance: The role of strategy, industry structure, and the entrepreneur. *Journal of Business Venturing, 2,* 5-28.

Sandberg, W.R., Schweiger, D.M., & Hofer, C.W. (1987). *Determining venture capitalists' decision criteria: The ues of verbal protocols.* Paper persented at the Babson College Entrepreneurship Research Conference. Malibu, CA.

Sapienza, H.J. (1989). *Variations in venture capitalist-entrepreneur relations: Antecedents and consequences.*Unpublished doctoral dissertation. University of Maryland.

Sapienza, H.J., Smith, K.G., & Gannon, M.J. (1988). Using subjective evaluations of organizational performance in small business research. *American Journal of Small Business, 12* (3), 45-53.

Say, J.B. (1827). *A treatise on political economy* (3rd Ed). (American Edition). Philadelphia: John Grigg.

Schere, J. (1981). *Tolerance of ambiguity as a discriminating variable between entrepreneurs and managers.* Unpublished Doctoral Dissertation. The Wharton School, University of Pennsylvania.

Schmidt, F.E. (1973). Implications of a measurement problem for expectancy theory research. *Organizational behavior and human performance, 10*, 243-251.

Schmidt, F.L., & Hunbter, J.E. (1981). Employment testing: Old theories and new research findings. *American Psychologist, 36* (10), 1128-1137.

Schmidt, F.L., Hunter, J.E., & Pearlman, K. (1981). Task differences as moderators of aptitude test validity in selection: A red herring. *Journal of Applied Psychology, 66*(2), 166-185.

Schoonhoven, C.B. (1981). Problems with contingency theory: Testing assumptions hidden within the language of contingency theory. *Administrative Science Quarterly, 26*, 349-377.

Schultz, T. (1975). The value of the ability to deal with disequilibria. *Journal of Economic Literature, 13*. 827-846.

Schultz, T. (1980). Investment in entrepreneurial ability. *Scandinavian Journal of Economics, 82*, 437-448.

Schumpeter, J. (1934). *The theory of economic development.* Cambridge, MA: Harvard University Press.

Schumpeter, J.A. (1935). The analysis of economic change. *Review of Economic Statistics*, (May), 2-10.

Schumpeter, J. (1939). Business cycles. New York: McGraw-Hill.Seligman, D. (1987). Brainstorms. *Fortune*, August 3, 206-208.

Sexton, D.L. (1982). Research needs and issues in entrepreneurship. In: Kent, C.A., Sexton, D.L., and Vesper, K.H. (Eds.), *Encyclopedia of entrepreneurship.* Englewood Cliffs, NJ: Prentice-Hall, 383-389.

Sexton, D.L. & Bowman, N. (1985). The entrepreneur: A capable executive and more. *Journal of Business Venturing, 1*, 129-140.

Shapero, A. (1975). The displaced, uncomfortable entrepreneur. *Psychology Today.* (Nov.), 83-88.

Shapero, A. (1981). Numbers that lie. *Inc.*, 3 May, 16-18.

Sharma, S. & Mahajan, V., (1980). Early warning indicators of business failure. *Journal of Marketing, 44*(Fall), 80-89.

Sharma, S., Durand, R.M., & Gur-Aire, O. (1981). Identification and analysis of moderator variables. *Journal of Marketing, 18*(Aug.), 291-300.

Sharma, S., Durvasula, S. & Dillon, W.R. (1988). *Some results on the behavior of alternative covariance structure estimation procedures in the presence of non-normal data.* Unpublished Paper.

Sharma, S., Shimp, T.A., & Fitzgerald, M.P. (1985). *Developing better measurement scales: The role of confirmatory factor analysis.* Unpublished paper.

Sims, R.R. (1983).Kolb's experiential learning theory: A framework for assessing person-job interaction. *Academy of Management Review, 8*(3), 501-508.

Singer, J.L. & Kolligian, J. (1987). Personality: Developments in the studyof private experience. *Annual Review of Psychology, 38*, 533-574."

Smith, A. (1963). *An inquiry into the nature and causes of the wealth of nations* (Vols. 1 & 2). Homewood, ILL: Richard D. Irwin.

Smith, J.E., Carson, K.P., & Alexander, R.A (1984). Leadership: It can make a difference. *Academy of Management Journal, 27*(4), 765-776.

Smith, N.R. (1967). *The entrepreneur and his firm: The relationship between type of man and type of company.* East Lansing, MI: Bureau of Business and Economic Research, Michigan State University.

Spearman, C. (1910). Correlation calculated from faulty data. *British Journal of Psychology, 3*, 271-295.

Spearman, C. (1927). *The abilities of man.* New York: MacMillan.

Steinmetz, L.L. (1969). Critical stages of small, business growth: When they occur and how to survive them. *Business Horizons* (Feb), 29-36.

Sternberg, R. J. (1977). Component processes in analogical reasoning. *Psychological Review, 84*, 353-378.

Sternberg, R.J. (1979). The nature of mental abilities. *American Psychologist, 34*(3), 214-230.

Sternberg, R. J. (1985). *Beyond I.Q.* Cambridge, England: Cambridge University Press.

Sternberg, R. J. & Wagner, R.K. (Eds.) (1986). *Practical intelligence.: Nature and origins of competence in the everyday world.* Cambridge, England: Cambridge University Press.

Stevenson, H. & Gumpert, D. (1985). The heart of entrepreneurship. *Harvard Business Review, 63*(2), 85-94.

Stewart, R. (1982). A model of understanding managerial jobs and behavior. *Academy of Management Review, 7*(1), 7-13.

Stoner, J.A.F. & Wankel,C. (1986). *Management* (3RD Ed) Englewood Cliffs, NJ: Prentice-Hall.

Stuart, R. & Abetti, P.A. (1986). Field study of Start-up ventures - part II: Predicting initial success. In: Ronstad, R., Hornaday, J.,Peterson, R., & Vesper, K. *Frontiers of entrepreneurship research.* Wellesley, MA: Babson College, 21-39.

Stuart, R. & Abetti, P.A. (1987). Start-up ventures: Towards the prediction of initial success. *Journal of Business Venturing, 2*, 215-230.

Susbauer, J.C. (1979). Commentary. In Schendel, D. and Hofer, C.W. (Eds.). *Strategic Management.* Boston: Little, Brown. 327-332.

Szilagyi, A.D. & Schweiger,D.M. (1984). Matching managers to strategies: A review and suggested framework. *Academy of Management Review, 9*(4), 626-637.

Teel, J.E., Bearden, W.O., & Sharma, S. (1986). Interpreting LISREL estimates of explained variance in nonrecursive structural equation models. *Journal of Marketing Research*, 23(May), 164-168.

Thompson, A.A. & Strickland, A.J. (1987). *Strategic management: Concepts and cases*. Plano, TX: Business Publications.

Thurstone, L. L. (1931). Multiple factor analysis. *Psychological Review, 38*, (406-427).

Thurstone, L. L. (1938). *Primary mental abilities*. Chicago: Chicago University Press.

Tichy, N.M. (1983). *Manageing strategic change: Technical, political, and cultural dynamics*. New York: John Wiley.

Tichy, N.M., Fombrun, C.J. & Devanna, M.A. (1982). Strategic human resource management. *Sloan Management Review,23*(2) 47-61.

Timmons, J.A. (1978). Characteristics and role demands of entrepreneurship. *American Journal of Small Business, 3* (1), 5-17.

Timmons, J.A. (1982). New venture creation: Models and methodologies. In Kent, C.A.,Sexton,D.L., and Vesper,K.H.,(Eds). *Encyclopedia of entrepreneurship*. Englewood Cliffs, NJ: Prentice-Hall, 126-139.

Timmons, J.A. (1985). *New venture creation*. Homewood, IL: Richard D.Irwin.

Timmons, J,A., Muzyka, D.F., Stevenson, H.H., & Bygrave, W.D. (1988). Opportunity Recognition: The core of entrepreneurship. *Frontiers of Entrepreneurship Research*. Wellesley, MA: Babson College. 109-123.

Toffler, A. (1980). *The third wave*. New York: Random House.

Tyebjee, T.T. & Bruno, A.V. (1984). A model of venture capitalist activity. *Management Science, 30*(9), 1051-1066.

Bibliography

Tyler, L.E. (1986). Back to Spearman? *Journal of Vocational Behavior*, 29, 445-450.

Van De Ven, A.H., Hudson, R., & Schroeder, D.M. (1984). Designing new business startups: entrepreneurial, organizational, and ecological considerations. *Journal of Management, 10* (1), 87-107.

Venkatraman, N. (1989). The concept of fit in strategy research: Toward verbal and statistical correspondence. *Academy of Management Review, 14* (3), 423-444.

Venkatraman, N. & Camillus, J.C., (1984). Exploring the concept of "fit" in strategic management. *Academy of Management Review, 9* (3), 513-525.

Venkatraman, N. & Grant, J.H. (1986). Construct measurement in organizational strategy research: A critique and proposal. *Academy of Management Review, 11*(1), 71-87.

Vernon, P.E. (1971). *The structure of human abilities.* London: Methuen.

Vesper, K.H. (1979). Commentary. In Schendel,D. & Hofer,C.W. (eds.) *Strategic Management.* Boston: Little, Brown, 333-338.

Vesper, K.H. (1980). *New Venture Strategies.* Englewood Cliffs, NJ: Prentice-Hall.

Vesper, K.H. (1983). *Entrepreneurship and national policy.* Heller Institute for Small Business - Policy Papers:USA

Virany, B., & Tushman, M.L. (1986). Top management teams and corporate success in an emerging industry. *Journal of Business Venturing, 1*(3), 261-274.

Von Mises, L. (1966). *Human action*, 3rd Ed. Chicago: Henry Regnery Co.

Wagner, R.K. (1987). Tacit knowledge in everday intelligent behavior. *Journal of Personality And Social Psychology, 52*(6), 1236-1247.

Wagner, R.K. & Sternberg, R.J. (1985). Practical intelligence in real-world pursuits: The role of tacit knowledge. *Journal of Personality And Social Psychology, 49*(2), 436-458.

Warren, R.D., White, J.K., & Fuller, W.A. (1974). An errors in variables analysis of managerial role performance. *Journal of the American Statistical Association, 69*, 886-893.

Webster, F.A. (1976). A model for new venture initiation: A discourse on rapacity and the independent entrepreneur. *Academy of Management Review, 1*(1), 26-37.

Webster, F.A. (1977). Entrepreneurs and ventures: An attempt at classification and clarification. *Academy of Management Review, 2*(1), 54-61.

Widaman, K. F. (1985). Hierarchically nested covariance structure models for multitrait-multimethod data. *Applied Psychological Measurement, 9* (1), 1-26.

Williams, R.D. & Thomson, E. (1986). Normalization issues in latent variable modeling. *Sociological Methods & Research, 15* (1-2), 24-41.

Wissema, J.G. Van der Pol, H.W., & Messer, H.M. (1980). Strategic management archtypes. *Strategic Management Journal, 1*(1), 37-47.

Woo, C.Y. & Cooper, A.C. (1981). Strategies for effective low share businesses. *Strategic Management Journal, 2*, 301-318.

Woo, C.Y. & Cooper, A.C. (1982). The surprising case for low market share. *Harvard Business Review*, (Nov-Dec), 106-113.

Wright, R.V.L. (1974). *A system for manageing diversity.* Cambridge, MA: Arthur D. Little.

Zaleznik, A. & Kets de Vries, M.F.R. (1976). What makes entrepreneurs entrepreneurial? *Business and Society Review, 17*(Spring): 18-23.

Index

Ability, 17, 18, 25, 26, 32, 37, 39, 43, 46, 49, 51-53, 121, 186, 189, 193, 209, 211, 212, 214, 215
Allport and Odbert, 35
Anderson, 36, 37
Aptitude, 43, 45-48, 50-54, 56, 76, 87, 91, 95, 96, 101, 115, 173, 176, 186, 199, 206, 209, 210
Austrian school of economics, 14, 16

Bandura, 39
Baudeau, Abbé Nicolas, 13
Begley and Boyd, 20-23, 28
Behavior, 12, 19, 25-29, 31-33, 35-39, 41, 45, 49, 51, 53, 54, 56, 77, 208, 210
Böhm-Bawerk, 15, 16
Borland, 21
Brinberg and McGrath, 73
Brockhaus and Nord, 21, 24, 25
Brockhaus, 20-22, 28
Buchele, 24

Cantillon, Richard 12, 14, 15, 17
Cattell, 45-47
Clark, J.B., 14, 15, 16, 17
Cohen and Cohen, 118
Cohen, 117
Collins and Moore, 23, 24
Cost, 4, 13, 16, 207, 213

Differentiation, 84, 213
Drucker, Peter, 25, 26

Eastlack & McDonald, 31
Economic literature, 6, 11-14, 17, 18, 20, 25, 29, 54, 213
Entrepreneurial characteristics, 5-7, 11, 12, 18-20, 22, 23, 25-29, 54, 74, 75, 84, 96, 101, 179, 199, 203-205, 208, 210-212, 214, 215
Epstein, 36, 37

Factor analysis, 35, 45, 74, 78, 81, 84, 87, 91, 92, 97, 105, 107, 111, 116, 117, 135, 140, 146, 149
Factor score: See Factor Analysis
Feigl, 74

Galton, 46
Gartner, 26, 27, 208
Growth, 21, 23, 24, 78, 81, 84, 105, 107, 135, 140, 192
Guilford and Hoepfner, 87
Guilford, 45, 46, 48, 50-54, 76, 77, 87, 91, 96, 103, 173, 206
Gupta and Govindarajan, 31, 92
Gupta, 31

Hambrick, 41
Hawley, 14, 15
Hébert and Link, 17
Hoad and Rosko, 23, 24
Hofer & Schendel, 31
Hollenbeck and Whitener, 37, 39, 43, 204
Hornaday and Aboud, 22
Hoselitz, 12
Hull, Bosley, and Udell, 21
Hunt, 45

Industry life cycle, 31, 84, 207
Industry product homogeneity, 84, 87
Industry structure, 4-6, 27, 29, 31, 33, 48, 52, 54, 74-76, 78, 81, 84, 87, 91, 95, 97, 107, 115, 116, 118, 121, 134, 140, 146, 149, 158, 173, 179, 186, 192, 194, 196, 198, 199, 203-205, 208, 211, 213, 214
Intelligence, 25, 43, 45, 46, 47
Interaction, 75-77, 115-117, 121, 140, 146, 149, 158, 173, 176, 179, 181, 185, 189, 192, 194, 196, 198, 199, 204, 206, 207, 209, 211, 212, 214

Jensen, 45

Katz, 32, 48, 49, 50, 53, 87, 205
Kaynes, John Maynard 14
Kirzner, 14-17, 206
Knight, Frank, 15-17
Kogan-Wallace, 20
Komives, 21, 22
Kotter, 32

Lamont, 24
Leontiades, 31
LISREL, 107, 111, 140
Locus of control, 21, 22, 28, 33, 35-37

MacMillan, 24, 25, 27
Maidique, 28
Maier, 37, 43, 53, 206
Management implementation literature, 7, 11, 27, 29, 31, 33, 41, 54, 84
Marshall, Alfred, 14
McClelland, 21
Meeker, 46, 50, 51
Menger, Carl, 14, 15
Meyer, Walker, and Litwin, 20
Miles and Snow, 31
Mill, John Stuart, 13
Mintzberg, 32
Motivation, 37

Naisbitt, 4
Need for achievement, 21, 22, 35
Nunnally, 105

Personality traits, 19, 22, 23, 25, 27, 28, 33, 35-39, 41, 54, 56, 74, 96, 204, 208, 210, 213
Pigou, 14
Porter, 31
Price, 12, 87
Psychological literature, 7, 12, 27, 33, 35, 41, 56, 206, 208, 210

Quesnay, 13

Reagan, Ronald, 3
Ricardo, David, 13

Index

Risk, 12-20, 23, 26-28, 31, 32
Roberts, 24
Robinson, et al., 107, 140
Rotter, 37
Roure, 23, 28, 33, 212

Sandberg and Hofer, 27
Sandberg, 5, 24, 29, 33, 204, 208
Say, Jean-Baptist, 13, 16
Schmidt, 117
Schultz, 14, 16-18
Schumpeter, Joesph, 16, 17, 19, 26
Scope, 78, 81, 105, 107, 135, 140, 192, 194, 196, 198, 207
Shackle, 16, 17
Shapero, 21
Shultz, 15, 16
Skill, 13, 18, 23, 26, 31-33, 35, 39, 41, 43, 47-50, 52-54, 56, 75, 76, 87, 91, 96, 97, 101, 102, 111, 115, 116, 118, 121, 134, 140, 146, 149, 158, 173, 176, 179, 181, 185, 186, 189, 192, 194, 196, 198, 199, 204-215
  Administrative, 32, 49, 53, 76, 77, 121, 123, 134, 158, 161, 173, 186, 198, 199, 205, 207
  Entrepreneurial, 50, 53, 56, 76, 77, 121, 134, 158, 161, 173, 176, 186, 189, 192, 194, 196, 198, 205-208, 212, 213, 215
  Human, 49, 77, 121, 161
    Leadership, 49, 75, 77, 121, 123, 158, 161, 173, 186, 205

  Networking, 49, 76, 123, 158, 161, 173, 186, 189, 192, 194, 196, 198, 205, 207
  Technical, 48, 52, 205
    Business, 49, 52, 75, 77, 121, 123, 158, 161, 173, 186, 194, 196, 198, 205, 207
    Industry, 49, 52, 75, 77, 121, 123, 158, 161, 173, 186, 189, 192, 205, 207, 214
    Product/service, 49, 52, 75, 76, 121, 123, 146, 158, 161, 173, 179, 189, 192, 194, 196, 198, 205, 207, 214
Smith, Adam, 13
Smith, N.R., 23
Spearman, 45, 46
Sternberg, 45, 47, 48
Stevenson and Gumpert, 18, 26
Steward, 32
Strategy, 4-6, 27, 29, 31-33, 48, 54, 74-78, 81, 84, 87, 95, 97, 107, 115, 116, 118, 121, 134, 135, 140, 146, 149, 158, 173, 179, 192, 194, 196, 199, 203-209, 211, 213, 214
Strategy implementation literature: See Management implementation literature
Stuart and Abetti, 28, 33
Substrategy, 31, 32, 81
Szilagyi and Schweiger, 32, 37, 41, 43, 48, 49, 205

Teams, 26-28, 33, 210, 212
Thurstone, 45

Tichy, 31
Timmons, 25, 27
Toffler, 4
Tolerance for ambiguity, 22, 23
Turgot, Anne-Robert, 13

Van de Ven, 4
Venkatraman and Grant, 78

Venture capitalists, 5, 25, 27, 199, 203, 208, 209, 212
Vesper, 78, 81
von Mangoldt, 13
von Mises, Ludwig, 15-17
von Thünen, 13

Wissema, 31
Wright, 31